Charismatics and Postmodernity

Charismatics and Postmodernity

Modernism, Postmodernism, and Premodernism
in the Church of England's Charismatic Movement

JITESH K. PATEL

☙PICKWICK *Publications* • Eugene, Oregon

CHARISMATICS AND POSTMODERNITY
Modernism, Postmodernism, and Premodernism in the Church of England's Charismatic Movement

Copyright © 2025 Jitesh K. Patel. All rights reserved. Except for brief quotations in critical publications or reviews, no part of this book may be reproduced in any manner without prior written permission from the publisher. Write: Permissions, Wipf and Stock Publishers, 199 W. 8th Ave., Suite 3, Eugene, OR 97401.

Pickwick Publications
An Imprint of Wipf and Stock Publishers
199 W. 8th Ave., Suite 3
Eugene, OR 97401

www.wipfandstock.com

PAPERBACK ISBN: 979-8-3852-4027-2
HARDCOVER ISBN: 979-8-3852-4028-9
EBOOK ISBN: 979-8-3852-4029-6

Cataloguing-in-Publication data:

Names: Patel, Jitesh K. [author].

Title: Charismatics and postmodernity : modernism, postmodernism, and premodernism in the Church of England's charismatic movement / by Jitesh K. Patel.

Description: Eugene, OR: Pickwick Publications, 2025 | Includes bibliographical references.

Identifiers: ISBN 979-8-3852-4027-2 (paperback) | ISBN 979-8-3852-4028-9 (hardcover) | ISBN 979-8-3852-4029-6 (ebook)

Subjects: LCSH: Pentecostalism—Church of England—History. | Great Britain—Church history. | Church renewal. | Evangelicalism—Church of England.

Classification: BX5125 P384 2025 (print) | BX5125 (ebook)

Scripture quotations are from New Revised Standard Version Bible: Anglicized Edition, copyright © 1989, 1995 National Council of the Churches of Christ in the United States of America. Used by permission. All rights reserved worldwide.

Jemimah and Keren, may you know the love of Christ and the power of the Spirit as you are led in worship to God our Father.

Contents

Acknowledgements ix

Abbreviations xi

CHAPTER 1. Introduction and Methodology 1

CHAPTER 2. Postmodernism in the Charismatic Church 22

CHAPTER 3. Exploring the Charismatic Movement in the Church of England 55

CHAPTER 4. Sociological and Anthropological Insights 91

CHAPTER 5. Postmodernism and the Early Movement 116

CHAPTER 6. Postmodernism and the Later Movement (I): Postmodern Characteristics 159

CHAPTER 7. Postmodernism and the Later Movement (II): Models and Trajectories 192

CHAPTER 8. Conclusion and Challenges 224

Appendices 257

Bibliography 261

Acknowledgments

THIS BOOK IS A modified version of my PhD thesis and finds its life through the encouragement, support, and influence of several people to whom acknowledgement and thanks are due. To begin with, I am deeply grateful to my two successive doctoral supervisors. Firstly, Professor Allan Anderson rapidly brought me up to the doctoral level of writing and research with great skill. Secondly, Reverend Dr. Andrew Lord, whose tireless reading, commenting, critiquing, and encouragement have been a source of much wisdom and guidance and without whom this book would be much poorer.

I am grateful for the support of the two worshiping environments in which this book was written: the church community of Holy Trinity Church, Leicester, and the theological community of St. Mellitus College (especially its staff team in the East Midlands). Thank you to both for releasing me to research and enabling me to ground my findings in the living communities of Christ that I am called to serve.

Special thanks go to the following: Reverend Dr. Phil Weston for his first read-through; Dr. Anna Weston for her comments on my philosophical work; Dr. Brian Stiller for his early correspondence; those interviewed as part of this study who graciously gave of their time and energy; and to the Diocese of Leicester and PCC of Holy Trinity Leicester for their gifts of financial support.

Thank you to the team at Wipf and Stock and especially to my editors, Professor Charles Tieszen and Reverend Dr. Robin Parry, who were helpful founts of knowledge for this first-time author.

Whilst this book was being formed and written, I married my wife Bridget, and together we had the joy of two daughters being born to us. To Bridget, the greatest thanks are due; without your encouragement, love, and understanding this work simply would not exist. To Jemimah and Keren, this book is dedicated.

Soli Deo Gloria

Abbreviations

Alpha	The Alpha Course
CEEC	The Church of England Evangelical Council
HTB	Holy Trinity Church, Brompton
The Movement	The Charismatic Movement in the Church of England
TTB	The Toronto Blessing

1

Introduction and Methodology

1.1 INTRODUCTION

THIS BOOK FINDS ITS genesis in the observations of several contemporary Christian commentators who have commented on a relationship between charismatic renewal and postmodernism, yet with little to no substantiation of this relationship, nor elucidation of its dynamics. The study this book inscribes helps rectify this through the investigation of a specific, rich, and localized example of charismatic renewal, the Charismatic Movement in the Church of England—hereafter "the Movement." The results of this are important, both for the way in which such renewal movements should be understood and for the Movement's own self-understanding and ongoing life.

The main contention this study gives rise to is that while the Movement exhibits many clear postmodern characteristics throughout its life, which vary in strength and nature over time, it is incorrect to call the Movement a postmodern one. A better narrative demonstrates that these characteristics come about through a more complex interaction with modern, postmodern, and premodern themes—whereby they are generated through a reaction to modernism, retrieve premodern emphases that look postmodern in nature, and subsequently are amplified in size through their seen appeal to elements of wider culture. Appearances can be deceiving, and what looks postmodern is in fact subtly but importantly more complex.

This study explores several areas to substantiate this better narrative. Of primary importance, it explores whether the Movement can be said to have postmodern characteristics, discovering how valid observations made about its postmodern tendencies and nature are. However, simultaneously, this study investigates the paucity of evidence for the direct shaping of the Movement by postmodern ideas and culture that could explain such observed characteristics. Rather, three other responsible dynamics, existing in complex interplay in the Movement, are elucidated and substantiated. Firstly, such characteristics came about through a reaction to the felt deficiencies with modernism within the church that led to anti-modern emphases that overlap with postmodern ones, paralleling how this occurred in the history of philosophical enquiry that led to philosophical postmodernism. Secondly, this anti-modern impulse leads to a sustained recovery of premodern emphases, some of which have significant similarities and overlaps with postmodern ones, such that the two are sometimes identical in nature—as the way forward past modernism is found to be the way back to before modernism. Thirdly, the Movement's interaction with elements of its surrounding cultural context, especially through missional outreach, helped encourage the subsequent growth of these postmodern characteristics due to their perceived resonances and parallels with both modernistic and postmodern elements of it.

Reflection upon these findings enjoins a nuanced range of reactions and transformative inferences for the Movement in response, which ought to be rightly received and incorporated into its ongoing praxis. These will be drawn out in this book's last chapter, but the main substance of this study is dedicated to substantiating the above narrative that impels them, a narrative itself impelled by the need to explain observations of postmodernity made about charismatic renewal generally and the Movement specifically. Thus, it is to these observations this study first turns.

1.1.1 Initial Observations

Several general observations have been made about the postmodern nature of Pentecostal-Charismatic movements. Popular Christian writer Ajith Fernando writes, "The explosion of the charismatic movement is one expression of the postmodern thirst for spiritual experience to replace dry, ultrarationalistic religion."[1] Fernando notes that he has ar-

---

1. Fernando, *Sharing the Truth*, 25.

rived at this thesis by applying an idea gleaned from a set of lectures on Pentecostalism given by Brian Stiller.[2] Stiller, in the first of these, writes,

> Pentecostal ideas . . . [are] centered in a view that truth could be learned by way of experience and intuition, classic characteristics of post modernity. This heart impulse was deeply desirous of discovering life in the Spirit, beyond the cognitive search that characterized both liberal and conservative methodologies. . . . Ignoring epistemological assumptions of the Enlightenment, it is not a stretch to say they were postmodern. They acted as postmoderns, seventy years ahead of the mainstream culture. . . . It was a postmodern movement years ahead of its time.[3]

Fernando perhaps over-simplistically transposes Stiller's analysis of Pentecostalism's birth to charismatic renewal, which occurred in most mainline denominations decades later. Additionally, analyses like Stiller's, describing early Pentecostalism as antithetical to Enlightenment epistemology, have recently been found wanting.[4] However, it is telling that a casual observer such as Fernando feels able to make this leap in good faith based on his observations of charismatic renewal movements.

With greater insider experience Michael Green, a key leader in the Movement, makes similar observations. He opines,

> It is not hard to see that the charismatic movement has significant parallels with postmodernism and speaks powerfully to the postmodern scene. It too was a revolt—against the dryness of evangelical and Anglo-Catholic Christianity. Like postmodernism, it placed a high-value on community, and had a disdain for hierarchy and tradition. And like postmodernism it valued experience more than intellectual achievement. . . . This movement provided exactly the right emphasis, in the providence of God, for the times in which it was born.[5]

Here it is telling that a leader and theologian from within the Movement, who gained much of his understanding of charismatic renewal from within its specific context,[6] is moved by his experiences to speak about similarities with postmodernism with greater nuance—highlighting the

---

2. Fernando, *Sharing the Truth*, 35.
3. Stiller, "Growing up Pentecostal," 3–4.
4. See Poirier, "Pentecostalism."
5. Green, *When God Breaks In*, 136.
6. Green, *Adventure of Faith*, 261–70.

parallels between charismatic renewal and postmodernism without simply labelling the former as an expression of the latter, hinting that the relationship between the two is more complex than Fernando surmises.

The Church of England itself touched on this question with tantalizing uncertainty when its General Synod published in 1981 *The Charismatic Movement in the Church of England*, a report on the rapid rise of the charismatic movement among its ranks. Amid six identified causes, the report observes,

> It is arguable that the charismatic movement reflects a form of Christianised existentialism. . . . It would be hard to show that there has been a direct causal link, but the secular and charismatic trends have moved synchronously, and the less satisfactory expressions of the charismatic movement look remarkably like Christianised existentialism. If there is a seed of the rise of the movement in this, there is also cause for alarm.[7]

As will be seen later when looking at this report in greater depth, the existentialism understood here is perhaps better understood as postmodernism in a stricter and later definition.[8] The key question provoked by the simple word "if" points to the need for a deeper investigation of the nature of the possible relationship between the Movement and such postmodernism. However, such investigation has yet to be undertaken, leaving the self-awareness of both the Movement and the Church of England more widely poorer as a result.

Reflecting on the report's above observation, John Maiden suggests, "Charismatic renewal . . . may have little to do directly with Sartre, Derrida, and Foucault, but it undoubtedly reflected developing notions of authenticity from the mid-century."[9] The latter two philosophers are key postmodern ones,[10] and in this statement Maiden seems to posit that while there probably is no direct link between postmodern philosophy and the Movement, there is certainly a link between the Movement and a general cultural mood formed from such philosophical influences. However, this is posited without proof. Martyn Percy's similar but more scathing analysis of charismatic renewal is also without evidence; writing from his experience of charismatic renewal in the Church of England, Percey

---

7. Buchanan, *Charismatic Movement*, 41–42.
8. See §3.3.3.
9. Maiden, *Age of the Spirit*, 233.
10. Explored in §2.3.2 and §2.3.3, respectively.

says that renewal "holds up a mirror to postmodern trends: it copies and competes with healing movements, the New Age, materialism, pluralism, and, as I shall suggest later, contemporary eroticism."[11] Such a strong suggestion impels a need to investigate its veracity.

This book examines the question of the relationship between charismatic renewal and postmodernism by specifically examining the Charismatic Movement in the Church of England. Given the more general observations of Fernando and Green, the rationale for narrowing examination to this specific context is four-fold. Firstly, talk of Pentecostal-Charismatic renewal is best located in a local context due to its local variation that makes any generalized assessments difficult to perform without such grounding.[12] Conversely, results from localized studies not only help enable other such studies, but also allow some generalizable observations to be tentatively made. Secondly, such a study completes the unfinished line of analysis found in the 1981 General Synod report, which is important given the potential "alarm" it expressed might be warranted for both the Movement and the Church of England more widely if a clear relationship is established. Thirdly, the context of this writer himself, an ordained priest in the Church of England shaped by charismatic renewal, gives energy to such an investigation. This appreciates an approach that values subjective experience and import, congruent with the nature of a question dealing with postmodern ideas that contain such subjective emphases.[13] Lastly, though this question might also be fruitfully investigated in the context of charismatic renewal in other denominations, focusing on the Church of England both pays attention to how charismatic renewal in Britain first flowed from its experience of it[14] and also offers a local boundaried context with a size and local variation that enables rich analysis. Results from this will enable similar research questions to be asked of other contexts, both in Britain and further abroad, providing some initial hypotheses to them yet not claiming universal similarity.

Given the observations above, an initial question arises as to what Pentecostal-Charismatic scholarship has already said about this question. Sadly, there is a relative dearth of analysis to date in answer. As early

---

11. Percy, "Sweet Rapture," 79.

12. See Droogers, "Essentialist." The fruitfulness of this approach has been seen in numerous recent studies, e.g., Frestadius, *Pentecostal Rationality*; Alvarez, *Pentecostal Orthodoxy*.

13. See §1.2.1 for further discussion.

14. See §2.1.

as 1965, Michael Harper, one of the Movement's founding figures, traces its historical development and reasons for success yet does not mention any specific philosophical or sociological context as important. However, he does tantalizing opine, "The climate of opinion in Britain was against such a movement until the sixties. . . . [F]rom 1962 onwards there has been a steady increase in interest and support. Minds previously shut completely to this subject have become open."[15] Philosophical and related cultural movements may be part of the context for such change, yet Harper fails to engage in deeper analysis that elucidates this.

In more academic analysis, Peter Hocken looks at the factors behind the historical rise of the charismatic movement in Great Britain, which he divides into "Seeking Factors" that caused people to seek charismatic renewal and "Finding Factors" that enabled what was sought to be found.[16] However, none of these factors include philosophical or cultural climates in the church or nation, and other more general historical treatments of Pentecostal-Charismatic movements do not look at this aspect as well.[17] For example, in Simon Coleman's survey of global charismatic renewal, he explains, "One of the aims of this study of Protestant charismatics is to show that many features of their ideology and practice are well adapted to modern and even postmodern cultural conditions,"[18] yet surprisingly fails to investigate or specifically identify what is meant by "postmodern" in this aim. This dearth of analysis continues to the present day, with a recent work on charismatic renewal in both Britain and America opining on its back cover, yet failing to substantiate or investigate within, that "'charismatic renewal' or 'revival' was a key response to globalization, modernity and secularization."[19] As shall be seen, the question of a response to modernity is key to understanding the Movement's postmodern character, but here this is simply assumed as fact.

An exception to this dearth is Richard Quebedeaux's older work on the charismatic movement, which looks at reasons for its success and speaks of the spread of secularism leading to a desire for the "non-rational" as part of a continuing religious adherence that longs for experience.

15. Harper, *As at the Beginning*, 84.
16. Hocken, *Streams of Renewal*, 156.
17. For example, Walter Hollenweger's authoritative analysis examines every major reason the Church of England report highlights for the Movement's rise apart from the potential cultural-philosophical one. Hollenweger, *Pentecostalism*.
18. Coleman, *Globalisation of Charismatic Christianity*, 3.
19. Atherstone et al., *Transatlantic Charismatic Renewal*, 264.

He comments, "Charismatic Renewal, which clearly can be interpreted as a movement of countersecularization . . . owes its growth and spread, emergence and success, in part, to the new enthusiasm for religious experience in Western culture today.[20] Quebedeaux further explains the pervasiveness of an "Anti-Institutionalism" that inputted into the charismatic movement's success:

> The prevalence of such anti-institutional sentiment makes Charismatic Renewal attractive as a movement of spiritual unity in diversity that seeks to revitalize ("renew") existing church structures rather than to tear them down to build new ones.[21]

Without identifying them as such, these two trends of desire for the non-rational and anti-institutionalism are key postmodern characteristics, as will be seen in chapter 2. Herein, Quebedeaux comes closest to pertinent analysis for the needs of this question. Overall, however, greater depth is still needed, and the lack of appropriate scholarship to investigate this question adds additional impetus to this study, filling a noticeable void in Pentecostal-Charismatic studies.

1.1.2 Key Questions and Models

The above observations help suggest three key central research questions (CRQs) to be explored in this study, which will repeatedly energize and direct its investigation:

1. CRQ-1: To what extent does the Movement display postmodern characteristics?

2. CRQ-2: What models of relationship between the Movement and its wider cultural context help explain these characteristics?

3. CRQ-3: Are these characteristics caused by other trajectories and influences in the Movement, and whence do they come from?

While CRQ-3 is open-ended in nature, CRQ-1 and CRQ-2 are not, and require clear frames of analysis. The derivation of a frame to enable CRQ-1 to be answered via a Postmodern Analytic is the main subject of the next chapter. In investigating CRQ-2, which is especially energized by

---

20. Quebedeaux, *New Charismatics*, 181.
21. Quebedeaux, *New Charismatics*, 189.

the General Synod's concern noted in §1.1.1, three proposed models of relationship frame its enquiry:[22]

1. A *Direct Influence* model: postmodern thought is directly received into the Movement through its cultural context, and thus its postmodern characteristics formed under its influence.

2. A *Mutual Origins* model: the Movement reacts to forms of modernism in a similar fashion to the reaction to modernism found within postmodernism,[23] causing postmodern-looking characteristics to be generated within the Movement.

3. A *Cultural Catalysis*[24] model: the Movement's postmodern characteristics are encouraged in growth due to the positive appreciation of them by elements of the wider cultural context the Movement encounters.

Investigating CRQ-2 using these models requires a cautionary note; such models cannot fully represent the complexities of the Movement's lifeworld.[25] However, in a similar use of models, Stephen Bevans explains that models "are nevertheless *useful*. Though they do not capture, and do not pretend to do so, the whole nuanced reality that they explain, they do grasp a particular thrust which may very well be at the heart of . . . system."[26] Such is true for the nature of the models proposed here. The size, complexity, and variegation of the Movement's lifeworld necessitates an organizing ability to describe central dynamics within it, yet without purporting to describe it exactly and exhaustively.

---

22. This three-fold model approach is original to this study yet has resonances with other model-based approaches to the question of church and culture, most notably Stephen Bevans's work referenced below and throughout. Additionally, CRQ-3 covers the investigations of other potential relational dynamics not described by these three models in their non-exhaustive nature.

23. Both philosophical and cultural postmodernism; see discussion of §2.1 on how these are linked.

24. Here, an understanding of *catalysis* from the physical sciences is apposite. Catalysis of a chemical reaction by an outside agent speeds up that reaction, while the outside agent is not overall responsible for the initial reaction or altered by it. It is in this context that it is theorized that wider cultural elements sped up the growth of the Movement's postmodern characteristics while not being responsible for them in the first place.

25. This study understands the term "lifeworld" as used in the work of Mark Cartledge: a praxis stemming from an imbedded manner of being in the world that expresses wider worldviews and value systems. See §1.2.1 for further discussion.

26. Bevans, "Models," 187.

1.1.3 Key Definitions

Before exploring how these three questions might be answered, it is helpful to define some terms that will be used. This study will use several terms in a general manner as understood by wider scholarship. However, some key terms have a range of understandings, and it is useful here to clarify this study's usage of some of them.

1.1.3.1 *Charismatic*

The term "charismatic" is often used in combination with "Pentecostal" and indeed the two are sometimes seen as interchangeable. For example, Allan Anderson's authoritative work, *An Introduction to Pentecostalism*, is subtitled *Global Charismatic Christianity*.[27] However, the historical exploration of the Movement's birth undertaken in §3.1 shows the initial relative independence of it from Pentecostal influence, the two only coming into more significant conversation subsequently. Therefore, it is unhelpful to sublimate the term "charismatic" under "Pentecostal."

Work by Mark Hutchinson et al. has recently theorized five specific "traits" of charismatic renewal taking a non-phenomenological approach, which is helpful for this study's purposes given overlapping areas of focus.[28] Firstly, *primitivism*, an emphasis on the recovery of the charismatic heritage of the early church focused on the activity and work of the Holy Spirit. Secondly, *emergence*, emphasizes propagating this recovery to the wider church for its greater good. Thirdly, *experimentalism*, by which charismatics infer truths from experiences of the Spirit's work, voice, and leading, which comes into creative conversation with more objectively based theology. Fourthly, *expressionism* emphasizes the expression of personal spiritual dynamics in a holistic and often physical or emotional way. Lastly, *presentism* seeks to focus on what the Spirit is doing now, today.

This five-fold model helps to circumscribe some of what is meant by the term "charismatic" and enables analysis of present-day charismatic movements discerned through the inhabitation of these traits—especially when they are not easily distinguishable via self-identification.

---

27. Anderson, *Introduction to Pentecostalism*. Anderson discusses this sublimation on page 157.

28. Hutchinson et al., "Introduction," 14–18.

Yet this explicitly non-phenomenological approach[29] has weaknesses. Mark Cartledge, a prominent interlocutor in this study, defines the essence of charismatic spirituality as "encountering the Spirit,"[30] which, if true, implies that something of the phenomenological aspect of this needs to be included in a definition. The solution this study takes is to notice the word "charismatic" itself, whereupon its etymological origin, *charismata*, speaks of the primacy of expectation of the reception of God's grace through spiritual gifts mentioned in the New Testament (NT).[31] Such a mode of definition has recently been given by Helen Collins,[32] and here is not proposed here in opposition to the above five-fold model, but together with it. Indeed, emphasis on the charismata fits each of the five traits, uniting them: spiritual gifts that are to be recovered, released in the wider body of the church, and often reveal the speaking voice of God, accompanied by physical and emotional manifestations, bringing clarity to the "now" work of God. Thus, though charismatic renewal is not defined by spiritual gifts, nor is it here defined without reference to them. As a result, this study locates the "charismatic" in an integration of Hutchinson et al.'s non-phenomenological approach with a phenomenological approach that focuses on the charismata.

1.1.3.2 Postmodern

The unresolved argument about what defines postmodernism is extensive and is discussed in chapter 2—which discerns what postmodernism in an ecclesial lifeworld looks like. This study argues for a philosophically rather than culturally defined postmodernism in §2.1, the narrative of which finds a subsequent four-fold definition in §2.4: (1) in contrast to the foundationalistic epistemology of modernism, a non-foundational epistemology that values non-rational means of knowledge; (2) a splitting of signifiers from signified in language; (3) a new concentration on micronarratives together with macronarratives; and (4) an emphasis on the value of community as opposed to just the individual. This definition of postmodernism is one directed towards ecclesial context; it is not an

---

29. Hutchinson et al., "Introduction," 14.
30. Cartledge, *Encountering the Spirit*, 16.
31. Especially the "gift lists" of Rom 12:6–8; 1 Cor 12:7–11, 28–30.
32. Collins, *Charismatic Christianity*, 10.

objective universal definition—which would be to misunderstand postmodernism's inherent nature that argues against such a possibility.

1.1.3.3 Experience and Emotion

In the analysis of the Movement's lifeworld, it will become clear that different views are held about the epistemological significances of experiential and emotional aspects of an individual's life within the Movement. The two from the lifeworld perspective are distinguishable in the writings and comments of those considered, yet within wider discussions, the delineation between the two is not straightforward.[33] In this study, *experience* is understood in epistemological terms to correlate to an individual's knowledge and understanding gained through later reflection (often theological) on actions and events that occur either in the personal or corporate context. Conversely, *emotion* is understood to speak of the immediate, often sudden, cognition based on feelings such as peace, joy, love, fear, sadness, etc. Though the two may overlap, as initial emotions become part of later experiential processing, the difference drawn here is temporal.

1.2 INVESTIGATIVE METHODOLOGY

1.2.1 Cartledge's Spirit-Dialectic Model

To investigate the CRQs, this study chooses to employ a version of Mark Cartledge's Spirit-dialectic model, as outlined in *Practical Theology: Charismatic and Empirical Perspectives*,[34] yet modified for the needs of this particular study. Here, Swinton explains that, unlike other fields, "we only come to know what practical theology is as we do it, and we all do it differently,"[35] and Cartledge agrees with such an analysis, speaking of a flexibility of approach that is "heuristic not absolute,"[36] implicitly welcoming adaption of his practical theology model.

---

33. Cartledge, *Mediation of the Spirit*, 29, 168. In his summative conclusion, Cartledge proposes that practical theology has failed to explore these areas and needs to, implying his contribution is not seen as definitive.

34. Cartledge, *Practical Theology*, 11–39.

35. Swinton, "What Comes Next?," 164 (emphasis in original).

36. Cartledge, "Can Theology Be Practical?"

There are several reasons why this methodological model is apt for this study's purposes. Firstly, as an inhabitant of charismatic renewal, from the beginning of his methodology's construction, Cartledge seeks a hermeneutic that is helpfully located within a charismatic spirituality which "provides the theological and spiritual milieux in which and from which it functions in a critical way."[37] In application, this approach emphasizes that God is involved in theological enquiry, drawing people into Triune relationship with himself such that "trust is not simply doxological and theological (orthodoxy), nor simply action based (orthopraxy), but is also affective (orthopathy)," coming about via a dialectic relationship with God that enables the discovery of truth to be God's gift to the church in a journey of "search-encounter-transformation."[38]

Cartledge's dialectic methodology specifically focuses on the movement between the poles of two dialectics. One dialectic pays attention to a methodological requirement of this study to notice postmodern critiques that adjure the need for a space for the interrelation between subject matter, researcher, and wider theological context, some of which will be explored in §2.3. In an open and non-realized dialectic, research moves between the two poles of "lifeworld" and "system." By "lifeworld" Cartledge means a praxis that denotes a "way-of-being-in-the-world that is part and parcel of someone's worldview, beliefs and values,"[39] which denotes the concrete setting of the circumstance. This stands in tension with the "system," which is the confession constellation of beliefs and values in a tradition that is historically and culturally mediated, and trans-contextual.[40] Borrowing ideas from Anthony Thiselton and Jürgen Habermas, a dialectic interaction back and forth between these two poles avoids the error of practical theologians who either stay in the horizons of the lifeworld or sublimate the system into it. Though an appropriate postmodern critique could be levelled against the metanarrative nature of the trans-contextual system in this, Cartledge rebuffs this by appealing to the fact that such critiques are often a form of metanarrative claim themselves, thus finding space to perform research within a postmodern context.[41]

---

37. Cartledge, *Practical Theology*, 4.
38. Cartledge, *Practical Theology*, 19.
39. Cartledge, *Practical Theology*, 17.
40. Cartledge, *Practical Theology*, 18. Here "lifeworld" is in opposition to "trans-contextual," indicating that the contextual is included in the idea of "lifeworld."
41. Cartledge, *Practical Theology*, 24. Cf. §2.3.1.

As will be seen, Michal Foucault's rejection of a disinterested knower is an important aspect to this study's postmodern focus[42]—a rejection that enjoins that its methodology takes into account the personal insight of the researcher, namely this author, yet not to the extent that it cannot be objectively critiqued. Cartledge's methodology does exactly this by adding to the first dialectic a second, which is the incorporation of a non-realized faith-driven dialectic tension which seeks to include the life of "The Practical Theologian" at one end, and the "Charismatic Spirituality" to which they relate on the other. This dialectic presumes that "the person in the theological tradition is also a member of a doxological and missiological community: the local church . . . which supports and facilitates charismatic spirituality,"[43] and which receives the insights and understanding of the theologian while simultaneously investigating and critiquing them, resulting in dialectical growth of the Kingdom of God. This second dialectical dynamic is an apposite gift to this study's telos—which is one of the church's life directed back towards it, aiming to feed into its scholarship and praxis in a developed response to the observations of §1.1.1.

Cartledge helpfully adds granular detail in how to apply his methodological proposal to specific contexts. Firstly, he explains that movement back and forth between the two poles of this second dialectic generates a triad of specific questions to be attended to amid the study's journey:

> (1) What is the Holy Spirit doing in this context?; (2) how does this activity relate to the work of the Holy Spirit revealed in Scripture; (3) what is the Spirit saying to the church (Revelation 2:11)?[44]

Secondly, Cartledge helpful illustrates how the outworking of both dialectics simultaneously can be practically diagrammed as motion within two sets of orthogonal axes, with the journey of search-encounter-transformation occurring within this space.[45]

---

42. See §2.3.3.
43. Cartledge, *Practical Theology*, 26.
44. Cartledge, *Practical Theology*, 30.
45. Cartledge, *Practical Theology*, 28.

FIGURE 1. MARK CARTLEDGE'S SPIRIT-DIALECTIC METHODOLOGY.

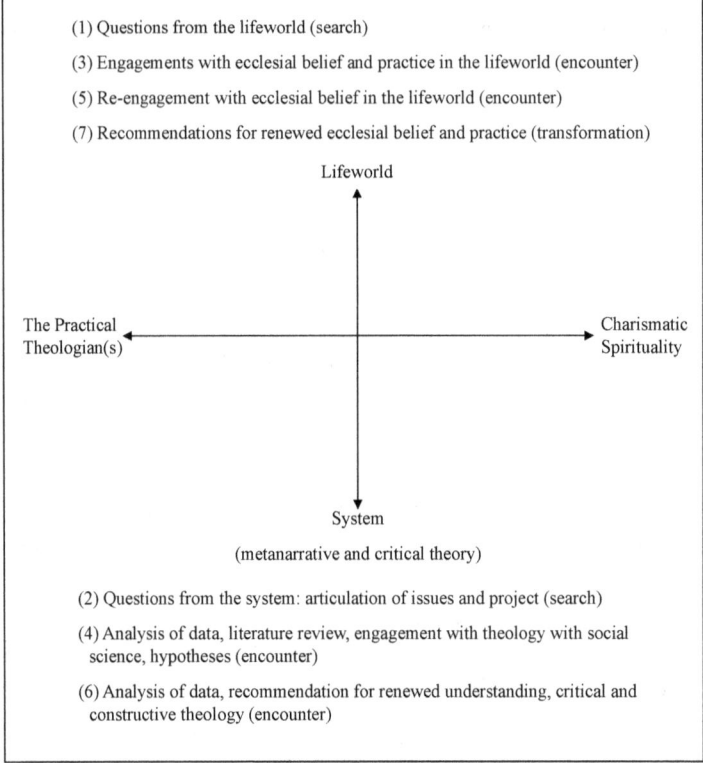

1.2.2 Adaption of Cartledge's Methodology

Cartledge's methodology clearly fulfils the basic requirements for an employable methodology appropriate for this study's task. However, there are important modifications needed for it to be fully usable. Firstly, Cartledge sees his approach as part of the empirical strand of practical theology,[46] which is "theology arising from contemporary practice, as it is explored and is tested by means of empirical research methods."[47] Thus his understanding of practical theology does not allow for an investigation of anything but present-tense practices and realities. However, in doing empirical research into a phenomenon as broad and rich as the Movement, there is a need to understand it on its own terms, a *movement*—which

---

46. Cartledge, "Practical Theology," 278.
47. Cartledge, *Practical Theology*, 269.

indicates the need to analyze historical progression over time, especially in its historical context.[48] Here, Gijsbert Dingemans notes the general concern of some "practical theologians [who] think that the empirical approach does not pay sufficient attention to the historical backgrounds of churches and individual believers," failing to access what lies "behind" religious acts.[49] Exemplifying this, in a similar ground-up Pentecostal-Charismatic study, Simo Frestadius comments, "Methodologically it is insufficient for Pentecostal philosophical theologians to talk about Pentecostal rationality without firmly rooting it in the historical practice of Pentecostal communities";[50] the same is true here. Though it is possible to analyze the Movement's lifeworld in its present or near-present tense alone, such an approach is insufficient given the rich historical contexts and influences on present practice.

A second modification is needed in considering the appropriate "system" for this study. Cartledge's method allows for *any* appropriate theological system to be employed and does not define a "correct" system as such. It therefore potentially suffers by limiting the contextually variant elements in practical theological research solely to the lifeworld side of the dialectic and allowing something potentially abstracted from it to be its system conversation partner. However, the breadth of possibilities this freedom enables is of benefit to this study, as the central research questions can define the system to be employed for this study. Congruent to the postmodern orientation of this question, the postmodern critiques of power explored in §2.3 mitigate against using an imposed external doctrinal system to analyze the lifeworld. The system must stem from the crucial first question of the Movement's postmodern character (CRQ-1) from which the others take their cue, and therefore must be rooted in the question of postmodernism in action in the ecclesial sphere, thus creating a congruent interface between the Movement's lifeworld and the postmodern orientation of this study by allowing the shaping of methodology by what is being studied.

This study therefore must first define its own system as a starting point rather than choose a pre-existing one, an *ecclesial postmodernism*, which constructs a clear set of criteria from first principles that enables appropriate lifeworld analysis. It defines what postmodernism could and would look like in the ecclesial context in order to analyze the postmodern

48. See §3.1 on the contextualized situatedness of the description "movement."
49. Dingemans, "Practical Theology," 88–89.
50. Frestadius, *Pentecostal Rationality*, 217.

character of the Movement, and this system must be first constructed before being used, which takes up the majority of chapter 2. In the dialectical methodology of Cartledge employed here, this system is expanded in nature in chapter 4 to include a broader set of postmodern manifestations to be searched for in further interrogation of the lifeworld as a result of "critical dialogue with the contributions of the social sciences,"[51] whereby this postmodern-sensitive methodology values insights from a plurality of disciplines to richly analyze a lifeworld.

One last adaptation needed addresses a weakness of Cartledge's methodology that lies in its horizontal dialectic and the triad of questions which cover the pneumatological aspects important to the investigation. For Cartledge, such questions are not worked into the stages of the investigation but "free float" over it, running the danger of missing their vital contribution to it. Here, instead, these questions will be explicitly addressed in the last stage of this study's dialectical methodology, as the work of the Spirit is not to be separated from the transformative effect of the Spirit if this methodology is to be true to the charismatic spirituality that Cartledge highlights. Thus, this study's last chapter explicitly explores what the Holy Spirit may have been doing through observed insights into the lifeworld in a critical manner. This indeed is a methodological structure that Cartledge uses in his later work, *The Mediation of the Spirit*,[52] suggesting that he later realized the same weakness and sought to crystalize these questions in a structurally comparable manner.

1.2.3 The Journey of this Study

Incorporating the above modifications into a heuristic shaping of Cartledge's methodology, the structure of this study is as follows with reference to his 7-stage schema.[53] This current chapter begins its "search" phase and explores "(1) Question from the lifeworld (search)," namely the observations made in contemporary literature of the postmodern nature of charismatic renewal, resulting three questions to be answered in this study (CRQs), and proposing models of the relationship between

---

51. Cartledge, *Testimony in the Spirit*, 15.

52. Where Cartledge offers an end personal "manifesto" to practical theology, both as the series he produces this work in may require—"Pentecostal Manifestos"—but also in fulfilment of the full integration of the horizontal dimension of his methodological dialectic. Cartledge, *Mediation of the Spirit*, 167–70.

53. Cartledge, *Practical Theology*, 28–30.

renewal and postmodernism. Within this search phase, an appropriate research methodology is discerned—Cartledge's Spirit-Dialectical approach itself.

Chapter 2, "Postmodernism in the Charismatic Church," explores "(2) Questions from the system: articulation of issues and project (search)," and derives a system of *ecclesial postmodernism* to be used through the creation of a set of criteria by which an ecclesial lifeworld can be described as postmodern in character. Chapter 3, "Exploring the Charismatic Movement in the Church of England," moves on to "(3) Engagement with ecclesial belief and practice in the lifeworld," which here is specifically a historical investigation into the Movement's lifeworld that aims to map its key thrusts and create elements of a working hypothesis that begins to answer the CRQs in a preliminary fashion, which acts as a guide to more in-depth analysis that follows.

Returning to the system pole of the dialectic, chapter 4, "Sociological and Anthropological Insights," moves the methodology on to "(4) . . . engagement of theology with social science, hypotheses," whereby the system of *ecclesial postmodernism* is expanded by critical dialogue with relevant sociological and anthropological research, while simultaneously contextualizing and therein further substantiating conclusions reached at the end of chapter 3 to create a full working hypothesis to bring to a more detailed lifeworld examination that follows.

From this hypothesis, the next three chapters move to "(5) Re-engagement with ecclesial belief and practice in the lifeworld," engaging in a phase of substantive qualitative research to investigate the validity of this hypothesis and to create clear final answers to the CRQs of this study. Chapter 5, "Postmodernism and the Early Movement," examines the Movement's early lifeworld through the examination of the entire written corpora of two of its key early leaders: Michael Harper and David Watson. Chapter 6, "Postmodernism and the Later Movement I: Postmodern Characteristics," continues this methodological stage and concentrates on analyzing semi-structured interviews conducted with a range of leaders from the later and contemporary life of the Movement to make conclusions about its postmodern character in answer to CRQ-1, fulfilling the first part of "(6) *Analysis of data*, recommendations for renewed understanding." Chapter 7, "Postmodernism in the Later Movement II: Models and Trajectories," concludes the investigation into the Movement's later and contemporary lifeworld, analyzing the aforementioned semi-structured interviews to answer CRQ-2 and 3, discerning the models of relationship between the Movement and culture, and its premodern impulse in reaction to modernism. This completes the first part of "(6) *Analysis of data.*"

Chapter 8, "Conclusions and Challenges," completes "(6) Analysis of data, *recommendations for renewed understanding, critical and constructive theology*" by bringing the answers of the CRQs into dialogue with the initial observations of §1.1.1. From this, the study moves into the final stage of "transformation," "(7) Recommendation for renewed ecclesial belief and practice." Questions of the work of the Holy Spirit in the Movement's life considering the conclusions of this study are explored to explicitly satisfy the "Practical Theologian-Charismatic Spirituality" dialectic of exploration, as well as how the results of this study help transform the Movement's ongoing praxis.

1.3 PRACTICAL RESEARCH METHODS

Chapters 5–7 of this book concentrate on using qualitative research methods to intensively investigate the Movement's lifeworld. These methods hinge on the inter-disciplinary approach that Cartledge's methodology enables, which he speaks of as more appropriately "intra-disciplinary," the "idea of borrowing concepts, methods and techniques from other disciplines and integrating them into another science."[54] Thus, while these are not specifically theological apparatuses, they are co-opted for the theological endeavor. While this finds initial expression in chapter 3's usage of interviews with David MacInnes and Colin Buchanan to help understand historical events, more substantive usage occurs in this study's deeper qualitative research phase: chapter 5's usage of documentary content analysis and chapter 6's and 7's usage of semi-structured interviews with later Movement leaders. The specific usage of these specific methods in this latter analytical phase of the study requires some justification.

Here, the means of investigating the Movement must fit the questions being asked of its lifeworld. The CRQs and relatedly proposed models do not lend themselves to *quantitative* methods; ideas such as "character," "trajectories of movement," and "influences" do not easily beget numerical analysis, especially given the lifeworld complexity of investigating a charismatic movement in its national breadth, even if

---

54. Cartledge, *Practical Theology*, 16.

confined to one denomination.⁵⁵ In this study's constructivist approach, the emphasis is on gaining an understanding of the Movement, rather than objective universal and generalizable knowledge, creating space for non-quantitative description and analysis. Thus, the methods employed are *qualitative* rather than *quantitative* in nature.⁵⁶

The qualitative methodologies employed in this study focus on analyzing the thoughts of selected key leaders in the Movement as this enables a boundedness that makes the research feasible in terms of source investigation, as well as generating a rich set of sources for analysis. The alternative of focusing on the Movement's participants, rather than leaders, is appealing. However, the lack of participant testimony from the earlier Movement precludes this possibility given the detail level needed for analysis. Relatedly, interviewing such participants today to generate this data suffers from the length of time that has passed, which combines with a probable lack of attention to the issues under investigation compared to leaders and instigators within the Movement. Simon Western suggests leaders are cultural avatars, both carrying and transmitting cultures, such that "leaders shape culture, and culture shapes leaders."⁵⁷ If true, this means a focus on key leaders allows some "normal" participant aspects to be accessed, ameliorating some of the loss of participant data, while also expositing important influences transmitted to the Movement through their leadership influence.

To investigate the Movement's six-decade period, it is helpful to bifurcate it into an early and later Movement, choosing appropriate methods to apply to each. This has the advantage of enabling dynamics within the Movement to be tracked over time until the present day by comparing the results of the analyses of the two periods. As there is no historical moment clearly splitting the Movement into two halves, inevitably overlap between these periods will occur in analysis, which is helpful in enabling continuous larger narratives to be described, free from sharp discontinuities.

For the early Movement, since many of its first leaders apart from David MacInnes have died, a rich approach is enabled through documentary analysis of literature produced by that period as a record of their

---

55. Cartledge's usage of quantitative methods gravitates towards investigations that have smaller geographic bounds, as seen in each of his studies in Cartledge, *Narratives and Numbers*.

56. Swinton and Mowat, *Theology and Qualitative Research*, 70–71.

57. Western, *Leadership*, 111.

thought. Choosing an interview approach with just MacInnes as a subject would not allow a rich enough analysis, only providing one perspective. Additionally, as indicated in his biographical note in §6.1, his most significant leadership in the context of charismatic renewal came mainly later in his ministry as rector of St. Aldates, therefore acting more appropriately as a source for analyzing the later Movement.

Two key leaders of the early Movement are chosen for analysis of their literary corpora: Michael Harper and David Watson. As explored in chapter 5, they are unparalleled figures in the early Movement in terms of literary output and, arguably, influence. Focusing on these two leaders brings helpful contrast: Harper a leader of a larger network of early renewal, while Watson of a key localized center of it in action, bringing universality and specificity through the analysis of both. Their corpora are large enough to generate thick analysis; indeed, consideration of more than these two leaders' corpora would become unmanageable in the bounds of this study because of their size.

Given how categories for analysis are generated through the earlier stages of this study's dialectical methodology, the documentary method selected for the analysis of the early Movement is specifically that of Content Analysis, with other potential methods being less helpful by contrast.[58] The categories used in the Content Analysis of Harper and Watson's literary works in chapter 5 are found in appendix 2.

For the later Movement, many of its key leaders can, however, be directly interviewed. Despite the strengths of the literary approach, an interview approach is preferable to an analysis of their writings, as specific questions generated by the enquiry trajectory of the CRQs can be asked of them and their praxis—preferable to gleaning answers to such questions from material not specifically written to answer them. Reasons for the selection of the nine leaders interviewed are given in §6.1,[59] which hinge on the variety of contexts and perspectives they encompass.

The method of interview used is that of the semi-structured interview, which meets key epistemological challenges raised in using interviews that are pertinent to this study's postmodern focus.[60] It does this by treading a line that gives space to explore the importance of subjectivities

---

58. For discussion of these methods, see Silverman, *Interpreting Qualitative Data*, 114–43. See also Padgett, *Qualitative Methods*, 31–53.

59. David MacInnes, David Pytches, Mary Pytches, Sandy Millar, Graham Cray, Charlie Cleverly, Alison Morgan, Nicky Gumbel, and Christian Selvaratnam.

60. See §§2.3–2.4.

peculiar to the interviewee—appreciating their understanding of reality and comparing it to others—and also helping interviewees feel that they are in control of the main flow of what emerges, while at the same time using a defined structure that enables a thorough investigation of the matters to be explored.[61]

In practical outworking, the categories used in the Content Analysis of chapter 5 are transferable to subsequent semi-structured interviews to formulate first-level lines of questioning into each of them. Through this, analyses of the early and later lifeworlds of the Movement can be compared, despite differing qualitative methods being employed to investigate them. However, following secondary questions in such a semi-structured interview approach—articulated in a form which yields rich answers in the interview context—are more open-ended in nature, allowing for unseen insights to emerge. In essence this entails targeted initial questions which are followed by non-targeted follow-up questions—the latter held flexibly, able to be dropped or replaced depending on the answers to the former.

With all this considered, this study now proceeds to its next stage, investigating ecclesial postmodernism.

---

61. For a deeper discussion about the methodological choices selected in this study, see Patel, "Postmodernism," 30–37.

2

Postmodernism in the Charismatic Church

To speak about the postmodern nature of a renewal movement, language is first needed to circumscribe what is meant by postmodernism in the church context. Herein, this chapter focuses on the transcontextual system pole of the dialectical investigation of the Movement's postmodern nature, deriving a base *ecclesial postmodernism* system via the creation of an Analytic tool. This Postmodern Analytic tool is comprised of four minimal criteria of postmodernism, and the wider system is their manifestation in the ecclesial sphere.

Justification will be made for the specifically philosophically derived nature of the Analytic from the work of four key postmodern thinkers combined with an exploration of the historical development of postmodern thought. The manifestations of the Analytic's criteria as a base system are elucidated through conversation with relevant wider Pentecostal-Charismatic scholarship that addresses ecclesial postmodernism. Though this base system finds further expansion in chapter 4 through dialogue with sociological and anthropological insights, it first enables an initial historical exploration of the Movement's lifeworld through dialectical conversation with it in the next chapter.

2.1 DEFINING POSTMODERNISM

To answer CRQ-1, and the other subsequent CRQs that take their cue from its answer, a clear transcontextual system must be created that enables an analysis of the Movement's lifeworld postmodern character. However, this runs into definitional problems of what postmodernism is, which need to be resolved. The variously used terms *P/postmodern*, *P/post-modern*, *P/postmodernism*, and *P/postmodernist* are recognized to be hard to define because of their historical emergence as catch-all terms for several different twentieth-century movements of thought in the arts, architecture, and literary theory, and more specific usage in philosophy—especially in epistemology and metaphysics. Its popular cultural usage in the 1980s and beyond stems from a disparate heritage of academic usage.

The term *postmodern* may have found its first modern usage in its Spanish cognate in the 1930s.[1] Its first English usage is found in literary theory of the 1950s and 1960s,[2] climaxing with the publication in 1972 of *A Journal of Postmodern Literature and Culture*.[3] Simultaneously, the mass vandalism of the ultra-modernist Pruit-Igoe housing project in St. Louis, Missouri, in the same year has also been seen as the explosive event that symbolized the "Death of Modernism/Rise of Post-Modernism."[4] Nevertheless, the more commonly recognized moment when the term became more widely accepted occurred in the publishing of Jean-François Lyotard's 1979 report commissioned by the Quebec government on the condition of knowledge in modern societies, *The Postmodern Condition: A Report on Knowledge*. Here, Lyotard contends that paradigm transformations have occurred in the major fields of science, literature, and the arts, which have an epistemological basis that can be categorized as postmodern. Lyotard defines his usage of the term postmodern in simplest form as the "incredulity towards metanarratives."[5]

However, the term's more varied usage before Lyotard's report, and subsequent usage in other ways, negates such a simple summary. Millard Erickson, expands on the difficulties of elucidation and suggests a way forward:

> There is no uniform, consistent, or thoroughly worked-out scheme of thought such that it could in any way be called a system.... That is not the nature of postmodernism... [instead] what we will attempt to describe in this work is a collection of

---

1. This and subsequent literary development of the term is discussed in Anderson, *Origins of Postmodernity*.
2. Huyssen, "Mapping the Postmodern," 44.
3. Anderson, *Origins of Postmodernity*, 15.
4. Anderson, *Origins of Postmodernity*, 24.
5. Lyotard, *Postmodern Condition*, xxiii–xxv.

elements, loosely clustered, but nonetheless lending their character to the movement.⁶

Such elements have one commonality, their rejection or critique of modernism. "They share in common the realization that there has been a fundamental shift within modern western culture. We have moved beyond and/or away from the culture identified with modernism."⁷ Hence, the simplest understanding of postmodernism is a negative one of critique and negation of modernism. However, such alone would be unhelpful in looking for positively distinguishable postmodern characteristics in a lifeworld. As noted in §1.1.3.2, this pragmatic need is a controlling paradigm for definitional work here given the multiplicity of options available. Further elucidation is needed.

Related to these difficulties, Keith Tester highlights the problem of what words to use, commenting that there is much at stake in the presence or absence of a hyphen in this discussion. Should the terms be "Post-modern" or "Postmodern," "Post-modernism" or "Postmodernism"? The absence of a hyphen implies a clear distinction between what is being discussed and modernity, while its presence implies it can only exist in a complex relationship with and from it. Tester posits that the latter is true, and therefore the hyphenated forms of the key terms are to be preferred.⁸ Similarly, Stephen Best and Douglas Keller commend speaking of a postmodern "turn" in modernism, rather than a departure from it, explaining, "Postmodern discourse as intensification of critical tendencies of such modern figures as Nietzsche, Heidegger, or Dewey rather than as a leap into a whole new mode of discourse altogether."⁹ Nevertheless, they speak of "four main thematic similarities that break with distinct modern concepts and themes,"¹⁰ indicating that in practice there is some clear measure of separability and distinction.

Here, given the need to analyze the Movement's specifically postmodern character, it is most helpful to talk in terms of such separable discontinuities with modernism, and in this vein the historical mapping work of §2.2–4 below enables some measure of separable postmodern

---

6. Erickson, *Truth or Consequences*, 14.

7. Van Gelder, "Postmodernism," 415–16.

8. Tester, *Life and Times*, 28–29. Hence Amos Yong, in deliberate contradistinction, uses the term "late modern" rather than "postmodern." Yong, "Radically Orthodox."

9. Best and Kellner, *Postmodern Turn*, 25.

10. Best and Kellner, *Postmodern Turn*, 255–58. Cf. Snyder, "Translator's Introduction"; Harvey, *Condition of Postmodernity*, 116.

characteristics to be defined and looked for in contradistinction to modernistic ones. Thus, the terms *postmodern, postmodernism,* and *postmodernity* will be used. However, they will be used as lower-case terms, to recognize that such terms are used with the understanding that the postmodern always exists with the modern in a complex relationship, and without a standalone identity apart from it.

A further definitional decision needed is whether the primary framing context of postmodernism should be understood as philosophical or cultural. Graham Cray, in his interview analyzed later in this study, argues for the latter understanding—that postmodernism should be understood on the grounds of its cultural manifestation—which would be in keeping with the term's earliest usage before Lyotard.[11] However, such an approach does not necessarily help understand *how* such manifestations arise and therefore is unhelpful in understanding how they might have arisen in the Movement, part of this study's enquiry.

A better approach is found by analyzing the philosophical roots behind cultural manifestation, and from this to derive a system that yields richer results when brought into conversation with a lifeworld. Supporting such an approach, sociologist Pierre Bourdieu argues that the various elements in an intellectual field participate in and influence the larger cultural field and consciousness in a "trickle-down" nature.[12] Fritz Ringer points out that while the role of secondary interpreters and the cross-fertilization and influence of other elements cannot be ignored in such a process, the direction of influence from primary thinkers to culture remains intact.[13] Similarly, Francis Schaeffer argues that current cultural phenomena especially reflect preceding philosophic movements of thought. The intellectual mapping might not be direct, and context shapes the cultural expressions of ideas strongly, but the link between cultural expression and philosophical antecedents can be traced through movement along the three axes of geography, class, and the arts.[14] Thus, James Smith argues that to understand postmodernism at any point of any of these axes of influence, one needs to "return back to philosophy itself in order to understand postmodernity."[15]

11. See also Cray, *Postmodern Culture*.
12. Bourdieu, "Intellectual Field," 91.
13. Ringer, "Intellectual Field, Intellectual History," 277.
14. Schaeffer, *Schaeffer Trilogy*, 234–35.
15. Smith, *Who's Afraid of Postmodernism?*, 21.

Such an approach is seen in the work of John Milbank, who concludes from the written works of philosophers such as Hegel, Nietzsche, Foucault, Heidegger, Lyotard, and others, "postmodernism, as represented by these texts, articulates itself as, first absolute historicism, second as an ontology of difference, and third as ethical nihilism."[16] However, Milbank does not show how he derives his triad of articulation from their works, giving little confidence in his application of them. A better approach is modelled by Bradley Noel in his work on Pentecostal and postmodern hermeneutics, who discusses the wider philosophical background to the rise of philosophical postmodernism, and the thought of key postmodern philosophers, leading to reflections on unique postmodern themes.[17] Noel's purposes are more descriptive than analytic, and he does not construct a means of discerning postmodernism's existence in given contexts. Nevertheless, his approach highlights how a robust approach that traces historical developments through key philosophical figures and texts is needed, the narrative of which enables a rich distinguishability between modernistic and postmodernistic characteristics in an ecclesial context.

2.2 THE JOURNEY TOWARDS POSTMODERNISM

2.2.1 The Background of Modernity

There are various narratives of modernity and the related idea of "the Enlightenment" that can be constructed; as will be seen, Foucault would argue this is not unrelated to the power dynamics underlying their creation.[18] Additionally, John Poirier has recently critiqued a lack of awareness of geographic variation in possible narratives—that American, French, and English stories are all differentiable.[19] Nevertheless, driven by a methodological need to construct an ecclesial system that uncovers postmodernisms in the Movement's lifeworld, these critiques are both acknowledged, yet partially ameliorated by the fact that the focus is on *postmodernism*, to which the background of modernity provides a reference frame. Thus, some measure of generalization of narrative is allowed

---

16. Milbank, *Theology and Social Theory*, 278.
17. Noel, "Pentecostal," 44–83.
18. See §2.3.3.
19. Poirier, "Pentecostalism," 503–4.

if greater specificity is employed when postmodernism begins to emerge from it.

In such a generalized narrative,[20] the Western modernistic worldview, "modernism," sprung from the Renaissance period of the fourteenth to seventeenth centuries. Recovering Greco-Roman philosophical ideals, humanity—and specifically its rational capacity—became the dominant locus of understanding. This can partially be seen as a rejection of medieval scholasticism, which often studied previous learning without attempts to innovate beyond it. In this "humanism," the modern scientific method emerged as the key means of accessing knowledge of reality, which assumed a regular and rational basis to both the universe and the human mind, such that new information about the former could be comprehended by the latter through repeatable experimentation. Thereby, Francis Bacon (1561–1626) explained that as the universe was tamed and brought under humanity's power through knowledge of it, a flourishing society results. Hence, *scientia potestas est*, "knowledge is power."

From this, the period later known as the Enlightenment, c .1650–1800,[21] saw an anthropocentric paradigm shift in Western thought. Important underpinning work by René Descartes (1596–1650) created a system of certain acquisition of knowledge based on the one irreducible fact of reality, the subject's existence: *cogito ergo sum*, "I think, therefore I am." Augmenting this came scientific corroboration from scientists such as Johannes Kepler (1571–1630), Galileo Galilei (1564–1642), and preeminently Isaac Newton (1642–1727). Newton's theories described an orderly universe comprehensible and predictable through human reason and observation alone. This confirmed the "empiricist" proposition of David Hume (1711–76), that objects and knowledge of objects are identical, as such knowledge could be reliably tested to see if it was accurate in Newton's ordered system.

The consequence of this period was a perceived human utopian trajectory of self-betterment via increasing comprehension of the universe. Reason as arbitrator of truth was more than just another human faculty, as the rational structure of the human mind cohered with and mapped

---

20. For cross-reference throughout this section, see the historical analysis found in Grenz, *Primer on Postmodernism*, 58.

21. Exact beginning and end points are debatable, but, as shall be seen, Kant's work in 1781 is a helpful pinnacle that also indicates the first stages of failure of Enlightenment ideals.

the same rationality present in all reality, resulting in an unadulterated flow of pure truth. Hence the period was also later known as "the Age of Reason." For a Postmodern Analytic, such themes imply that the critiques of rationality, individuality, and powerful controlling metanarratives of hope or "progress" are of key concern.

2.2.2 Kant and the First Existentialists

Karl Barth comments that Immanuel Kant (1724–1804) represents the spirit of the Enlightenment which has "come to terms with itself; it therefore knows where it stands, and it has thus acquired humility."[22] In *A Critique of Pure Reason* (1781), Kant applied reason to the age of reason itself, arguing, contra Hume, that it is impossible to know an object as it is. The human mind interprets all information of what he called *noumenal* objects along pre-formed categories of the mind, giving rise to a *phenomenal* knowledge of the object, which is always non-identical to the noumenal. This first fracture of Enlightenment axioms would be widened by philosophers over the next two centuries; the idea of the mind's active part in the knowledge of reality, rather than its passive intuition of it, opened the door for subjectivity and a dissolving of the objective, eventually leading to postmodern ideas.

Erickson identifies Søren Kierkegaard (1813–55) and Friedrich Nietzsche (1844–1900) as two key nineteenth-century philosophers integral to this.[23] For Kierkegaard, the objective approach of empiricism negates the importance of subjective truth where existence is situated. Because the objective approach can never reach complete certainty, it does not enable decisions on how to act based on reality; instead, actions must cohere with the subjective truth of an individual that has priority over objective truth, while retaining relationship with it. Thus, truth's locus shifts from object to subject, as what is believed to be true is more important than what is perceived to be objectively true. Such lies at the basis of what was later termed "existentialism."

In Nietzsche, existentialism developed in a sharper subjective manner. Arguing that the world is made up of fragments that differ completely, the human mind's active role in knowledge acquisition constructs concepts to force onto things to name and describe them, destroying

---

22. Barth, *Protestant Theology*, 254.
23. Erickson, *Truth or Consequences*, 75, 84.

their uniqueness and true knowledge of them. Additionally, concepts are combined to create edifices—laws of nature—that are human impositions on a world that transcends our intellectual constructions. Hence, what is commonly accepted as human knowledge is merely a self-contained set of illusions where truth is a function of the language employed, and thus only exists in certain linguistic concepts. Such "nihilism" argues that there is no access to reality whatsoever, only a perspectival appearance of it whose origins lie within the human mind. This perceived reality is the self-working itself out in self, creating a web of illusions, or sometimes positively, works of art. Consequentially, a rejection of any knowledge grounded in transcendent or universal moorings, including morality, follows. Nietzsche issues a lasting epistemological challenge: language not only distorts reality—it is reality itself.

Such existentialism not only emphasizes the subjective turn within epistemological fields but also questions the ability of language to describe reality itself, implying that a Postmodern Analytic must focus not just on questions about the knowledge of reality, but also on how language communicates it.

2.2.3 Preparers of the Way

Stanley Grenz comments, "Nietzsche brought Western philosophy face to face with the knotty issue of the nature of interpretation. He articulated the question and left other thinkers to seek the answers."[24] As philosophers sought answers, they especially focused on hermeneutical theory—the theory of interpretation of written texts—which could be applied to all language about reality, paving the way for twentieth-century postmodern philosophies.

Wilhelm Dilthey (1833–1911) sought to recover Kant's noumenal categories by proposing their development via a growing body of personal experience that enables construction of a coherent metaphysical system, a worldview. The individualistic nature of this is overcome through an inductive back-and-forth methodology between the individual interpreter and a larger community of interpreters, iteratively coming closer to actual truth, even if never fully found. As seen shortly, such communal activity is foundational for Richard Rorty's postmodernism.

---

24. Grenz, *Primer on Postmodernism*, 98.

Martin Heidegger (1884–1976) sought to rewrite base philosophical paradigms, therein overcoming Kantian and Nietzschean epistemological challenges. He opined that philosophy ought to start with "Dasein," the "Being-in," rather than the transcendental thinking self. This takes seriously our embeddedness in the world, dislodging traditional dichotomies of mind/self, self/world, subject/object, and subject/world. Here our "Being," in distinction to our "Presence," participates in all tenses of reality, allowing access to truth that occurs as it is revealed through "meditative thinking": artistic expression, including language. Thus, countering Nietzsche, experience of language is experience of thought, and through that of truth.

Ludwig Wittgenstein (1889–1951) responded to Nietzsche's challenge by freeing language from the sole function of describing truth. Rather, language is employed not only to state facts but also for multiple other purposes. Each employment occurs in separate self-contained systems with their own rules, like in playing differing games, "language games." All that is required to meaningfully employ language is an awareness of a particular game's rules. The games themselves may have little to do with each other and cannot be said to be connected to an objective reality. Truth is thus not about correspondence with objective reality, but rather truth within the internal function of language.

Similarly, Ferdinand de Saussure (1857–1913) proposed that language's structure neither maps thought's structure, nor is it the representation of independently given "facts." It is entirely internal to language itself. Hence the reason one cannot give logical reasons why words mean what they do. Therefore, the bond between the "signifier" (the linguistic expression) and the "signified" (what the expression connotes) is not logically derived. Signifiers can only be defined in terms of their relationships within language's structure, which is culturally and socially formed. In such a "structuralist" approach, universal cultural systems structure our mental processes and fundamental hermeneutics. This splitting of "signifiers" and "signified" becomes, as will be seen, fundamental in describing postmodernism—where the need for any link between the two is questioned.

2.3 FOUR KEY POSTMODERN PHILOSOPHERS

The above background provides the birthing context of postmodern philosophy. However, reflecting the challenges of defining postmodernism, no scholarly consensus exists on which twentieth-century postmodern philosophers need to be understood to surmise its key characteristics and manifestations. Smith considers Jacques Derrida, Jean-François Lyotard, and Michel Foucault as paradigmatic; Erickson considers Derrida, Foucault, Richard Rorty, and Stanley Fish; Grenz considers Foucault, Derrida, and Rorty.[25] Here Lyotard, Derrida, Foucault, and Rorty are examined because of multiple attestations in such sources, while recognizing that a broader set of philosophers could be exposited. Nevertheless, these four philosopher's ideas are central to what philosophical postmodernism is, even if they do not give an exhaustive mapping of it.[26]

2.3.1 Jean-François Lyotard

Hope in the Enlightenment story of human progress was severely shaken in the twentieth century by two world wars and millions killed; reason ought to have directed only good action. As mentioned, Jean-François Lyotard (1924–98), in his 1979 report, points to a key definitive feature of postmodernism, an "incredulity towards metanarratives"[27]—the rejection of any overarching historical-ideological narrative or claim. Therein metanarratives in fields diverse as modern rationalism (the Enlightenment Project), scientific naturalism (A Grand Unified Theory), and socio-biology (Darwin's Theory of Evolution), constructed through reason alone, are to be critiqued and rejected.

Lyotard contends transformations over the previous forty years had taken place that led to this crisis and birthed a new set of narratives. Focusing on Science as an example, before extrapolating outwards to society generally, he explains,

> The narrative function is losing its great functors. . . . It is being dispersed in clouds of narrative language elements . . . conveyed

---

25. Smith, *Who's Afraid of Postmodernism?*, 21; Erickson, *Truth or Consequences*, 113–84; Grenz, *Primer on Postmodernism*, 123–60.

26. These are complex thinkers, whose writings can be understood in multiple ways from differing angles. Therefore, what is offered is a summary of their thought as it pertains to the goal of creating a Postmodern Analytic.

27. Lyotard, *Postmodern Condition*, xxiii–xxv.

with each cloud are pragmatic valencies specific to each kind. Each of us lives at the intersection of many of these. However, we do not necessarily establish stable language combinations, and the properties of the ones we do establish are not necessarily communicable.[28]

Lyotard takes up Wittgenstein's language games to explain that what exists in the postmodern age are self-consistent and self-referential micronarratives, held together by smaller groups socially bound together. Such narratives may have nothing to do with each other and do not fit into a larger metanarrative. A key mark of the postmodernism the Analytic must describe.

2.3.2 Jacques Derrida

The postmodern contribution of Jacques Derrida (1930–2004) is a conceptualization of new ways of reading texts and interpreting the history of literature. A grouping of new concepts that help encapsulate his thought emerges. Importantly, Derrida's own "system" of thought argues that his work cannot be systematized or ever called a method, as such would be subject to *deconstruction*, perhaps the most important of his contributions to postmodern thought.

"Deconstruction" is introduced in *Of Grammatology*, where Derrida outlines his science of grammatology, which examines logocentric concepts such as signifiers, speech, and writing, across the history of metaphysical considerations. Therein he makes two observations. Firstly, what is signified in language by words in writing cannot be separated by the references that constitute language, "there is not a single signified that escapes, even if recaptured, the play of signifying references that constitute language."[29] Influenced by Heidegger, and continuing Saussure's trajectory, words can never signify reality but are context dependent; language itself is a chain of signifiers defined by other signifiers and therefore entirely self-referential.[30] Secondly, Derrida argues that this play between signifiers has reached an epoch-changing moment,[31] whereby words and concepts undergo "deconstruction": a discourse that looks at

---

28. Lyotard, *Postmodern Condition*, xxiv.
29. Derrida, *Of Grammatology*, 7.
30. Derrida, *Of Grammatology*, 11.
31. Derrida, *Of Grammatology*, 6.

oppositions that are posited and allows them to no longer be brought into synthesis, nor remain in opposition—rather both overturn each other, simultaneously creating something new.

This unseen deconstructive motion has been present throughout the history of metaphysical writing. In *Of Grammatology*, he sees it in the artificial metaphysical hierarchy created historically between speech and writing, whereby the former has been seen as more representative of truth—phonocentrism—an idealization of the phonic that has no basis apart from historical pedigree.[32] This has unhelpfully created binary oppositions such as mind/body, spirit/matter, which are in opposition to each other and undergo deconstruction. In *Of Spirit*, Derrida shows how for Heidegger his desire to avoid the term "spirit" in his work changed to an acceptance and then promotion of it, indicating that Heidegger is "citing or borrowing a word he wanted to put to another use"[33] and thus is being used in a deconstructed sense to be understood in the "discourse of the other."[34] In *Given Time/The Gift of Death*, Derrida shows how deconstruction operates in even simple concepts such as a "gift" in religious literature, arguing that the idea of "gift" is an "impossibility" because as soon as a gift is identified as such, "the donee knows it is a gift, he already thanks the donator, and cancels the gift."[35]

These examples are part of a wider opening of hermeneutical possibilities that Derrida suggests occurs as readers engage and enter continual conversation with written words. Key here is another well-known yet hard-to-define concept of Derrida's, *differance* (deliberately misspelled): the reading of words in the difference to others contextually and their difference temporally as well, a double reading that ought to come before any other. Dawne McCance comments how this aspect of Derrida's work has caused lasting disruption to the reading of texts, as "part of the "difficulty" has to do with the "primordiality" of differance. We are accustomed to thinking of presence, or unity, first and differences as secondary," while Derrida swaps this ordering, upturning metaphysical and hermeneutical paradigms.[36] Grenz explains, "In the wake of Derrida's work, avant-garde postmoderns conclude that we can no longer

32. Derrida, *Of Grammatology*, 11–12.
33. Derrida, *Of Spirit*, 30.
34. Derrida, *Of Spirit*, 35.
35. Derrida and Marion, "Gift," 59.
36. McCance, *Derrida on Religion*, 28.

assume an ontological ground for certain knowledge,"[37] as what applies to the hermeneutics of texts subsequently applies to all aspects of reality, as reality is known through language.

The consequences of Derrida's postmodern contribution are significant. He pluralizes and relativizes knowledge, enthrones the subjective epistemological turn in postmodernism, and detaches signifiers from signified completely—key ideas to be described by the Postmodern Analytic.

2.3 Michel Foucault

Michel Foucault's (1926–84) work is neither purely philosophical nor historical, but in admixture of both he looks at history to deduce key philosophical themes,[38] refusing to take standard lines of interpretation to expose what has been previously hidden, agreeing with Derrida and Lyotard that a time has come for a new movement of thought.

In *Madness and Civilization*, Foucault examines the history of the treatment of the insane in society, and what can be concluded from this with regards knowledge and truth. He concludes from the history of separating the abnormal from normal—the former in minority and the latter in majority—that the majority defines the truth of normalcy based on numbers and a wielding of truth rather than inherency of it. However, Foucault stats that the "insane" man separated from society

> rediscovers a truth he had forgotten, though it was manifest: what desire can be contrary to nature, since it was given to man by nature itself. . . . The madness of desire, insane murders, the most unreasonable passions—all are wisdom and reason, since they are a part of the order of nature.[39]

Thus, there is discovered truth, what Foucault later speaks of as a local truth, that has been subjugated to, or repressed by, the truth of the larger society. This is explained further in *Discipline and Punish*, where he looks at how society has engaged in punishment and discipline in the name of either justice (such as prisons) or training (such as schools and the military), to conform people to societal norms. "The power of normalization

---

37. Grenz, *Primer on Postmodernism*, 150.
38. On the difficulty of defining Foucault and his approach, see O'Farrell, *Foucault*.
39. Foucault, *Madness and Civilization*, 282.

imposes homogeneity,"[40] as individuals come under knowledge's power, a knowledge belonging to the larger norm-defining majority. From such examinations, Foucault later explains, "Truth isn't an outside power, or lacking in power.... [T]ruth is a thing of this world: it is produced only by virtue of multiple forms of constraint. And it induces regular effects of power."[41]

Here, Foucault's key contribution to the postmodern assault of Enlightenment epistemology is the rejection of the ideal of a "disinterested knower." A vantage point that offers certain and universal knowledge is impossible, as knowledge is embedded in the world and involved in its power struggles. Knowledge is the product of a desire to establish knowledge that systems of power find useful: "We should admit rather that power produces knowledge ... that power and knowledge directly imply one another."[42] Thus Bacon's idea transforms: "knowledge is power" but only for those who control it, with specific purposes of their choosing. Part of Foucault's life-long work was to expose these controlling systems of knowledge to achieve liberation.[43]

This liberation is more than enabling human freedom. The agenda is deeper: to alter the view of reality itself, where one is no longer a subject in reference to an object, rather within history's matrix, "one has to dispense with the constituent subject ... to arrive at an analysis which can account for the constitution of the subject within a historical framework."[44] In this framework, reality is not *understood* by subject-object discourse, but *created* by this discourse within societal context. Hence, there is no objective body of knowledge to be discovered, but rather knowledge is created in historical power dynamics, creating multiple knowledges.

Again, Foucault, like Derrida, contributes to the enthronement of subjective elements of epistemology over objective ones, leading to a pluralistic outlook. Additionally, he suggests that a suspicion against larger structures and institutions which mediate "objective knowledge" must be central to the Analytic's understanding of postmodernism.

---

40. Foucault, *Discipline and Punish*, 182.
41. Foucault, *Power/Knowledge*, 131.
42. Foucault, *Discipline and Punish*, 27.
43. One could apply Foucault to Foucault, asking what his agenda in this lifelong battle was, and how this changes reception of his thought.
44. Foucault, *Power/Knowledge*, 117.

2.3.4 Richard Rorty

Not as prominently recognized, Richard Rorty (1931–2007) espoused a philosophy and method notably different to those considered thus far. His postmodern pragmatism shifts the question from what is true and knowable about reality, to what works as true. Similarly to others, Rorty rejects that language describes reality, as it is a human construction of context dependence, created through a web of inner linguistic relationships. However, in application of Wittgenstein, statements can be true if they cohere with entire sets of beliefs, as beliefs cause language, shaped by the community inhabiting it. It is not that beliefs are caused by objects they represent (realism), or by our minds rather than external objects (idealism), but rather an anti-realistic epistemology based on language is described.

This epistemology's vocabulary is found through what works more than what is theoretically correct—how all human endeavors work. For philosophy, this means that modernistic logo-centric philosophy does not need to be fully rejected as Derrida argues, but rather the parts that may be helpful for given inhabited contexts must be discerned. Grenz comments thus, "Truth becomes in essence truth for us,"[45] as all systems of truth are self-referential and created in community. Cultural or temporal context cannot be transcended to find objective truth, rather pragmatically we speak of what ought to be true as the truth about what is within a larger system formed in community. This confronts the Enlightenment's idolization of the individual knower, promoting instead the importance of community:

> Our identification with our community . . . is heightened when we see this community as ours rather than nature's, shaped rather than found, one among many which men have made. In the end, the pragmatists tell us, what matters is our loyalty to the other human beings clinging together against the dark, not our hope of getting things right.[46]

Rorty's communal pragmatic epistemology represents a meeting between the wider American Pragmatic tradition and a philosophical postmodernism which eschews objective truth. John Ryder argues that the American philosophical tradition has been long overlooked as a

---

45. Grenz, *Primer on Postmodernism*, 155.
46. Rorty, *Consequences of Pragmatism*, 166.

"positive alternative to philosophic modernism,"[47] and its development away from Continental philosophy enabled it to come to a place whereby it has "contributed immensely . . . to the philosophic achievements of postmodernism."[48] Rorty and other's contributions expand postmodernism beyond being a Eurocentric affair and suggest that this study's Analytic must encompass communal and pragmatic emphases in its criteria, especially in how knowledge is interpreted and first known.

2.4 A POSTMODERN ANALYTIC

The scene is now set to create a Postmodern Analytic, which forms the core of the ecclesial postmodernism system when brought into dialogue with ecclesiological themes. The Postmodern Analytic employed in this study is here proposed as four broad criteria. This is done with acknowledgment that these criteria are not exhaustive but rather result from key base themes in the postmodern conversation, acting as a minimal set of criteria that emerge out of the trajectories of thought described above. They do not encompass all postmodern characteristics, "to give a full definition of postmodernism is virtually impossible."[49] However, if an ecclesial lifeworld is to be described to have postmodern character, these four criteria are likely to be observable in some form.

2.4.1 Criterion One: A Non-Foundational Epistemology

There is a rejection of reason as the only way to knowledge of reality, it is only one of the ways. There is also an emphasis on subjective and pragmatic discovery as routes to access knowledge of reality alongside it, as the subjective participant in knowledge is a key factor in knowledge itself and there is no direct mapping of reality onto rational thinkers. Consequently, there is an inherent level of relativism as no one individual or community can claim definitive objective knowledge of the truth, and thus multiple truths are allowed to sit alongside each other in pluralistic fashion.

---

47. Ryder, "Use and Abuse," 93. See also Stuhr, *Pragmatism, Postmodernism, and Future*. Stuhr parallels Ryder's argument, though argues that American Pragmatism is to be seen as a way beyond postmodernism in a constructive philosophy that goes beyond modernism.

48. Ryder, "Use and Abuse," 98.

49. McGrath, *Passion for Truth*, 184.

The line of questioning of the nature of how we interpret reality, begun with Nietzsche, comes to a place of deconstruction with Derrida's mistrust of every act of reading reality. Beforehand there was an assumption that epistemology "consists of either a set of unquestioned beliefs or certain first principles on the basis of which the pursuit of knowledge can proceed . . . universal, context-free, and available—at least theoretically—to any rational person."[50] However in postmodernism, "philosophically, nonfoundationalism (or antifoundationalism) is certainly one of the most important roots or resources of postmodernism. Non-foundationalists deny that we have any of those alleged strong foundations for our belief-systems."[51]

Pauline Rosenau comments that within postmodern circles, "Most sceptics call for a "definitive farewell" to reason."[52] For some postmodernists, as Foucault showed, the foundationalist worldview was part of the time when "unspoken political and ideological assumptions exert a greater influence than reason itself on the construction of reigning paradigms of knowledge."[53] Reason's context is never neutral, hence it ought to have never been lionized. Instead, there is an emphasis on the validity of subjective intuition and knowledge of reality, a levelling of the epistemological playing field. In some stronger postmodernism, "all life is subjective and the distinctions between truth and falsehood, essence and appearance, fact and interpretation are dissolved. What matters is not whether a belief is true, but whether it is "'life-affirming,' that is, capable of providing feelings of power or freedom."[54] Heidegger's reorientated epistemology which focuses on the *experience* of embeddedness flows into this view. Furthermore, taking Rorty's pragmatism to heart, *pragmatic* truth thus has validity in understanding the universe.

This opens an inherent relativity, as movement is seen "from unique truth and a world fixed and found . . . to a diversity of right and even conflicting versions or worlds in the making."[55] Zygmunt Bauman comments, "The plurality of interpretations (coexistence of rival knowledges) ceases thereby to be seen as a regrettable yet temporary and in principle rectifiable inconvenience . . . becoming instead the constitutive feature of

50. Grenz and Franke, *Beyond Foundationalism*, 30.
51. Huyssteen, *Essays in Postfoundationalist Theology*, 3.
52. Rosenau, *Post-Modernism*, 128.
53. Lints, *Fabric of Theology*, 219.
54. Brown, "Theology," 160.
55. Goodman, *Ways of Worldmaking*, x.

being."⁵⁶ The emphases of diverse types of non-rational epistemologies, combined with a relativistic and pluralistic view of truth, feed into the criteria that follow below and lie at the heart of them. Thus, this criterion's postmodernism likely figures most strongly in *ecclesial postmodernism*.

2.4.2 Criterion Two: Discontinuities Between Signifiers and Signified

There is an allowance for discontinuity between signifiers and that which is signified, as language does not necessarily describe reality as it is, but rather words can have meanings self-referentially defined in their own contextually shaped systems and communities. As a result, language becomes somewhat a reality in itself.

The epistemological reorientation in postmodernism causes an especially sharp break between signifiers and what they are thought to signify. Through Nietzsche's influence, and philosophers who reacted to his work, the hermeneutics of reality becomes a fluid concept in which the subjective dominates. Grenz explains,

> Considerations such as these lead postmodern thinkers to abandon the realist view in favor of a nonrealist or constructivist view.... They contend that what we call the "real world" is actually an ever-changing social creation. Ours is a "symbolic" world, a social reality that we construct through our common reality... because our social context is always changing, meanings—and, as a consequence, the world as we see it through language—are constantly shifting as well.⁵⁷

As a result, there is a recognition that signifiers can be detached from what is signified, with a new emphasis on the former over the latter; a deconstruction program seriously applied to reality generates a need to completely re-orientate to signifiers to construct what is signified. Richard Tarnas comments, "The inherent human capacity for concept and symbol formation is recognized as a fundamental and necessary element in the human understanding, anticipation, and creation of reality.... Reality is in some sense constructed by the mind, not simply perceived by it."⁵⁸

---

56. Bauman, *Intimations of Postmodernity*, 132.
57. Grenz, *Primer on Postmodernism*, 42. See also Veith, *Postmodern Times*, 51.
58. Tarnas, *Passion*, 396. See also Tarnas, *Passion*, 406.

This outlook outworks itself in every field of study and strata of social reality, creating a focus on immanence, "the growing capacity of mind to generalize itself through symbols . . . a patina of thought, of signifiers, of 'connections,' now lies on everything the mind touches in its gnostic (noo)sphere."[59] Consequently, as with other postmodern characteristics, while the signified reality is still directly mediated in the modernistic sense by signifiers, it is also constructed by the self-same signifiers which take a reality of their own disconnected from one that was previously signified by them—in the life of the individual perceiver and social interpretive community. As will be seen, this potentially manifests in a multitude of manners in ecclesial settings.

2.4.3 Criterion Three: Metanarratives and Micronarratives

Large-scale metanarratives of reality sit alongside smaller-scale narratives of individuals, communities, geographical areas, and interpretations of historical events. In this, the story of an individual or community is as important as, and often more important than, the universal stories that are told. Experience and testimony are as valid as passed-down narratives; tension, conflict, and contradiction between these and larger metanarratives is allowed.

Through the confluence of several philosophical voices, modernist overarching stories are no longer completely trusted or authoritative in the postmodern paradigm.[60] Combining with Lyotard's postmodernism as incredulity towards metanarrative, the philosophy of Derrida has had a catalytic effect: "This aspect of postmodernism has been reinforced by the activities of the deconstructionists. In their suspicion of any narrative that aspires to coherence, and in their rush to deconstruct anything that even looks like meta-theory, they challenged all basic presuppositions."[61] Foucault's influence is seen in the postmodern suspicion of metanarratives, "whose secretly terroristic function is to ground and legitimate the illusion of a 'universal' human history. We are now in the process of awakening from the nightmare of modernity, with its manipulative reason and fetish of the totality."[62] More softly, Gary Phillips comments

---

59. Hassan, *Postmodern Turn*, 172.
60. See Adams, "Toward," 522.
61. Harvey, *Condition of Postmodernity*, 350.
62. Eagleton, "Awakening," 194.

that for postmoderns "no single metanarrative is possible because none is large enough to encompass the experiences of all people, marginalized or not."[63]

Resultantly, there is a new emphasis on the smaller stories of individuals and communities, whereupon the grand narratives have been deconstructed, and the voice of the repressed, marginalized, and unheard, is now heard and given legitimacy. Snyder comments,

> What was traditionally referred to as "history" is now perceived as having broken down into an infinity of "histories" that can no longer be (re)combined into a single narrative governed by a central theme such as "the march of progress" or "the triumph of enlightenment." This is accurately reflected in the explosive growth of "microhistory" in the past decades.[64]

A mark of ecclesial postmodernism therefore will be an emphasis on micronarratives, personally or communally generated; a Non-Foundational epistemology present generates a pluralism which allows these micronarratives to sit in tension, and even contradiction, with other micronarratives and with surviving larger metanarratives. For the creation of an *ecclesial postmodernism* system, it will therefore be important to identify important micronarratives that show this character.

2.4.4 Criterion Four: The Importance of Community

The idea of an autonomous individual knower of modernism sits alongside the need for an interpretive community in which truths about reality are held corporately and self-consistently, even though such communities themselves may not overlap with each other. Thus, a multiplicity of interpretative communities, which may differ by only slight measures, may exist. In these communities, there can be both an emphasis on what is pragmatically true, and a suspicion of what is authoritatively declared to be true rather than communally discussed and discerned.

Gene Veith explains, "The postmodern worldview operates with a community-based understanding of truth."[65] With distrust of traditional epistemology and over-arching stories, the community becomes foundationally important in postmodernism, and suspicion is directed against

63. Phillips, "Religious Pluralism," 133.
64. Snyder, "Translator's Introduction," vi.
65. Veith, *Postmodern Times*, 79.

institutions and individual authority holders. It is within the community's agreed language game that reality can be spoken about and understood, and that moments of existential crisis created by the destruction of the previous edifices of modernity can be tempered and processed to find new meaning. Bauman comments,

> For the philosophers and the ordinary folk alike, community is now expected to bring the succor previously sought in the pronouncements of universal. . . . Communities are imagined: belief in their presence is their only brick and mortar, and imputation of importance their only source of authority. An imagined community acquires the right to approve or disapprove. . . . [T]he approval seeking individual invests it with the arbitrating power and agrees to be bound by the arbitration.[66]

In regards to their epistemology, J. Wentzel van Huysseen explains, "In a strong reaction against modernist and generic notions of rationality, nonfoundationalism also highlights the crucial epistemic importance of community. . . . [E]very community and context has its own rationality, and that any and all social activities may in fact function as a test case for human rationality."[67] Within communities, truth is found through Rorty's maxims of what is "good" for it, the aforementioned pragmatic question, which occurs through conversations within it. Rorty argues,

> If we see knowing not as having essence, to be described by scientists or philosophers, but rather as a right, by current standards to believe, then we are well on the way to seeing conversation as the ultimate context within which knowledge is to be understood.[68]

Such implies that for *ecclesial* postmodernism, the presence of such conversations in church communities is an important factor.

2.5 ECCLESIAL POSTMODERNISM SYSTEM

2.5.1 Approaches to System Construction

The next stage in the construction of the needed transcontextual system of ecclesial postmodernism is to bring the above Analytic into conversation

---

66. Bauman, *Intimations of Postmodernity*, xix.
67. Huyssteen, *Essays in Postfoundationalist Theology*, 3.
68. Rorty, *Philosophy and Mirror*, 389.

with relevant ecclesiological themes. By doing so the shape of ecclesiological practice shaped by such postmodernism is discerned, enabling a base description of the system.

One approach here is seen in Grenz, who engages with this need via surprising reduction. Perhaps recognizing the daunting breadth of what could be understood as postmodernism, he chooses to limit his discussion: "At the heart of a post-modern Christian ecclesiology is the concept of church as community . . . a particular community marked by certain characteristics," leading him to "outline an ecclesiology that incorporates postmodern and communitarian insights."[69] Grenz, despite grasping the breadth of themes within postmodern thought,[70] chooses to reduce his discussion to just one—community. Such an approach is inappropriate for this study. Choosing one of the criteria to focus on in system creation both undervalues the variety of postmodern thought seen in this chapter and forces a hierarchical approach. Grenz is helpful, however, in suggesting that the ecclesiological system for this study may be formed by looking at how the church might be "marked by certain characteristics" because of postmodernism, highlighting how this study's system can primarily focus on potential manifestations of seen postmodernisms in the ecclesial sphere for it to be helpfully brought into subsequent conversation with potential lifeworlds such as the Movement's.[71]

In this vein, the sociologist James Beckford gives a more fully orbed approach. Paralleling this study's Analytic, he defines four criteria of postmodernism as follows:

> 1. A refusal to regard positivistic, rationalistic, instrumental criteria as the sole or exclusive standard of worthwhile knowledge.
> 2. A willingness to combine symbols from disparate codes or frameworks of meaning, even at the cost of disjunctions and eclecticism.
> 3. A celebration of spontaneity, fragmentation, superficiality, irony, and playfulness.

---

69. Grenz, "Ecclesiology," 252.

70. See Grenz, *Primer on Postmodernism*, 161–74.

71. Another approach would be to theorize how each key postmodern idea affects the church's internal vision of praxis. However, this is unlikely to generate a clear system that enables the lifeworld analysis needed by the CRQs because of the multiplicity of divergent possibilities. For example, Caputo's application of deconstruction to the church creates no clear ecclesial vision but rather ends with "two case studies [that] describe what a church might look like after deconstruction," the dissimilarity between which is pronounced. Caputo, *What Would Jesus Deconstruct?*, 135.

4. A willingness to abandon the search for over-arching or triumphalist myths, narratives, or frameworks of knowledge.[72]

Based on these criteria, Beckford explains his expectations, which could be viewed as a basic form of an ecclesial postmodernism system:

> My expectation would be that putatively post-modern forms of religion would embrace diversity of discourse and the abandonment of unitary meaning systems; cross-references between, and pastiches of, different religious traditions; collapse of the boundary between high and popular forms of religion; and an accent on playfulness of cynicism.[73]

Applying this to Christian religion in the United Kingdom in the latter half of the twentieth century, Beckford sees no postmodern tendencies observable. Importantly, regarding Pentecostal-Charismatic Christianity,

> Even the cultivation of ecstatic experiences and heightened emotion in, for example, Pentecostalism or charismatic movements, is based on principles derived from the Bible, presumably a source of ultimate truth. The fashion for "house churches" and Christian communities also reflects much greater continuity than discontinuity with the strong Christian meta-narrative about hope, heaven on earth and salvation.[74]

If Beckford's analysis is true, then CRQ-1 has been simply answered, and the Movement—covered within its description—has no postmodern character. However, Beckford's analysis suffers from two major flaws, which can be learnt from. Firstly, its simplism; Beckford does not consider the historical development of postmodernism, and, like Milbank, his criteria suffer from being posited without substantiation, rather than emerging out of an analysis of the historical emergence of postmodern thought, leading to over-simple criteria. This is partially why Valdis Teraudkalns, applying Beckford's criteria to new Latvian charismatic churches, can only conclude "new charismatic churches in Latvia are in complex relationships with postmodern culture."[75] Here the Analytic's criteria shine, as they inscribe more complex nuanced descriptions of

---

72. Beckford, "Religion," 19.
73. Beckford, "Religion," 20.
74. Beckford, "Religion," 20.
75. Teraudkalns, "New Charismatic Churches," 452.

postmodernism through their narrative formation, enabling deeper understanding and elucidation.

Secondly, Beckford's analysis uses strong definitive verbs and adjectives to judge if something is postmodern in a binary fashion, such as "refusal," "sole," "exclusive," and "abandon." However, this misses an important aspect of what postmodernism can be seen to be from its historical progression, namely that postmodern thought always contains an element of modernism within it in dialectic nature, as it seeks to react to it and construct a new way forward. This was highlighted in the definitional discussion of §2.1. In an ecclesial postmodernism system, expected manifestations must be allowed to sit alongside, even in contradiction to, more modernistic ecclesial aspects.

Beckford's analysis provokes discussion of what a fuller and more nuanced version of a postmodern ecclesial system looks like—to which the work of Rebecca Jaichandran and B. D. Madhav suggests a helpful way forward. To explore what postmodern philosophy would look like in Pentecostal worship and spirituality specifically, they construct a five-fold base description of postmodernism: "anti-foundationalism," "deconstruction of language," "denial of truth," "Virtual Reality," and "disorientated self."[76] This description is used to create three sets of likely manifestations in religious spirituality:

1. Higher Experience: a rejection of rational foundations leads to an increased draw to religious movements such as the New Age movement that emphasize a higher supra-rational and mystical experience of "the Ultimate" and similar metaphysical concepts.

2. Silence: the deconstruction of language leads to an inability to speak about metaphysical reality, and therefore an increased emphasis on silence.

3. The Voice Within: with a loss of external objective reality, the only reality that matters is the one constructed by the individual, leading to an exploratory journey within to find reality.[77]

76. Jaichandran and Madhav, "Pentecostal Spirituality," 45–49.

77. Jaichandran and Madhav, "Pentecostal Spirituality," 51–54. Here, "Silence" is not contained within the Analytic's likely ecclesial manifestations outlined below yet finds some confirmation in §4.1.3 where William Kay discerns that this postmodern context energized some of the manifestations within "the Toronto Blessing." §5.2.1.2 explores how instead of silence, the postmodern breakdown of the connection between signifiers and what is signified by them also opens the space for forms of postmodern communication. See §6.2.2 for analysis of Criterion Two manifestations in the Movement's communicative language.

From this, they conclude that there are two observable effects of postmodernism on Pentecostal spirituality and worship. Firstly, emphases on individual experiences which prize the ecstatic and supernatural. Secondly, experiences of worship which create their own reality, where symbols (signifiers) create the ground of a reality that appeals to a culture lacking in connection to a signified reality. In Pentecostalism, this can function as a form of postmodern escapism into a "virtual reality." However, at its best, in Pentecostal worship this is not an escapism from the real world into unreality, rather into the ultimate reality of God facilitated by a sensory-immersive experience.[78] Jaichandran and Madhav conclude such above effects and manifestations are largely seen in the Pentecostal lifeworld, though significantly they note that "while postmodern spirituality emphasizes silence, Pentecostal spirituality emphasizes the audible."[79]

Unlike Beckford, Jaichandran and Madhav's approach notices and appreciates contradiction, and employs a more detailed nuanced analysis, modelling a more expansive and nuanced approach to system creation than Beckford. Some of their insights are important for both integration into this study's system below, and future conversations precipitated by investigation of the Movement's lifeworld. However, two key weaknesses can be seen. Firstly, their construction relies on summaries of what postmodernism is, rather than an analysis of postmodern philosophy itself as performed in construction of this study's Analytic, which therefore does not have this weakness. This is why—in an opposite manner to Grenz—their version of postmodernism does not include anything like *Criterion Four* aspects,[80] betraying a certain lack of rigor to their understanding of postmodernism given how often communal emphases are seen as a mark of it. Secondly, in their funneling approach of turning a five-fold description of postmodernism into a three-fold postmodern spirituality, leading to a two-fold description of its effects on Pentecostal worship and spirituality, there is a sequential loss of a wider scope of possibilities. For example, how might the "denial of truth" affect Pentecostal worship

---

78. Such an emphasis might underlie the observations of narrative discontinuities in §4.2.2—a call to break with cultural narratives to enter the true story and reality of God facilitated through such worship. Similarly, in the reflections of §8.2.2.2 such "escapism" could be understood as part of the playful interface between the world and church whereby the world comes into the reality of God through the church that is shaped to enable this through charismatic renewal.

79. Jaichandran and Madhav, "Pentecostal Spirituality," 57.

80. Perhaps because of the Eurocentric bias discussed in §2.3.4.

directly? Could it lead to a worship that minors in doctrinal truth, or one that holds contradictory ideas about God?

Both learning from and ameliorating this latter potential weakness, this study's ecclesial postmodernism system is here constructed through the following:

1. Exploratory conversations with appropriate wider scholarship that exposits Pentecostal-Charismatic movements and postmodern ecclesial manifestations, enabling a full range of specific ecclesial manifestations to be theorized. In the dialectic methodological journey of this study, while this first occurs here below in conversation with general Pentecostal-Charismatic scholarship to define a base system, it is furthered by chapter 4's return to system questions through interaction with specific sociological and anthropological insights to fill out a richer system to enable lifeworld analysis in chapters 5–7.

2. Judiciously receiving additional possible ecclesial manifestations from initial and later explorations of the Movement's lifeworld, as well as a nuancing of existing ones by the same process, enabling this study's methodology to be truly dialectic in conversation—whereby the lifeworld illuminates aspects of the system. Such partly incorporates Foucault's understanding of locally discovered truths,[81] yet without collapsing the difference between system and lifeworld in the methodological dialectic.

To avoid a funneling effect which misses possible manifestations, these manifestations are described as direct ecclesial manifestations of the Analytic Criteria, such that a one-to-one correspondence can be found between each of the four criteria and proposed manifestations. Indeed, instead of a funneling down in number, it will be seen how this approach leads to a wide range of potential manifestations of *each* of the four Analytic Criteria, the opposite result.

2.5.2 Insights from Scholarship

Through exploratory conversations with wider Pentecostal-Charismatic scholarship on postmodernism in ecclesial settings, a wide range of potential ecclesial manifestations of postmodernism can be theorized.

81. See §2.3.3.

While discussions in scholarship highlight a variety of potential manifestations of each of the Analytic Criteria, *Criterion One* manifestations are most prominently seen. This is unsurprising given the central precipitative importance of epistemological changes in the narrative of postmodernism described earlier in this chapter, something which wider Pentecostal-Charismatic scholarship likely discerns when investigating postmodern themes.

Smith's work highlights a personal and corporate *experiential* knowledge of God as a potentially key *Criterion One* manifestation, as well as a focus on *personal testimony* as a *Criterion Three* manifestation, noticing the importance of personal testimony at the heart of the Pentecostal worldview which gives rise to an understanding of knowledge as something that is known personally through experience—in contrast to modernistic rationalism. He explains,

> I want to suggest that at work here is a kind of proto-postmodern intuition about knowledge that constitutes a performative critique of modern criteria for knowledge—a pentecostal critique of the rationalism (or cognitivism or "intellectualism") that characterizes modern accounts of knowledge. Pentecostal practice can function as a sort of countermodernity. Thus there are elements of a pentecostal worldview that resonate with a "postmodern" critique of autonomous reason such that we might see Azusa Street as a postmodern revival.[82]

Smith goes on to develop this insight and others to argue that a distinct Pentecostal philosophy has value in wider philosophical conversations, especially the postmodern one, because of such characteristics. However, this is not without critics who question if such an approach seals knowledge in hermeneutical bubbles of affective storytelling,[83] and is not properly Pentecostal because it neglects wider Pentecostal theology and history,[84] as well as other historical contexts.[85]

On this latter weakness, a more global approach to Pentecostal epistemology is needed than Smith gives, especially given other centers of early Pentecostal experience that cannot be framed in terms of modernistic rationalism. Here Anderson highlights the leader of the Mukti

---

82. Smith, *Thinking in Tongues*, 52.
83. Davis and Franks, "Against a Postmodern."
84. Frestadius, *Pentecostal Rationality*, 20–32.
85. Poirier, "Pentecostalism," 499. For a constructive, reparative defense to many of these critiques, see Shin, *Pentecostalism, Postmodernism, and Reformed Epistemology*.

revival, Pandita Ramabai, who critiqued, "Let revival come to Indians so as to suit their nature and feelings. . . . [L]et the English and other Western Missionaries begin to study the Indian nature, I mean the religious inclinations, the *emotional* side of the Indian mind."[86] She suggests the indigenous mind, which had never conformed to Western rationalism, had to be reached in another way, a premodern way—which Pentecostalism therefore flourished in, as such emphases were contained in its focus. As will be suggested through CRQ-3's enquiry, the premodern and the postmodern perhaps are two sides of the same coin here, the latter a return to the former.[87] Some global contexts perhaps never needed such a "return," as the influence of Western modernism had never been fully received by them to cause a departure from premodern ideals. If such an equivalence is true, here an *emotional* experience of God is seen as another potential *Criterion One* manifestation of ecclesial postmodernism given historical and global Pentecostalisms. Buttressing the importance of this supposition, from sociological perspective Karel Dobbelaere and Liliane Voyé view the emotional aspects of the charismatic movement as the key reason for its success in postmodern cultural contexts.[88]

Frestadius's study of the Elim Pentecostal church[89] articulates the "Pentecostal Rationality" of "Biblical Pragmatism," which combines a tradition-specific biblicism with experientialism and experimentalism, such that "human (spiritual experiences) are central in forming and justifying Elim's Pentecostal beliefs, and these beliefs are further corroborated and tested in light of experimental practices."[90] Sadly, Frestadius sublimates terms in his analysis, explaining that "in terms of terminology, throughout the book the terms "rationality," "epistemology" and "philosophical hermeneutics" are used more or less synonymously."[91] Having quickly rejected postmodern ideas early in his work,[92] Frestadius seems unable to see that he describes an epistemology broader than one defined

---

86. See Anderson, "Revising Pentecostal History," 155 where he quotes Ramabai's article, "Stray Thoughts on the Revival, which appeared in *The Bombay Guardian* on November 4, 1905.

87. See especially §7.2.4.

88. Dobbelaere and Voyé, "From Pillar," S8–S9. This observation finds expansion in the discussion of deprivation models in §4.1.2.2.

89. Frestadius, *Pentecostal Rationality*, 201–13.

90. Frestadius, *Pentecostal Rationality*, 189.

91. Frestadius, *Pentecostal Rationality*, 5.

92. Frestadius, *Pentecostal Rationality*, 2.

under the paradigms of modernistic rationality. Ameliorating this weakness, his analysis implies that a *pragmatic* justification of praxis is a potential additional epistemological element that constructs the system under *Criterion One*.

Combining the insights of Smith, Anderson/Ramabai, and Frestadius, shows how the broad range of epistemological elements of *Criterion One* find likely expression in ecclesial postmodernism. Hence, a *pluralism* is likely to be seen due to different "truths" found through different epistemological emphases, sitting alongside each other in faith discourse and worship. Relatedly, an ecclesiological relativism described by *Criterion One*, which in the ecclesial sphere manifests as *relativity* in the same discourse, is therefore likely in strongest postmodern manifestations when multiple truths indicate an inaccessibility to what is true about reality.

Turning attention to *Criterion Two* manifestations, Karla Poewe argues that the Pentecostal-Charismatic worldview's emphasis on signs and symbols shows that

> Charismatic Christianity is post-modern. It regards the whole universe and the whole of history . . . as consisting of signs. These signs are available to explore the meaning of life in a concretely meaningful way. In other words, these signs are metonymic. That is, signs are current manifestations of the creative activity of the Creator.[93]

Poewe sees visions, dreams, and internally heard voices as signs that are interpreted as the activity of God, and comments that in new religious movements the hunger for experience through such signs cannot be explained in the *modern* world.[94] Here the Analytic explains some of what Poewe sees, as such metonymic signs rely on a discontinuity between signifier and signified in the interpretive moment where meaning is revealed, explainable in the *postmodern* context as *Criterion Two* underscores. Thus, Poewe's analysis highlights likely *Criterion Two* ecclesial manifestations in signs of God's activity, and it can be argued that in charismatic contexts this occurs especially in the usage of *spiritual gifts*.[95]

The philosophical background to the *Criterion Two* split between signifiers and signified has been seen to be rooted in changed approaches to hermeneutics. Therefore, it is unsurprising that new biblical

---

93. Poewe, "On the Metonymic Structure," 361.
94. Poewe, "On the Metonymic Structure," 375.
95. See §1.1.3.1.

hermeneutics constitute key elements of ecclesial postmodernism under this criterion. This is an aspect of Pentecostalism that has been seen in scholarship, especially in *spiritual* and *allegorical exegesis*.[96] Timothy Cargal opines that the grassroots Pentecostal exegetical method, which sees multiple simultaneous meanings in the same text, is indeed postmodern in nature—and something not to be rejected. He explains, "if Pentecostals in particular and Christians more generally do not find ways of interpreting the Bible which are meaningful to people living in this postmodern age, their interpretation of the Bible will increasingly be perceived as irrelevant."[97] Corroborating this view, Noel points out that in early Pentecostal hermeneutics the

> similarities between early Pentecostalism and current Postmodern thought are striking. From the earliest times, as evidenced by her initial leaders, Pentecostalism has not taken the Modern approach to faith and the Scriptures. . . . Like the Postmodernists reacting to the tenets of Modernism, so Pentecostals could no longer apply a rationalistic outlook to their new experience with the Holy Spirit.[98]

Furthermore, Noel notes three marks of early Pentecostalism which created a very different hermeneutical environment to modernistic academic approaches, all of which can be understood as manifestations of the Analytic Criteria in the ecclesial sphere: (1) the importance of individual story, *testimony* (*Criterion Three*); (2) the role of *experience* in determining what is true (*Criterion One*); and (3) the significance of *community interpretation* of truth (*Criterion Four*). These factors created a participatory style of reading scripture, whereby the early Pentecostal communities entered into the biblical narratives and placed individual's stories, experiences, and expectations in it, such that "the truth communicated was that of their place within the larger narrative of God's redemptive plan."[99] As will be seen in §3.1.1, Noel's analysis of early Pentecostalism, which shows a full range of manifestations of the Analytic Criteria, demands investigation under CRQ-3's enquiry of later Pentecostalism's influence in the Movement's observed postmodern character.

---

96. For a helpful survey see Noel, *Pentecostal and Postmodern Hermeneutics*.
97. Cargal, "Beyond," 165.
98. Noel, "Pentecostal," 119–20.
99. Noel, "Pentecostal," 120.

Noel's work, like Smith's, highlights *Criterion Three* manifestations seen in relevant scholarship, emphasizing the importance of *personal and communal testimony* in ecclesial postmodernism, ideas that will be expanded upon in chapter 4. Focusing on further *Criterion Four* manifestations beyond that seen in Noel, Thomas Csordas's work on the Charismatic Movement in the Catholic Church argues that while it is "not accurately described as a postmodern cultural phenomenon because of marked impulses toward traditionalism and centralism," there are three features of the postmodern condition that help clarify the context by which it flourishes, the second of which is "the decentering of authority in meaning, discourse, and social form," which the movement feeds off.[100] This can be understood as an ecclesial manifestation of *Criterion Four*. Following this impulse to logical conclusions, in ecclesial spheres the obverse of *Criterion Four*'s emphasis on community and communal interpretation under a Foucauldian suspicion of power leads to a *suspicion of authority and authority holders* and a *de-emphasizing of institution*, and conversely what Thomas Csordas calls in charismatic renewal an emphasis on "closely interacting *networks* of groups."[101] Taking this impulse further, such ecclesial manifestations might include the creation of entirely *new structures* of church, competing with, and even replacing, traditional denominations.

2.5.3 Ecclesial Postmodernism in Action

The above conversation highlights probable manifestations of ecclesial postmodernism, mapping the base ecclesial postmodernism system used in this study:

1. *Criterion One*: experiential, emotional, and pragmatic knowledge of God and spiritual truth; epistemological pluralism and relativism in faith discourse.

2. *Criterion Two*: discontinuities between signifiers and signified in the usage of spiritual gifts, and in exegesis of Scripture.

3. *Criterion Three*: a strong emphasis on the authority of personal and corporate testimony in the knowledge of God.

---

100. Csordas, *Language, Charisma, and Creativity*, 44.
101. Csordas, *Language, Charisma, and Creativity*, 52 (emphasis added).

4. *Criterion Four*: communal interpretation of truth; suspicion of authority; de-emphasizing of institution; new organizations and structures that sit in parallel or distinct from previous ones.

This base system will be added to through the dialectical integration of anthropological and sociological insights in chapter 4. However, a basic framework is now in place, enabling initial explorations of the Movement under the CRQs.

In application, Ihab Hassan suggests that postmodern characteristics form a catena whereby one builds upon and flows from another in the manifestation of postmodernism in action.[102] Applying this idea to ecclesial postmodernism potentially suggests a progressive "trickle-down" pathway of ecclesial manifestations, whereby manifestations of a non-foundational epistemology creates those of discontinuities between signifier and signified in language about reality, creating the context for manifestations of micronarratives held in communal identity. In such, a flow exists from *Criteria One* to *Four* where *Criterion One* manifestations would be primary and most strongly seen, while *Criterion Four*, being at the end of the chain, the least. However, such would be one possible catena, and others placing the criteria in different orderings may be feasible as well—for example, *Criterion Three* emphases on testimony forming out of *Criterion Four* discoveries of the importance of it in community.

Whichever route, ecclesial postmodernism, if controlled by an internal postmodern drive that is epistemological in first nature, contains *Criterion One* manifestations in greater strength than any other criterion manifestation subsequently generated; *Criterion One* ecclesial manifestations stand at the head of all generation chains. This is a reasonable assumption given the primacy of epistemological development in the historical trajectory of postmodernism's birth described in this chapter, which, as has been noted, may be reflected in the weight of *Criterion One* manifestations highlighted in Pentecostal-Charismatic scholarship which discerns this. In application of this, if a given lifeworld shows such a *Criterion One* priority in dialectic conversation with the ecclesiological postmodern system, evidence is seen that its postmodern characteristics[103] are generated by an internal postmodern-like drive working itself out over time within the lifeworld.

102. Hassan, *Postmodern Turn*, 168–72.

103. Hereafter, the language employed is that when such system *manifestations* are brought dialectically to the Movement's lifeworld in analysis, they reveal its postmodern *characteristics*.

2.6 CONCLUSION

Much ground has been covered in this chapter and the scene is now set for initial explorations of the Movement's lifeworld in pursuit of answers to the CRQs of this study. Through utilizing a historical narrative approach that focuses on philosophical postmodernism, a robust Postmodern Analytic has been derived from first principles. Through bringing this into conversation with Pentecostal-Charismatic scholarship, the transcontextual system of this study's dialectic methodology, *ecclesial postmodernism*, has been mapped at a base level as a set of manifestations of the Analytic Criteria in the ecclesial context, and a relationship of relative strengths between them has been suggested.

Beyond the specific bounds of this study, the Analytic and ecclesial postmodernism system are gifts to wider scholarship. Rigorously derived from first principles, they give the ability to analyze any given Pentecostal-Charismatic ecclesial lifeworld for postmodern character. The Analytic itself gives a coherent set of minimal postmodern criteria that allow a well-defined discussion of postmodernism—unlike some of the approaches seen in §1.1.1—and the method of system construction in this chapter provides a more rigorous means of analysis than other parallel approaches highlighted. As this study turns to its first explorations of the Movement's lifeworld under the enquiry of the CRQs, it does so well-equipped for the task.

ID # 3

Exploring the Charismatic Movement in the Church of England

Now equipped to speak clearly about what postmodernism in the ecclesial context looks like, this chapter explores the Movement's lifeworld under the enquiry of the CRQs, analyzing four key historical moments within the first orientating "search" phase of this study's methodology.[1] Resultantly, initial answers to each of the CRQs are found which both orientate more in-depth lifeworld analysis later in this study and enable a contextualized return to system questions in the next chapter.

The historical nature of the Charismatic Movement in the Church of England has received little academic interest and has often been sublimated into historical analyses of the charismatic movement more generally in Britain. For example, no equivalent work to McBain's history of the Charismatic Movement in the British Baptist Church exists.[2] However, the works of Hocken[3] and James Steven[4] give a rich overview of events surrounding the rise of the Movement, including specifics unique to the Church of England; there is little need for a detailed historical presentation of the Movement, nor would it be helpful for this study's purposes. Instead, key moments within the history of the Movement are examined. Some warn of "the futility of attempting to write the history of charismatic

---

1. See §1.2.
2. McBain, *Fire Over the Waters*.
3. Hocken, *Streams of Renewal*.
4. Steven, *Worship in the Spirit*; Steven, "'Worship.'"

renewal from within a single denominational framework"[5] due to its globalized trans-denominational nature. However, by intensively examining four singular events and periods, a narrower denominational focus is enabled aware of larger contexts.

The four moments considered sample the Movement's nature along its timeline and explore different yet complementary aspects of it under the CRQs: examination of the Movement's birth explores foundational contexts and influences on its genesis; examination of the Fountain Trust allows investigation of a key structural facilitator of the Movement's early growth; analysis of the self-reflective nature of a report on the Movement generated by the Church of England explores mid-life contemporary understanding; lastly, consideration of later North American influences examines events centered on the lived experience of Movement participants.[6]

3.1 THE BIRTH OF THE MOVEMENT

Though many of its early pioneers sought to justify the Movement's agenda by referencing the re-emergence and recovery of past experiences,[7] it was a clear "birth" of a new movement in the specific context of the Church of England, which, as will be seen, had previously rejected Pentecostal-Charismatic possibilities. In this birth, numerous contexts must be understood to rightly analyze it. Firstly, that the Charismatic Movement in Britain was part of a bigger picture of similar movements on a global scale in a similar period;[8] secondly, that in Britain it began in the Anglican sphere and moved to others through a process of gentle "osmosis";[9] and thirdly that in this sphere, it originated largely, though not exclusively, in Evangelical churchmanship.

This latter context explains the Movement's heavily Evangelical nature in its early life,[10] and is important in precisely contextualizing

---

5. Hutchinson et al., "Introduction," 6; cf. Maiden, *Age of the Spirit*, 218.

6. The location of these events solely in the period 1950–2000 is supported by recent work that sees this period as of defining significance for charismatic renewal. See Hutchinson et al., "Introduction," 2.

7. For example, Harper, *As at the Beginning*, 17–22. Cf. Mather, "Theology," 43, 47.

8. Hocken, *Streams of Renewal*, 4; Anderson, *Introduction to Pentecostalism*, 157–75.

9. McBain, "Mainline Charismatics," 46.

10. Stanley, *Global Diffusion of Evangelism*, 181–82; Bebbington, *Evangelicalism in Modern Britain*, 229.

its birth. John Gunstone comments that of the twenty-one attendees of one of the first major charismatic conferences at Stoke Poges in 1964, "Seventeen were clergy of the Church of England and fifteen of those were Evangelicals; Michael Meakin and I were the only Catholic Anglicans."[11] Hocken comments, "It is also clear from the data . . . that the greatest impact of the nascent movement at this stage was upon the world of the Anglican evangelicals."[12] Though it is incorrect to claim no other Anglican churchmanships were present at the Movement's birth, Hocken's tracing of it centers on the early 1960s events in three Evangelical churches: All Souls' Langham Place, St. Mark's Gillingham, and St. John's Burslem.[13] MacInnes explains this Evangelical context was vital to the Movement's early success:

> Previously when a person had these sorts of experiences, they were regarded a little bit off the scale and therefore to be avoided at all costs. But . . . essentially here were, the sort of leaders of the Evangelical world, finding that this was something that was really important in their lives. It inevitably carried weight.[14]

This context helps situate a date and place of the Movement's birth in events in these interconnected parishes, suggesting a birthdate between 1962 and 1963. With greater specificity, the meeting on April 9, 1963, between Martyn Lloyd-Jones and four clergy who had come into charismatic renewal from two of these parishes—John Collins, David Watson, David MacInnes and Michael Harper[15]—is seen by Teddy Saunders and Hugh Sansom as perhaps "the moment when the Charismatic Movement in Britain was born."[16]

In the below, analyzing the Movement's birth in awareness of this context, added to its wider global and Anglican contexts, enables a fruitful examination of influences that precipitated it under the enquiry of the CRQs. This birth did not occur *ex nihilo*, and it is in analysis of how the

---

11. Gunstone, *Pentecostal Anglicans*, 11. Cf. Hocken's different record of the names, traditions, and theological emphases of these attendees, of whom only eight out of twelve Anglicans are called "Anglican (Evangelical)." Nevertheless, Gunstone's recollection of the event is telling of the perceived feeling of Evangelical weight at the Movement's birth. Hocken, *Streams of Renewal*, 118.

12. Hocken, *Streams of Renewal*, 105.

13. Hocken, *Streams of Renewal*, 65–69, 70–79, 91–97.

14. David MacInnes, interview by Jitesh K. Patel, May 1, 2020.

15. Atherstone et al., "Lloyd-Jones," 116.

16. Saunders and Sansom, *David Watson*, 71.

Movement was born within these contexts and formative influences that insights are found pertinent to this study's enquiry.

Richard Forster, constructing a subjective history of the Charismatic Movement's birth in Britain, speaks of tributaries flowing into flood, giving no historical precedence to one contribution over another.[17] This model helps illuminate the overlapping influences flowing into the Movement's birth, yet not all these "tributaries" illuminate aspects relevant to the CRQs. Those that do can be split into two broad categories: outside influences and internal frustrations.

3.1.1 Outside Influences

In §2.5.2, Noel's analysis suggested that early Pentecostalism displayed a range of postmodern characteristics, which here generates questions as to whether later Pentecostal influence on the Movement's birth—retaining some of these characteristics—might cause some of its seen postmodern character through transference, thereby being part of an answer to CRQ-3 which asks about non-cultural trajectories and influences within the Movement responsible for its postmodern characteristics. However, examination of historical evidence renders this possibility largely unlikely.

Historically, Pentecostalism's rise in the first half of the twentieth century had limited effect on Britain's historic denominations before the emergence of charismatic renewal. This was despite the influence of Alexander Boddy's pentecostal ministry in Sunderland and subsequent leadership of early British Pentecostalism.[18] Boddy desired pentecostal renewal of historical denominations including his Anglican one, which he never left.[19] Early in his ministry, he explained that he did "not feel that the Lord's leading in these days is to set up a new church, but to bless individuals where they are."[20] However, this did not translate into pentecostal renewal within the Church of England, and conversely saw little success in bringing Anglican clergy into the early British Pentecostal movement.[21] Several political factors that weakened Boddy's later influ-

---

17. Foster, "Rise."
18. Blumhofer, "Alexander Boddy."
19. Anderson, *Introduction to Pentecostalism*, 100.
20. Wakefield, *Alexander Boddy*, 126.
21. Wakefield, *Alexander Boddy*, 183.

ence might be behind this failure.[22] However, so was the realization by many early Pentecostal leaders that "revival within the churches had not happened and pressure was growing for a new direction,"[23] leading to the formation of offshoot Pentecostal organizations. Harper views the opposition of leaders in historical denominations, who violently expelled its Pentecostal members, as an additional factor.[24]

However, despite the witness of this earlier failure, many see Pentecostalism as the key influence giving rise to the Movement. Stephen Hunt proposes, "In the 1950s, a number of principal Pentecostal bodies opened up dialogue with the historical churches, and from this initiative neo-Pentecostalism in the shape of the Charismatic Renewal movement was seemingly born."[25] He further argues, "Given the impact of Pentecostalism in both countries [Britain and USA] by this time, its role in precipitating the Renewal movement is indisputable."[26] Such an analysis perhaps coheres with Hollenweger's wider analysis of global macro-trends wherein Pentecostals return to their ecumenical roots in dialogue with historical denominations after having originally split from them.[27] Key individuals are identified in this. Gunstone, an early leader and commentator on the Movement, defines its participants as "Pentecostal Anglicans," explaining, "Pentecostal Anglicans are those who are influenced by classical Pentecostal teaching and practice,"[28] highlighting the central figure of David du Plessis in this.[29] Similarly, Quebedeaux highlights the influence of Leslie Newbigin's challenge to Protestant churches to acknowledge Pentecostalism as a new third stream of God's work alongside Protestantism and Catholicism, and his call to learn from their emphasis on the Spirit's work.[30]

Given Noel's analysis in §2.5.2, such Pentecostal birthing could be the cause for the Movement's postmodern characteristics. Postmodern characteristics present in the Pentecostalism of the day, derived from

---

22. Wakefield, *Alexander Boddy*, 198–99.
23. Wakefield, *Alexander Boddy*, 199; cf. 212.
24. Harper, *As at the Beginning*, 44–47.
25. Hunt, *History*, 102.
26. Hunt, *History*, 144.
27. Hollenweger, *Pentecostalism*, 363.
28. Gunstone, *Pentecostal Anglicans*, 46.
29. Gunstone, *Pentecostal Anglicans*, 65.
30. Quebedeaux, *New Charismatics II*, 213.

those seen in its earlier life in Noel's analysis, are transferred in some form to the Movement it helps birth.

However, this view overlooks historical details about the Movement's initial birth which makes this answer to CRQ-3 unlikely. Pentecostal influence is neither as early nor as important as the above scholarship suggests. Though Hunt is correct in seeing that key individual Pentecostals played subsequent important roles in the later growth of the early Movement,[31] in Britain no formal overtures are recorded to have happened in the 1950s between Pentecostals and Anglicans, and there is evidence Pentecostal denominations initially regarded charismatic renewal with suspicion because of its ecumenical nature and resulting doctrinal impurity.[32] MacInnes explains a similar attitude of suspicion was held by Anglicans towards Pentecostals after the Movement's birth:

> We turned to them [Pentecostals] to some extent because we were trying to discover more about the meaning of this, this experience we were having. At the same time, we were very uncomfortable about some of the expressions of it and some of the doctrines that they had behind it. . . . As far as we were concerned, there was very little preliminary Pentecostal influence.[33]

Additionally, if Hocken is correct, and events at Langham Place, Gillingham, and Burslem formed a central nucleus of the early Movement by 1964, then the chronology of Pentecostal influence does not fit with how charismatic renewal arose in the lives and ministries of its earliest leaders such as Harper, Collins, Watson, and MacInnes.[34] In his autobiography, Harper explains his "earth shaking" event of renewal came from study of Ephesians in preparation for a weekend conference in September 1962, which evoked personal prayer leading to an experience of renewal;[35] in her biography of her husband's ministry Jeanne Harper

---

31. As did individuals from other denominations who had been renewed through past Pentecostal contact, acting as a bridging influence of Pentecostalism. See Hunt, *History*, 165.

32. Walker, *Restoring the Kingdom*, 58. See also evidence of friction in §3.1.2 below.

33. MacInnes, interview.

34. Hocken, *Streams of Renewal*, 96. The parish St. Paul's Beckenham and its vicar George Forester had little discernible effect on the early Movement, especially after the resignation of Forester in late 1964 and his subsequent ministry as a Pentecostal rather than Anglican minister. At most, events in Beckenham created public interest yet had little ongoing influence on the early Movement. See Hocken, *Streams of Renewal*, 71–81.

35. Harper, *None Can Guess*, 22.

adds his subsequent exploration of other NT passages as key to his full entrance into renewal.[36] Initial renewal for Harper came about despite his public opposition to Pentecostal emphases on healing and was independent of Pentecostal influence. Only later did he encounter du Plessis, who, though an enormous catalyst for the fledgling Movement, counselled the Harpers to "receive Pentecost but not Pentecostalism."[37] Records of du Plessis's movements in the 1960s verify that his first visit to England occurred over 12th–17th of October 1963, after many central events of the Movement's birth, including the April 1963 Lloyd-Jones meeting.[38]

Such prayerful scriptural provocation also lay at the heart of the renewal of clergy associated with St. Mark's Gillingham.[39] For Collins, a period of inner turmoil preceded a kindling of renewal through his preaching through Romans 6, precipitated by Watson's initial journey towards renewal through study of the same passage. Subsequently, the key breakthrough moment of wider parish renewal was precipitated through prayer and another passage of Scripture, Luke 11:9–13.[40] For MacInnes, the decisive moment came on the same night, who—spurred by news of spiritual seeking in his former parish—testifies that after a time of wrestling in conversation with God about the possibility of renewal, "I just hit cloud nine and I found myself absolutely full of the Holy Spirit."[41] Later, Watson's full entrance into renewal came through his studies of the book of Acts which provoked his desperate seeking for the missing spiritual dynamic of the early church,[42] which, combined with his studies of revivals past and present—especially the "East African Revival"—drove him to desperate prayer and spiritual breakthrough.[43]

These accounts of the Movement's birth through these key individuals indicate little Pentecostal influence on the Movement's birth. The catalytic effect of individuals from a Pentecostal background, du Plessis being prominent among them, may have been a factor in the early *growth* of the Movement, but not in its *birth*. Even this must be tempered by

---

36. Harper, *Visited by God*, 12; Hocken, *Streams of Renewal*, 75.

37. Harper, *Visited by God*, 12.

38. Ziefle, *David du Plessis*, 193. However, Harper seems to indicate a brief visit by du Plessis in 1960 not recorded in his travel logs. Harper, *As at the Beginning*, 84–85.

39. Hocken, *Streams of Renewal*, 91.

40. Hocken, *Streams of Renewal*, 92.

41. MacInnes, interview.

42. Saunders and Sansom, *David Watson*, 65; Watson, *You Are My God*, 50.

43. Saunders and Sansom, *David Watson*, 62–65.

several ongoing stark differences between the Movement and Pentecostalism, which made such cross-over difficult throughout the Movement's timeline, as David Bebbington has recently explored.[44] Thus theorized Pentecostal influences are unlikely to be an answer to CRQ-3 in explaining the early Movement's postmodern characteristics.

In a similar vein, neither does an examination of the influence of renewal in the American Episcopal church suggest this observed external influence is part of an answer to CRQ-3, necessitating an investigation into its postmodern nature and influence. Though events and subsequent ministry related to Dennis Bennett's 1959 Van Nuys renewal experience are also seen by many to have helped precipitate the Movement,[45] again, as with suggestions of Pentecostal influence, the influence of renewed American Episcopalians is overstated, and does not fit historical details of the Movement's birth. The relatively brief period between 1959 and an early birthdate of the Movement in 1964 suggests some probable links, yet as Maiden explains, "The Bennett myth has limitations as a genesis story. Its linear, American-centric account obscured the complex and decentred nature of charismatic origins."[46] Anderson highlights a larger trend at work here: the mistaken assumption that the Van Nuys events are "often regarded as the commencement of the Charismatic Movement in the Western world."[47] The overemphasis on American influence perhaps arises from Harper's early historiography of the Movement, which emphasized it.[48] Conversely, his contemporary Watson comments that the news of American events came *after* his experience of personal renewal,[49] while MacInnes explains the news was more of an after-fact comfort, because "here was the story of people who we could to some extent identify with."[50] No American visitors from Episcopalian Renewal visited Britain before 1963,[51] and though subsequent mid-to-late 1960s American books were important in the growth of the Movement, they cannot be seen to be of foundational influence due to a later chronology.

44. Bebbington, "Introduction," 243–50.
45. Stanley, *Global Diffusion of Evangelism*, 189–92; Quebedeaux, *New Charismatics*, 59; Mather, "Theology," 48; McBain, *Fire Over the Waters*, 3.
46. Maiden, *Age of the Spirit*, 51.
47. Anderson, *Introduction to Pentecostalism*, 158.
48. Harper, *As at the Beginning*, 84.
49. Watson, *You Are My God*, 62.
50. MacInnes, interview.
51. Hocken, *Streams of Renewal*, 128.

These two overstated external influences, often wrongly weighted in their causative effect on the Movement's birth, are, with a more nuanced weighting, unlikely to yield a substantive answer to CRQ-3 in explaining the Movement's early postmodern characteristics, even if they have a place in later dynamics. More important to the Movement's birth—especially in the question of postmodern characteristics seen in it—was an outside influence which subsequently became a key internal motivator for charismatic renewal: the provocative witness of recent global revivals—which as seen was part of Watson's journey towards charismatic renewal. This outside provocation, internalized together with key frustrations within the church of the time, led to powerful cries which precipitated a charismatic renewal with some clear postmodern characteristics.

3.1.2 Internal Frustrations

3.1.2.1 *Frustrations with the Church*

Cultural changes in Britain in the run-up to charismatic renewal, and the corresponding state of the Church of England, played an important part in the Movement's birth; as society underwent huge changes in the aftermath of two World Wars, charismatic renewal emerged in parallel with such changes. Josephine Bax, commenting on renewal, suggests, "It is surely no accident that while this death and resurrection is taking place in the church, society at large is going through a similar kind of travail . . . we have passed the end of Renaissance man, and are now in the post-enlightenment age." Yet she cautions, "Though there are obvious parallels, the church, I believe, is not just a mirror of our society, and the renewal not simply a baptism of the counterculture."[52]

This counterculture against earlier cultural norms contained a plurality of emergent cultural emphases which challenged the church to its core.[53] To many, the traditional church was unable to respond to these changes because of its lifelessness and impotence;[54] from personal experience, Thomas Walker testifies,

---

52. Bax, *Good Wine*, 16–17.

53. For more on this time and the challenges faced by the church see McLeod, *Religious Crisis*, 60–214.

54. Maiden, *Age of the Spirit*, 16.

> In the 1960s many were becoming aware that something new and drastic was needed to bring Christians alive, before the church as an institution could change sufficiently to seem appealing to the multitudes who had forsaken it or never gone near it.[55]

Theologically there was frustration for many with a liberalism which was the established church's prevalent answer to the rapidly changing culture, especially when this, in turn, engendered the opposite reaction of intense fundamentalism in other church quarters.[56] New converts from Billy Graham's crusades in the 1950s, populating stale churches that did not match the Christianity they had been promised, added to these frustrations.[57] Additionally, the witness of participants in the East African Revival and similar revivals created a hunger for change and revival in the UK,[58] leading even John Stott into deep pneumatological exploration.[59] Hocken's analysis outlines "Seeking Factors" that precipitated the Charismatic Movement in Britain, the first being "Concern and Prayer for Revival,"[60] and in this Thomas Walker explains,

> Out of the cynicism following two world wars, and out of a dry, churchy formalism . . . new life was emerging. . . . Although the prayer "renew us by your Spirit" had not yet become part of Anglican liturgy, it was in fact the heartcry of many Christians who felt that their spiritual lives were dry and inadequate to face the challenge of an increasingly godless, secular society.[61]

From its very beginning, the Movement is birthed out of a context that viewed the institutional church in a somewhat negative manner, longing for something more real and authentic to human experience. Herein, a *Criterion Four* characteristic is seen, a soft anti-institutionalism within charismatic searching in its early identity. However, as shall be seen, this did not flourish long-term, perhaps because it was not engendered by a postmodern suspicion of institution, but rather exasperation about its state—a state changed by the advent of renewal. Nonetheless, if

---

55. Walker, *Renew Us*, 15, 19.
56. Mather, "Theology," 43–44.
57. Hunt, *Charismatic Movement*, 165.
58. Saunders and Sansom, *David Watson*, 56; Maiden, *Age of the Spirit*, 35–38.
59. McBain, *Fire Over the Waters*, 18.
60. Hocken, *Streams of Renewal*, 152.
61. Walker, *Renew Us*, 9.

some of this exasperation was partly due to the modernistic nature of the institutional church, which §3.3.2 will suggest was true for some, then early evidence is found here under CRQ-2 of a *Mutual Origins* generation of this postmodern characteristic.

3.1.2.2 Frustrations with Evangelical Hermeneutics

General frustrations with the state of the wider church at the time of the Movement's birth combined with some more particular frustrations within the Evangelical context of the Movement's initial birth in the decades running up to 1962–63. Such frustrations precipitated an anti-modernistic impulse that rejected over-rational hermeneutics, opening the door to *Criterion One* emphases on subjective experience.

Alister McGrath comments that between the 1940s and 1950s, Evangelicals developed a siege mentality against growing Anglo-Catholicism and liberalism in the Church of England, becoming combative in theology and outlook.[62] With an emphasis on Scripture, the means of defense was highly rationalistic due to the "historic connection of evangelicalism with the intellectual legacy of the European Enlightenment... its preference for the acquisition of knowledge from written texts over untested intuition or illumination."[63] More widely, Brian Stanley comments, "Mid-twentieth-century evangelicalism has undoubtedly reacted to the ascendancy of Protestant liberalism with a form of defensive textual scholasticism that left too little room for the freedom and enjoyment of the Spirit."[64] Ian Randall suggests such observations should be tempered by the presence of Evangelical groups that emphasized a more subjective emotional spirituality in the early twentieth century, such as those of a Keswick platform.[65] Nevertheless, MacInnes explains that by the 1960s the influence of Stott's challenge to Evangelicals to take Scripture seriously in the face of liberalism had resulted in unintended spiritual consequences, as "there was a tendency with that, to become slightly dry

---

62. McGrath, "Evangelical Anglicanism," 16.

63. Stanley, *Global Diffusion of Evangelism*, 209.

64. Stanley, *Global Diffusion of Evangelism*, 210. Castelo suggests American Evangelicalism adopted rationalistic methodology both as defense and appeal, which may parallel the same in British Evangelicalism. Castelo, *Pentecostalism*, 84.

65. Randall, *Evangelical Experiences*, 276–78.

... and so there was the beginnings of a readiness to say we are looking for something else."[66]

Into such a context an experiential hermeneutic of Scripture was born. Andrew Walker comments that with hindsight charismatic renewal can be seen as an "overreaction" to "the rationalism of evangelical scholasticism,"[67] while in gentler tones Colin Buchanan concludes it was about "reasserting a traditional evangelical emphasis which could get lost behind the equally traditional but more rationalistic interest in doctrine."[68] Thomas Walker, commenting on his experience, explains, "I had a sense that if God was great as the Bible showed him to be, there should be great success in serving him, and I should know more of his triumph and victory in my life and ministry and it was evident that this change had happened in the lives of my friends who had come to renewal."[69] As explored above, early pioneers of the Movement came into an experience of charismatic renewal through an spiritual seeking engendered in part from a new experiential reading of scripture, something that can be viewed as a departure from a rationalistically controlled approach to Scripture to one informed by experience (or lack thereof).

Analysis of this under the CRQs reveals much. CRQ-1's enquiry suggests signs of *Criterion One* and *Two* postmodern characteristics mark the Movement's birth: an epistemology broadened to include experiential elements, leading to a new hermeneutical approach to scripture that reads it with personal experiential desires read into and out of the text. Importantly, this is a reaction against a modernistic climate internal to Evangelicalism, tentative evidence in response to CRQ-2 of the *Mutual Origins* model. This, in addition to signs of *Criterion Four* characteristics seen in frustrations with the institutional church, indicates a wide set of postmodern characteristics present at the Movement's birth, partially generated out of a reaction to modernism in its formative context. Under CRQ-3's enquiry, testimonies such as those of the early renewal pioneers, highlighting a new hermeneutical approach, can be seen as a generative desire to recover a premodern experience of God found in the NT; as will be seen, a desire that runs throughout the Movement's life.

---

66. MacInnes, interview.
67. Walker, "Recovering," 8.
68. Buchanan, *St. John's College Nottingham*, 167.
69. Walker, *Renew Us*, 12.

3.2 EARLY DEVELOPMENT AND THE FOUNTAIN TRUST

The Movement's early development is intertwined with the establishment of the Fountain Trust on September 29, 1964, by Michael Harper, who resigned from his position at All Souls Langham Place on July 2, 1964. A growing leadership role within early charismatic renewal, combined with a growing sense of distance from his incumbent Stott's view of the Movement, led Harper to seek to serve the perceived growing work of God full-time without restriction, resulting in the Trust's formation. Its subsequent influence as an organizing force bringing leadership to renewal is of critical importance in understanding the Movement's nature in the 1960s and 1970s, and in a key sense the Trust acts as the embodiment of the Movement in this period. Buchanan called the Trust's formation "a milestone in England"[70] for the Movement; likewise, McBain expresses from a Baptist viewpoint that "the Fountain Trust was by far the most responsible body in the renewal scene at the time."[71] Walker tellingly comments, "the closure of the Fountain Trust in 1980 left the Renewal without a clear focus."[72]

Under CRQ-1's enquiry, the Trust's life helps reveal some of the potential postmodern characteristics of the Movement's early development. As theoretically predicted, of largest weight are *Criterion One* characteristics—yet revealed to be held in tension with ongoing modernistic emphases—leading some to seek to reintegrate postmodern and modernistic emphases, therein suggesting limits to the operation of the *Mutual Origins* model in the Movement under CRQ-2's enquiry. However, expected *Criterion Four* characteristics are absent—and indeed opposed—despite their presence at the Movement's birth.

3.2.1 The Fountain Trust and Church Structures

It would be expected that the organization critically responsible for leading renewal in the 1960s and 1970s, if postmodern in character, would bear a suspicion of traditional ecclesial structures and institutions as *Criterion Four* manifestations, resulting in a new structure that competes with denominational ones, continuing the soft anti-institutionalism seen

---

70. Buchanan, *Charismatic Movement*, 7.
71. McBain, *Fire Over the Waters*, 31.
72. Walker, *Renew Us*, 60.

at the Movement's birth. However, this is not seen; rather, the Trust actively sought to emphasize the opposite.

With the need for personal financial support and a means of publishing literature, the Trust was created by Harper and a few sympathetic friends as a small community formed around pre-existing friendships, rather than denominational structures.[73] In founding the Trust, Harper spoke of his "horror" of "organisation" and his ability to "see so many dangers and misunderstandings that I really wondered if it was right to set up any structure at all."[74] The Trust was not set up to replace existing structures but rather out of pragmatic necessity, something reflected in its initial aims as a service agency: "We feel called to serve every section of the Church, without fear or favor. We are seeing the Holy Spirit moving in unlikely places today, and we rejoice in His power to bring men of different traditions together."[75]

Throughout the Trust's lifetime, it kept close to its second of three aims stated in 1967: "To encourage local churches to experience renewal in the Holy Spirit."[76] To this end, Harper highlighted the measures initially taken to make sure they were not seen as a parallel organization to existing churches:

> Right from the start we were determined not to attract "followers." . . . [W]e have never had a "membership." . . . [W]e have never had a regular meeting in London. . . . [W]e have deliberately changed the frequency with which they are held—the venues and the days on which they held, to make it as hard as possible for people to become regular customers. We have never advertised our meetings—other than in our own magazine and letters.[77]

Thomas Smail, the Trust's second director, commented on this continuing vision in a 1976 editorial of *Renewal* magazine, which was published by the Trust: "This magazine and the ministry it represents are not concerned with something called the Charismatic Movement, if that means something apart from the life and fellowship of the local church."[78]

73. Harper, *None Can Guess*, 60–63.
74. Harper, *None Can Guess*, 63.
75. See Hocken, *Streams of Renewal*, 119, where he quotes Michael Harper's December 1964 newsletter.
76. Harper, "Editorial: Ministry."
77. Harper, *None Can Guess*, 64.
78. Harper, "Editorial: Simplicity."

Several issues reveal the authenticity of this vision to bless structures and denominations as they are. Firstly, Hocken explains that the Trust's tumultuous relationship with Pentecostal denominations was partially because "local Pentecostals were never invited to speak at conferences promoted by the Fountain Trust . . . [as] there was some concern that Pentecostal speakers might urge the newly Spirit-baptised to join their own denomination."[79] Likewise, the Trust overtly criticized the emergent charismatic House Church Movement "as an anti-denominational and anti-historic church movement" that called people out of existing denominations to it.[80] A second witness is found in the Trust's 1967–68 failure in becoming a community-based organization,[81] taking a lead from a Houston-based example of renewed charismatic community[82] whose example helped engender other charismatic communities in Britain, such as the Community of Celebration, the Post Green Community, the Barnabas Fellowship,[83] and those emerging from St. Michael-le-Belfrey.[84] Connie Au comments that this arose from what Harper called "a deep-seated disunity" in the face of the prospect, despite "a time of sharing together in love."[85] The level of this failure, despite examples of success elsewhere, exposes the depth of the Trust's feelings about separate structures and organizations.

The greatest witness, however, is the Trust's self-closure on December 31, 1980.[86] According to Michael Baring, its last director, this was "a unanimous decision taken after some months of prayer and listening to the Lord,"[87] likening the Trust's closure to the seed that dies to bear much fruit in John 12:24. Later opinion critiqued this purely spiritual take on the decision,[88] yet as far back as a Trust advisory meeting of December 1968, Campbell McAlpine expressed the sense that in God's will there

79. Hocken, *Streams of Renewal*, 140–41.
80. Ho Yan Au, "Grassroots," 59.
81. Maiden, *Age of the Spirit*, 140.
82. Steven, "'Worship,'" 32.
83. Steven, "'Worship,'" 32–33.
84. Saunders and Sansom, *David Watson*, 151–60.
85. Ho Yan Au, "Grassroots," 42.
86. *Renewal* and *Theological Renewal* magazines continued to be published by others, the former up until 2000.
87. Baring, "Editorial."
88. Ho Yan Au, "Grassroots," 88–89; McBain, *Fire Over the Waters*, 73–74; Walker, "Pentecostal Power," 99.

might come a time when the Trust's work would be at an end, and the Trustees who reviewed the Trust's work every eighteen months asked the continual question of whether the Trust should continue.[89] Such ability to repeatedly ask of its death, and to subsequently enact it, speaks to the Trust's core belief that it did not exist as a replacement or parallel structure to historic church denominations, and strongly evidences against related *Criterion Four* postmodern characteristics of the Movement over the Trust's lifetime, despite early manifestations of them in the Movement's birth.

3.2.2 Experiential Ecumenicalism

In contrast, the Trust's history witnesses to suggestions of clear *Criterion One* manifestations in the Movement's experiential emphases, primarily seen in how the Trust enabled a radical ecumenical and cross-tradition inclusivity through them. In 1971, Harper commented, "This particular movement is characteristically unifying rather than divisive. . . . In fact it is no exaggeration to claim that this movement is the most unifying in Christendom today."[90] The evidence is clear that from an initial beginning in the Evangelical quarters of the Church of England, the Movement rapidly spread to Anglo-Catholic quarters—though less so in what were called "Radical" sections of the church (which now might be called Liberal)—and that the Trust was a key enabler of this.[91] This must be nuanced, however, by renewal experiences that were independent of the Trust's ministry, for example Colin Urquhart's in the Anglo-Catholic parish of St. Hugh's Church, Luton.[92]

Organizational factors enabled this inclusivity. The Trust was set up with a clear ecumenical agenda; Harper's aforementioned 1964 statement of intent was for it to "rejoice in His [God's] power to bring men of different traditions together."[93] The Trust implemented this vision well: forming an advisory council with representatives from all strands of the Movement,

---

89. Ho Yan Au, "Grassroots," 72.

90. Harper, *None Can Guess*, 149.

91. Gunstone tracks the spread of renewal in these three sections of the Church of England in Gunstone, *Pentecostal Anglicans*, 69–126.

92. See Urquhart, *When the Spirit Comes*. Important also are the influential charismatic experiences of Michael Meakin in 1963 and John Gunstone in 1964.

93. See Hocken, *Streams of Renewal*, 119, where he quotes Michael Harper's December 1964 newsletter.

inviting a Roman Catholic speaker to its first international conference in 1971, and seeking to be in constant dialogue and relationship with the various denominations touched by renewal.[94] Au records Smail's lament that with the Trust's closure the Movement's ecumenical dimension "got lost . . . and never came back again."[95] While figures external to the Trust were influential in enabling ecumenicalism, such as initially Lloyd-Jones for the Baptists,[96] and Michael Ramsey for Anglo-Catholics,[97] the Trust's ministry was critical to this aspect of charismatic renewal.

Underlying this unifying capacity was the role of experience. Harper, when asked what renewal was about in 1973, simply answered, "It's about an experience of God";[98] Hocken argues that the unity found in renewal hinged on such experience being shared:

> Those baptized in the spirit could now praise God together in free composition or tongues; and the fact that they could recognise each other in the same ability to hear the Lord in their inner spirit and act in his power, showed that their unity in the Spirit was not a matter of mere feelings and joyous emotions. It had an objective basis in themselves and in what they could observably do.[99]

Gunstone comments how the experience of "charismatic manifestations such as tongues, interpretations, prophecies and healings,"[100] found resonance with the Catholic sacramental tradition of God working through signs. Commenting on the Fountain Trust's five major conferences, Au explains that both Protestants and Catholics "found themselves having similar experiences in the Spirit and realised that, in fact, they were all members of the body of Christ despite doctrinal differences."[101] Moments of disunity in these conferences centered on doctrinal disagreements over the celebration of the Eucharist, leading some to weep,[102] and perhaps

---

94. Hocken, "Fountain Trust."

95. See Ho Yan Au, "Grassroots," 76, where she quotes an interview with Thomas Smail. As will be seen in chapters 6–7, Nicky Gumbel and Alpha's ministry shows Smail was perhaps premature in this assessment.

96. McBain, *Fire Over the Waters*, 45.

97. Gunstone, *Greater Things Than These*, 94.

98. Buchanan, *St. John's College Nottingham*, 167.

99. Hocken, *Streams of Renewal*, 161.

100. Gunstone, *Pentecostal Anglicans*, 95.

101. Ho Yan Au, "Grassroots," 187–88.

102. Ho Yan Au, "Grassroots," 168.

showed early signs of the limits of a unity based on subjective experience. Nevertheless, the fact that the Movement's newfound unity did not collapse under such differences shows the power of the experiential focus that maintained unity amid conflict.

Such experiential unity highlights signs of a *Criterion One* experiential and perhaps pragmatic epistemology at work, as a unity focused on experience is seen to work, bringing it legitimacy and life. This is a development of similar *Criterion One* characteristics seen at the Movement's birth, and the fact such unity overcame strong historic doctrinal disunity perhaps indicates a priority of experiential and pragmatic emphases over rationalistic ones in the Movement—highlighting the strength of these early postmodern characteristics. However, this priority was also quickly challenged.

3.2.3 Receiving Critique

From early in the Movement's life, its nearest critics lambasted its overemphasis on experience, especially when at the cost of doctrinal purity in the ecumenical context. Despite the Evangelical pedigree of many of the Movement's early pioneers, Stott led the Evangelical establishment's first response to the Movement negatively, setting the tone for the following years. In his Islington Clerical Conference address of January 1964, Stott—clearly aiming at experiences such as those of his former curate Harper—critiqued "special experiences":

> They should not, if they are true to scripture, refer to any of them as the baptism of the Spirit. Nor should they urge the same experiences upon others as if they were the spiritual norm. Nor should they suggest that such unusual spiritual experiences are the secret of either holiness or usefulness. . . . [L]et your experience lead you to worship and praise; but let your exhortation to others be grounded not upon your experiences, but upon scripture.[103]

Similarly, Lloyd-Jones, while initially sympathetic to charismatic renewal, expressed suspicion about the influence du Plessis had on it,[104] worrying that it had led to the downgrading of doctrine in favor of experience.[105]

---

103. Stott, *Baptism and Fullness*, 37–39.
104. Lloyd-Jones, *Knowing the Times*, 313.
105. Murray, *David Martyn Lloyd-Jones*, 278–80.

Gunstone recalls that because of such critiques "the Oxford Diocesan Evangelical Fellowship was one of several that warned its members that the Movement was divisive. Books about the renewal were banned from Scripture Union bookshops."[106]

Many initial disagreements centered on the idea of "baptism in the Spirit," which Evangelicals such as Stott believed that charismatics wrongly taught as a second experience, creating a distinction between first and second-class Christians,[107] a theology seen to have been naively absorbed by the Movement from Pentecostalism.[108] However, underlying such disagreements, the root issue was the Movement's theology, which seemed to have lagged behind its experiences. As MacInnes explained,[109] early charismatics had largely drawn on Pentecostal theology to help understand their new experiences. However, once it was realized that such naïve adoption was unwise, voices highlighted concern. In 1974, Green called for charismatics to engage in "more careful theological studies," which would show them "some interesting things"—especially in ideas about baptism in the Spirit.[110] Watson, in 1975, explicitly attributed the Charismatic-Evangelical division as due to a lack of theological study within charismatic renewal when it originally started.[111] As late as 1993 Smail called for charismatic renewal to gain a theology.[112]

Such a theological study was part of a "catch-up" that the Movement sought to engage in during the 1960s and 1970s. The "Eclectics Holy Spirit Study Group"—a subgroup of the Eclectics networks of local Evangelicals—regularly met from 1963 to 1971 to explore the NT basis to charismatic emphases;[113] Harper, Collins, Watson, and MacInnes, were all regular members of it.[114] The Trust ran a series of "Theological Workshops" throughout the 1970s that focused on the "Baptism in the Holy Spirit" and its "Pentecostal Doctrine," as well as other charismatic phenomena.[115] Importantly, out of concern for the theological foundations of

---

106. Gunstone, *Pentecostal Anglicans*, 72–73.
107. Harper, "Editorial: Narrowing."
108. Gunstone, *Pentecostal Anglicans*, 75–76.
109. §3.1.1.
110. Green, "Awakening."
111. Ho Yan Au, "Grassroots," 57.
112. Smail, "Cross," 49.
113. Fountain Trust, "Fountain Trust 1," 56.
114. Fountain Trust, "Fountain Trust 1," 4.
115. Fountain Trust, "Fountain Trust 2."

charismatic renewal, Smail—a theologian who trained under Barth—was recruited to be the Trust's general secretary between 1972–75, becoming its second director in 1975.[116]

Such actions led to a healing of the Charismatic-Evangelical divide in the mid-1970s. Buchanan comments that charismatics no longer insisted on the necessity of baptism in the Spirit and had generally become "slightly tamer"[117] due to, among other factors, greater theological reflection. A radical phase of reconciliation began at the end of 1974: Charismatic speakers were asked to give the Bible studies—and the charismatic music group Fisherfolk to lead sung worship—at 1976's Senior Evangelical Anglican Council; the Trust was asked to nominate seven people to correspond with the Church of England Evangelical Council (CEEC) chaired by Stott;[118] and capping this reconciliation was an invitation for Smail to participate in the April 1977 National Evangelical Anglican Conference, where the joint *Gospel and Spirit* theological statement between the Fountain Trust and the CEEC was ratified. Notably, this statement explained that previous division had occurred because "the main concern of the charismatic renewal, at least until recently, has been experimental rather than theological"; despite the power of experiential ecumenicalism, it lamented that "a unity based on experience at the expense of doctrine would be less than the unity envisaged in the New Testament and would be dangerous in the long term."[119]

These events reveal key details under the enquiry of the CRQs. Under CRQ-1's enquiry the first signs are seen that within the Movement's *Criterion One* broadened epistemology that over the Movement's lifetime—despite the experiential breakthrough the Movement enabled for many of its early participants—rational and experiential priorities are held normatively in parallel, such that when experiential emphases dominant through defining events and experiences, redress soon occurs. Such will be seen again in reactions to "the Toronto Blessing" and highlights the Movement's modernistic characteristics that its postmodern ones live in dialectical tension with, as suggested in §2.5.1.

Under the enquiry of CRQ-2, this in turn illuminates limits to the *Mutual Origins* model. When a strong *Criterion One* postmodern

116. Ho Yan Au, "Grassroots," 44–45.

117. Buchanan, *Encountering Charismatic Worship*, 21.

118. Fountain Trust, "Fountain Trust Advisory," 34.

119. Fountain Trust and Church of England Evangelical Council, "Gospel and Spirit," 3.

characteristic is initially generated through a reaction to modernism, and then encouraged by the pragmatic fruitfulness of its unifying effect to become dominant, this reaction is recognized to have gone too far, and redress is sought. This suggests there are limits to the *Mutual Origins* model when anti-modernistic reactions generating postmodern characteristics move the Movement too far from its more modernistic background.

3.3 A MOMENT OF SELF-UNDERSTANDING: THE 1981 GENERAL SYNOD REPORT

Critical reflection on the Movement found wider expression in the 1981 General Synod report, *The Charismatic Movement in the Church of England*.[120] Exploring its background and content through the enquiry of the CRQs again highlights signs of the Movement's clear *Criterion One* character, as well as potential manifestations of the remaining Analytic Criteria. Further evidence is seen for suggestions of a *Mutual Origins* model and for the importance of a premodern recovery impulse.

3.3.1 Context of the Report

Globally, report commissioning was the major instrument through which denominations sought to analyze charismatic renewal occurring within them. Killian McDonnell, in a 1980 compendium, captured 104 such endeavors, and a Church of England contribution is noticeably absent.[121] Within Britain, other mainline denominations had compiled reports, such as the Church of Scotland (1974) and the Baptist Union (1980).[122] In this context, Colin Buchanan, the instigator of the report, explains his reasoning for seeking it: "I thought I was in the middle of something happening in the Church of England which the General Synod was taking no interest of."[123]

---

120. Buchanan, *Charismatic Movement*. Recommendations made in the acceptance of this report by General Synod generated a chain of further reports not considered here. See Bax, *Good Wine*; The Doctrine Commission of the Church of England, *We Believe in God*; The Doctrine Commission of the Church of England, *Holy Spirit*.

121. McDonnell, *Presence, Power, Praise*.

122. Mather gives an overview of the varied official responses of mainline denominations in Britain in Mather, "Theology," 416–21.

123. Colin Buchanan, interview by Jitesh K. Patel, May 21, 2020.

The report began life in a private member motion proposed by Buchanan in July 1976, which eventually appeared before Synod in the last fifteen minutes of its July 1978 meeting. Buchanan gave eight reasons for its need, the first two suggesting *Criterion One* characteristics of the Movement: "An emphasis upon spiritual experience; A release of inhibitions—in witness, personal relationship."[124] Even stronger, upon the debate's resumption in November 1978's Synod, Edward Wickham, Bishop of Pontefract, commended the need for a report, warning of the Movement's "flight from rationality" like other contemporary movements in the world.[125]

Buchanan's motion passed, and Synod's Standing Committee convened a consultation in Ely on the 9th and 10th of October 1979, during which the Movement was intensively examined. Here several charismatic leaders were present, including Harper, Smail, Gunstone, and MacInnes, and a range of voices were represented: charismatic and non-charismatic; Anglican and non-Anglican; Evangelical, Anglo-Catholic, and Liberal; lay and ordained.[126] In records of this consultation, *Criterion One* aspects of the Movement are again notably suggested. A question from the first round of discussion groups asked, "What are the significant cultural factors in the renewal and in its appeal/lack of appeal to certain groups/classes—e.g. in the matter of non-rational communication?"[127] In response, Christian Howard "asked questions . . . about criteria for evaluating the non-intellectual in religion." The ensuing discussion raised issues such as *Criterion Three* emphases on "testimony rather than intellectual wrestling" and *Criterion One* emphases on the "not-rational rather than 'irrational.'"[128] Among final discussion groups "the reasons for this upsurge" included "the post-war world. . . . Reaction to an over-cerebral Western Christianity. The increasing of influence of existential philosophy."[129] A fascinating grappling with questions at the heart of this study, leading to suggestions akin to *Direct Influence* and *Mutual Origins* models.

---

124. Church of England, *Report of Proceedings*, 9:437.
125. Church of England, *Report of Proceedings*, 9:1192.
126. See throughout Fountain Trust, "Fountain Trust 1."
127. Fountain Trust, "Fountain Trust 1," 15.
128. Fountain Trust, "Fountain Trust 1," 66.
129. Fountain Trust, "Fountain Trust 1," 69.

Afterwards, Buchanan, seen as safely neither charismatic nor non-charismatic,[130] was asked to draft the report based on the results of the consultation and two smaller Working Group meetings in March 1980, and July 1981. In the presentation of the report to Synod in November 1981, Buchanan expresses that the opening debate "did not go well—there was ignorant abuse of what some charismatics were supposed to be up to, and little concentration by such critics on anything said in the report."[131] Such ignorance was partly due to a return to a critique of the Movement on the grounds of its epistemology. Debate minutes show Wickham lambasted Charismatic's "flight from rationality," calling the Movement "a very tame, Anglican, English equivalent" of "the "Moonies," the "Children of God," the "Family of Love," the Unification Church, Scientology."[132] Buchanan later felt this was very much "misdirected invective" not commonly held,[133] and one editorial's comments on the debate expressed how these views were clearly "wide of the mark";[134] these *Criterion One* characteristics were not perceived to be as strongly postmodern as a minority critiqued. Nonetheless, the foil in Wickham's argument, that the Church of England is "the most rational splinter of Christendom,"[135] highlights the wider context of his attack: if the Church of England is seen as a rationalistic creature shaped by modernism, the Movement's observed *Criterion One* postmodern characteristics contrast against this. Herein are indicators again of a *Mutual Origins* model if there is inherent causation within this friction.

3.3.2 Analysis of the Report

Turning to the report's contents, of particular importance are its third and fourth chapters. In chapter 3, "The Distinctive Phenomena of the Movement" are mapped. Following discussion of "Baptism in the Spirit" and "The Gifts of the Holy Spirit," it examines "Other features of the Charismatic Movement (The "Subculture")," generating a spread of observations cohering with predicted manifestations of the Analytic Criteria. Under

130. Buchanan, *Taking the Long View*, 192.
131. Buchanan, "What Are You Doing?," 26.
132. Church of England, *Report of Proceedings*, 13:1136–37.
133. Buchanan, interview.
134. Williams, "Editorial," 195–96.
135. Church of England, *Report of Proceedings*, 13:1137.

CRQ-1's enquiry, both *Criteria One* and *Two* characteristics are observed in "Biblical Interpretation": "from one point of view the charismatic movement is a form of Christianised existentialism" because "if people have been delivered from the dryness of their previous experience, and given the refreshing and life-conveying 'baptism in the Spirit,' then their present experience is crucial to them."[136] This transforms biblical hermeneutics to become subjectively centered, leading to the warning, "once anything can mean anything, then the movement becomes afloat on a sea of subjectivism. And there is always a tendency in that direction."[137] Here a *Criterion Two* characteristic in the exegesis of Scripture is potentially generated from a *Criterion One* experiential focus—witnessing to a potential internal postmodern-like drive within the Movement described in §2.5.3. Additionally, discussing the Movement's "Structures," the report notes the widespread notion of "lay eldership" found in new house churches, warning, "In places this has issued in a desire to *add* this element to Anglican structures."[138] Observations here of suggested ecclesial manifestations of *Criterion Four* in new structures of authority.

A potential CRQ-2 answer is seen in the last subcultural phenomenon commented on—"Romanticism?"—which "may express itself in the love of the miraculous, or in anti-intellectualism, or in many other ways. Such a mood has always accompanied a reaction to 'classicism.'"[139] Here the report focuses on a cultural mood some understand to have partly formed in reaction to the rational positivism of the Enlightenment period.[140] Such romanticism is explored in Charles Taylor's sociological work in the next chapter, and here the report might hint at a *Mutual Origins* model if "classicism" is read as "modernism" in this context.

Chapter 4 asks the question "What gave rise to the Movement in the Church of England?" and generates answers that speak directly to the enquiry of the CRQs. To CRQ-3, the first factor, "The Acts of Apostles?" reports on an impetus to recover the biblical description of the supernatural life of the first church as normative to ongoing Christian experience, which again can be seen as a desire for the recovery of the premodern world of the NT. To CRQ-2, the second factor, "A Missing Experience?" asks, "Is it possible that an institutionalised, intellectualised, formalized

136. Buchanan, *Charismatic Movement*, 38.
137. Buchanan, *Charismatic Movement*, 38.
138. Buchanan, *Charismatic Movement*, 37.
139. Buchanan, *Charismatic Movement*, 39.
140. Reardon, "Romanticism."

(and even fossilized) practice of Christianity has left a thirst in the inner being which only the springs of charismatic renewal could satisfy?"[141] Such was seen in §3.1.2.1, and here there are suggestions such frustrations are connected to a larger reaction against modernistic aspects, pointing towards a *Mutual Origins* model—something seen also in the reported answers of "A Reaction against Clericalism?" and "A Relief from Formalism?"

The report's fourth answer, "An Existentialist Atmosphere?" develops its previous observation of existentialism, asking whether the Movement's emphasis on "testimony"—a rare *Criterion Three* manifestation suggested in the report—might offer an alternative "trip" to a generation prone to such alternative "trips," like those given by drugs. The warning is sounded:

> It would be hard to show that there has been a direct causal link, but the secular and charismatic trends have moved synchronously, and the less satisfactory expressions of the charismatic movement look remarkably like a Christianised existentialism.[142]

As noted in §1.1.1, the posited potential link between a cultural philosophy and the Movement is important, but the usage of the term "existentialism" must be questioned. This description had profound effect, with Bebbington summarizing that the report correctly "diagnosed the movement as 'a form of Christianised existentialism.'"[143] However, the existentialism described in §2.2.2 does not perhaps quite correlate to the level of subjective formation of reality being suggested here. In interview, Buchanan explains the contextual understanding of the term:

> I think it was basically the living off the urges of the moment without, as it were, constant reference to Holy Scripture. . . . [P]eople who keep on having bright ideas they ought to do this, they ought to do that, without actually asking themselves whether it's scriptural [and] that [they're] sure they're being led by the Spirit.[144]

---

141. Buchanan, *Charismatic Movement*, 41.

142. Buchanan, *Charismatic Movement*, 42.

143. Bebbington, *Evangelicalism in Modern Britain*, 233. Bebbington later changes his mind on the term, replacing it with "expressivism." See Bebbington, "Epilogue," 249–50.

144. Buchanan, interview.

Put in these terms, this "trip"-like subjectivism is less *existentialism*, and more a *postmodern* direction of travel to a heavily subjectively weighted view of reality that ignores the objective completely, with a *Direct Influence* model behind this being theorized, or at least warned about. This redefinition is substantiated by the direct parallels between Synod's fear of drug-like "trips," and an immersive postmodern "virtual reality" that Jaichandran and Madhav posited as a manifestation of postmodernism in Pentecostal worship.[145]

Overall, the report and its context suggest, weighted towards *Criterion One*, manifestations of all the Analytic Criteria. The Movement possesses a thoroughly perceived postmodern character. It additionally suggests CRQ-2 answers of a *Mutual Origins* model, with a suggestion of a type of *Direct Influence* model as well, and under CRQ-3 gives further indications of a deep desire for premodern recovery. The key question, answered through the lifeworld investigations of chapters 5–7, is the same Green asked upon the report's release, "Are they right?"[146] An additional question this study helps answer is also, "What did they miss?"

3.4 LATER NORTH AMERICAN INFLUENCES

After the Fountain Trust's closure, and a seeming plateau in the Movement's life, the next place of renewal impetus came from a simultaneously likely and unlikely source. Likely, as it continued a narrative of American influence; unlikely, as it centered on a non-denominational former musician turned church leader and theologian, John Wimber, and his Vineyard church network.[147] Analysis of both the influential reception of his ministry, and also later events emanating from a Vineyard church in Toronto, "the Toronto Blessing," reveals potential manifestations of *Criterion One* and *Four*, adds additional evidence for a *Mutual Origins* model at work while again highlighting its limits, and points again to a premodern recovery emphasis within the Movement.

---

145. See §2.5.1.

146. Green, Review, 20.

147. A detailed historical account of Wimber and the Vineyard Church Network is found in Jackson, *Quest*. For Wimber and Vineyard's relationship with the church in England, see the overview of Leach, *Encountering Vineyard Worship*.

3.4.1 The Wimber Effect

The impact Wimber had on the Charismatic Movement in Britain, and in the Church of England in particular, is well attested. One leading Anglican exclaimed, "Wimber has had a greater impact on the Church of England than anyone since John Wesley."[148] "New power for 'Bankrupt Britain'"[149] was the title of an *ARM Link* article explaining how Wimber's visits gave the Movement fresh vitality in a season of spiritual doldrums. Wimber had a significant effect on the ministry of clergy in the Church of England; Gunstone speculates, "My guesstimate is that Wimber probably influenced to greater or lesser extent around fifteen per cent of the Church of England parishes, though a higher proportion of the clergy, especially younger ones."[150] Twelve hundred Anglican clerics were at one point on the Vineyard's regular mailing list,[151] and numerous parish centers of Wimber-inspired ministry grew out of his influence, especially St. Andrew's Chorleywood, HTB, St. Thomas's Crookes, and St. John's Harborne, all of which experienced marked growth as a result.[152]

Such impact stands in contrast to what might be expected. Hunt comments, "One could be forgiven for thinking that the Church of England would be one of the last Christian institutions which was likely to accept and apply Wimber's ministry."[153] The cultural dissonance between Wimber's Vineyard, formed out of radical Californian counter-culture, and the more genteel institution of the Church of England, was pronounced.[154] Yet despite this dissonance two aspects of Wimber and his Vineyard Churches were particularly winsome at the time, both of which speak to the Movement's potential postmodern character.

3.4.1.1 *Wimber's Ecclesiological Appeal*

Wimber's ministry in Britain is in one sense the result of historical circumstances by which two of the Movement's key figures came to meet

---

148. Hunt, "Anglican Wimberites," 106. Hunt opines that this was said by Sandy Millar, the then vicar of HTB.
149. See Steven, "'Worship,'" 44.
150. Gunstone, "Anglican Evaluation," 225.
151. Hunt, "Anglican Wimberites," 107.
152. Steven, "'Worship,'" 45.
153. Hunt, "Anglican Wimberites," 107.
154. See Wimber, *John Wimber*, 163.

and become fascinated by Wimber and the ministry he modelled. Percy explains, "He has strongly influenced significant portions of the Anglican church since 1980, largely through his association with David Watson and David Pytches,"[155] figures who opened the door to his influence on the Movement and the wider Church of England.

Watson's 1981 encounter with Wimber at Fuller Seminary created a huge impression on him,[156] engendering deep personal affection[157] and through this opening the hearts of other Movement leaders to him.[158] However, Watson was won over both by the man *and* his church.[159] So was Pytches, who with Watson co-hosted Wimber in Britain for his first ministry tour. Both were especially attracted to Wimber's emphasis on "every person ministry." Pytches recalls in his encounter with Wimber's church,

> The most significant result . . . was that I had just seen modelled before me a missing link in the ministry of our so-called charismatic church. John Wimber had somehow discovered how to equip and activate these ordinary people for the work of ministry.[160]

Watson likewise was "thrilled" by this emphasis because he similarly saw that while in the British Charismatic Movement gifts such as healing were only for a select few, in Wimber's Vineyard model they were for all.[161]

Subsequent theological analysis affirms the centrality of this belief in Wimber's ecclesiology,[162] and at the time its genuineness was deeply moving. Seeing this "missing link" through the lens of CRQ-1, this longed-for practice could be seen as a *Criterion Four* manifestation, whereby communal participation authenticates the new truths being taught. Neither Watson nor Pytches exhibit any suspicion of authority in this, yet this does raise questions as to whether a postmodern mood reorienting the Movement towards the importance of communal discernment of truth helped play a part in Wimber's impact.

155. Percy, *Words, Wonders, and Power*, 14.
156. Watson, "Third Wave," 64.
157. Watson, *Fear No Evil*, 25.
158. Gunstone, *Signs and Wonders*, 62.
159. Watson, *Fear No Evil*, 52.
160. Pytches, "David Pytches," 21.
161. Saunders and Sansom, *David Watson*, 207.
162. Miller, "Routinizing," 145; Zichterman, "Distinctives."

3.4.1.2 Wimber's Theological Appeal

More significant, however, was Wimber's theological approach, which appealed to the wider Evangelical world and subsequently gave his ministry traction across the Church of England's breadth. One memorial article explains,

> Perhaps Wimber's greatest impact, however, was in reminding the larger evangelical community that certain "Pentecostal emphases" could also be found in the Bible. "He raised the level of expectation of divine action in the life of the church," says J. I. Packer of Regent College, who at times took issue with points in Wimber's teaching.[163]

Jim Packer, a doyen of Anglican Evangelicals, highlights Wimber's ability to reach and bring into renewal Evangelicals previously critical of the Movement through his literal reading of the miracles of Jesus for today. This was aided by a downplaying of other more off-putting charismatic emphases: emphasizing multiple "fillings" rather than a single "baptism" of the Spirit and the secondary nature rather than the primacy of glossolalia[164]—thereby espousing neither "consequence" nor "subsequence" views prevalent in classical Pentecostalism.[165] Such came about through "Wimber's quest to find the radical middle between his historic, doctrinal evangelicalism and his desire to have Pentecostal power,"[166] "consciously attempting a synthesis of charismatic ideas with traditional evangelical ones."[167] As such he was able to formulate teaching appealing to the Evangelical scene—including, but not limited to, many in the Movement who still considered themselves Evangelicals.[168] Under CRQ-2's enquiry, this synthesis was perhaps especially appealing for those who felt an antimodernistic impulse had led the Movement too far from its rationalistic Evangelical moorings, again highlighting potential limits of the *Mutual Origins* model at work.

Wimber's appealing theology might have been pragmatically driven, but it also flowed from a deeply premodern worldview Wimber inhabited and imparted to the Movement through his visits. This partially

---

163. Christianity Today, "Wimber's Wonders."
164. Thiselton, *Holy Spirit*, 423.
165. Anderson, *Introduction to Pentecostalism*, 183.
166. Jackson, "Short History," 135.
167. Bonnington, *Patterns in Charismatic Spirituality*, 7.
168. Bax, *Good Wine*, 135.

stemmed from Wimber himself, a keen disciple of figures such as the Venerable Bede. Don Williams comments, "Living much of this time in a premodern spiritual world, Wimber positioned the Vineyard with the potential to minister effectively in the antimodern ethos of the emerging post-modern age."[169]

This premodern inhabitation found focus in his theological system, which relied on the ancient past becoming radically present, utilizing the teaching of George Ladd.[170] In Springer's write-up of Wimber's Fuller Seminary teaching, Wimber quotes Ladd's description of the theology of the New Testament as orientated around the concept of "the Kingdom of God" in the synoptic gospels, which stands in opposition to and advances against the power of Satan, finds expression and focus in Jesus's life and ministry, and is the invasion of the future age into the present accompanied by signs and wonders. Then, in a pioneering step, Wimber takes Ladd's system describing Jesus's *past* activity and transforms it to become a description of the *present* ministry of the church through the Spirit.[171] He engages in explicit premodern recovery, something likely well received if this was, as previously suggested, at the heart of the Movement's life—probably in turn encouraging this desire further still.

In Wimber's explanation of what inhibits this theological system from being appropriated by the church, further evidence is seen of a *Mutual Origins* answer to CRQ-2, and how this connects to a CRQ-3 premodern recovery answer. Appropriation of this system depended on exposing the Western church's Enlightenment mindset, and an undoing of it to enable inhabitation of a premodern worldview. Utilizing the missionary experiences of Paul Hiebert, Wimber describes a three-tiered worldview: an upper supernatural divine realm governed by religion; a lower "normal" earthly realm governed by Science; and between them a biblical worldview where these two intersect in a third middle realm that contains "the Holy Spirit's intervention in divine healing, signs and wonders, and spiritual gifts."[172] This "excluded middle" is what non-Westerners often inhabit, but Westerners do not due to Enlightenment rationalism: "*Rationalism* seeks a rational explanation for all experience, making reason the chief guide in all matters of life. . . . [E]verything that cannot be explained by human reason is rejected, especially supernatural

169. Williams, "Theological Perspective," 167.
170. Ladd, *Theology*.
171. Wimber and Springer, *Power Evangelism*, 29–48.
172. Wimber and Springer, *Power Evangelism*, 136.

events such as miracles," meaning, "Rationalism, therefore, is a non-Christian philosophy."[173] Wimber concludes, "Most Western Christians must undergo a shift in perception to become involved in a signs and wonders ministry."[174]

Evidence suggests not all received this idea well.[175] Nevertheless, Wimber's teaching had lasting impact on the Movement, and this is perhaps rooted in its appeal to the observed anti-modernism present in the Movement from its birth, in turn giving fresh energy to this impulse. If so, Wimber's system, received by the Movement into its praxis, shows initial evidence in a single place of how all the answers to this study's CRQs may be linked. A *Criterion One* experiential emphasis, an active seeking of the experience of the miraculous today (CRQ-1), while rationally rooted in Scripture, is energized by a *Mutual Origins* anti-modernistic reaction (CRQ-2), which leads to a radical recovery of a premodern—though largely only biblically-focused—worldview, which contained such *Criterion One* characteristics (CRQ-3). As will be seen, such a narrative suggests many postmodern characteristics seen in the Movement are better described as premodern in nature, the two converging as the way past unhelpful effects of modernism is found on the path back to times before it. Wimber was fond of saying "the way in is the way on," but perhaps also he should have added "the way on is the way back."

3.4.2 Insights from Toronto

Unlike the generally positive reception of Wimber's ministry, reception of events originating from a Vineyard church in 1994, later called by British media "The Toronto Blessing" (hereafter "TTB"),[176] was more mixed, highlighting the limits to some of the Movement's more potentially postmodern characteristics in this period. An account of the relevant events in Britain is given by Patrick Dixon in *Signs of Revival*,[177] which describes how events at the Toronto Airport Vineyard church in January 1994

---

173. Wimber and Springer, *Power Evangelism*, 140.
174. Wimber and Springer, *Power Evangelism*, 146.
175. Gunstone, *Signs and Wonders*, 106.
176. Poloma, "Toronto Blessing," 1149. Poloma highlights that John Arnott, then lead pastor of the Toronto Airport Vineyard, preferred the term "The Father's Blessing," as did others involved. However, the epicentric nature of Toronto makes the term apt for descriptive purposes.
177. Dixon, *Signs of Revival*, 12–112.

found replication in major Anglican churches, notably with relatively exotic new forms of charismatic manifestation such as animal sounds and unusual bodily sensations and actions, and without an accompanying theology to explain them.

Initially, British reactions to TTB were positive. Of weight was Wimber's reaction. Wimber's influence by 1994 had partially waned, due to his association with Paul Cain and "The Kansas City Prophets" and his planting of a Vineyard church in England in 1987 under the leadership of the ex-Anglican vicar John Mumford—despite previous assurances he would not seek to plant in the UK.[178] However, his reaction to "the Blessing" still gave a steering lead to the Movement, especially since they related to one of his own Vineyard churches.[179] Wimber was initially supportive of TTB,[180] which likely spurred an initially wider positive reaction within the Movement. In June 1994, Green was reported to have expressed the view that "what's going on is perfectly legitimate and people need encouraging,"[181] while the promotion of TTB at St. Andrew's Chorleywood, and especially at HTB, speaks self-evidently to the attitudes of David Pytches and Sandy Millar respectively, both of whom had travelled to Toronto. Millar particularly took to a regular defense of TTB and its outworking over the next few years.[182]

However, this occurred in the context of growing critical voices including the then Archbishop of Canterbury, George Carey,[183] a known sympathizer of the Movement. Wimber's support also turned into concern about the nature of the manifestations being seen and the emphasis on them, then from concern to warning,[184] and finally to ejection of the Toronto church from the Vineyard network, because Vineyard could not "endorse, encourage, offer theological justification or biblical prooftexting for any exotic practices that are extra-biblical."[185]

In this context, in December 1994 the Evangelical Alliance drew together Evangelical leaders from across the church spectrum, including some from the Movement. In the meeting's issued statement, they agreed,

178. Mumford, "Global Vineyard."
179. Elliott, "Worship Time," 67.
180. See Wimber and Association of Vineyard Churches, "Refreshing."
181. Dixon, *Signs of Revival*, 33.
182. See Atherstone, *Repackaging Christianity*, 49–56.
183. Dixon, *Signs of Revival*, 33–34.
184. Wimber, *John Wimber*, 180–81.
185. Association of Vineyard Churches, "Board Report," 4.

> We rejoice with those who have known genuine life-changing encounters with the holiness and majesty, power and love of the risen Christ. We reject any tendency to pursue manifestations as an end in themselves. . . . We recognise that historical, theological and cultural influences can unconsciously condition our Christian perspective. The existentialist spirit of our age emphasizes subjective experience and feelings over convictions and objective truth. We also recognise the equal and opposite danger of enlightenment rationalism, which has in the past resulted in dead orthodoxy which leaves no room for the direct intervention of the Spirit of God.[186]

Here two aspects of the potential postmodern character of the Movement in this period are illuminated. Firstly, the initial openness to TTB's more exotic spiritual practices, embraced by some, is rejected by others when emphasized for their own experience. Under CRQ-1's enquiry, again evidence is seen that normatively rational and experiential epistemological emphasizes run in parallel within the life of the Movement, such that when the experiential takes precedence above the rational, critique arises which helps renormalize the situation.[187] Similar was seen in the life of the Fountain Trust.[188] Given that this occurs again two decades later highlights how ingrained this parallelism is within the Movement.

Secondly, analyzing this statement under CRQ-2's enquiry reveals that leaders within the Movement were aware of the potential of a *Direct Influence* model to be at work in the reception of TTB,[189] rejecting it, while also expressing "the equal and opposite danger of enlightenment rationalism" which robs the church of the Spirit's work—the heart of the anti-modernistic impulse of a *Mutual Origins* model. Once again, this model is indicated by historical events as a primary answer to CRQ-2.

---

186. Recorded in Boulton, *Impact of "Toronto,"* 123–24.

187. This emphasis on experience, without accompanying theology, perhaps explains some of TTB's lack of lasting impact in the Movement compared with Wimber's ministry. A rational theological system was needed to explain the experiential.

188. See §3.2.3.

189. Again, as in §3.3.2, the period's usage of the term "existentialist" has overlap with, and perhaps better interpretation through, the term "postmodern."

3.5 CONCLUSION

Exploring the Movement through the investigation of four moments of its historical life under the CRQs yields a broad initial picture of its potential postmodern character. Under CRQ-1's enquiry, signs of ecclesial manifestations of all the Analytic Criteria are seen, showing the strength of this constructed means of analysis. As suggested if a postmodern-like drive is responsible for them, the most strongly seen are *Criterion One* manifestations, present in each of the four moments of the Movement's life explored.[190] At the Movement's birth, a frustration with Evangelical hermeneutics led to a broadened epistemology emphasizing experiential knowledge of God. The strength of this experiential emphasis, combined with the pragmatic fruit of its unity, overcame doctrinal differences in the Fountain Trust's ecumenicalism. However, its reaction to criticism about this exposes the normative parallelism within the Movement's epistemology, whereby the importance of the rational is recovered without rejection of the experiential, something seen again in reaction to TTB's experiential emphasis later. In both the background and content of the 1981 General Synod report, the Movement's experiential and non-rational natures are repeatedly highlighted, and such a context provided a good reception for Wimber's theological system which enabled a synthesis of experiential and rational epistemologies missing in the Movement's internal theology.

Manifestations of the other criteria are seen to a lesser extent. A new experiential reading of Scripture at the Movement's birth shows some signs of a hermeneutic that disconnects words from their original descriptive intent in a *Criterion Two* manner, a subjectively orientated approach the 1981 General Synod report also highlights. Discussion in the run-up to this report, and its contents, highlight the importance of testimony in a potential *Criterion Three* manifestation. At the Movement's birth, there seems to be a type of *Criterion Four* anti-institutionalism present yet not rooted in deeply held postmodern suspicion—verified by the Fountain Trust's subsequent attempts to avoid building new structures. However, the ready reception of Wimber's every-member emphasis perhaps indicates a manifestation of this criterion in another form.

Under CRQ-2's enquiry, no evidence is seen for a *Direct Influence* model. Both the General Synod report's working groups and content suggest its possibility, as does the Evangelical Alliance's statement on TTB, yet nothing beyond a suggestion is seen. In contrast, abundant evidence

---

190. See §2.6.3.

is seen for a *Mutual Origins* model throughout the Movement's timeline. An anti-modernistic reaction is seen at the Movement's birth in a reaction to over-rational Evangelical hermeneutics and the wider church's modernistic failings. General Synod's report comments on multiple aspects of this reaction, including explicitly naming the reaction against the modernistic nature of the church as part of the Movement's genesis. Wimber's theological system was both appealing to this anti-modernistic impulse and gave it fresh energy, articulating a need to break free from modernistic rationalism to experience the Spirit's work, and the Evangelical Alliance's statement in reaction to TTB also articulates some of the same. However, potential limits are also seen to the operation of a *Mutual Origins* model. The Fountain Trust's redressing of theological shallowness, and the positive reception of Wimber's hermeneutical approach synthesizing rational and experiential approaches, reveal how, when anti-modernistic impulses lead the Movement too far from its modernistic heritage, desires arise for a return to some of the Movement's modernistic heritage. The anti-modern impulse at the heart of these observations of *Mutual Origins* is perhaps the internal postmodern-like drive suggested by the prominence of *Criterion One* characteristics to be at work within the Movement above. As seen in §2.2, the rejection of modernism lies at the heart of the development of postmodernism, meaning that the manifestations of the former overlap strongly with manifestations of the latter.

Under CRQ-3's enquiry, the improbability of potential postmodern characteristics of Pentecostalism being imported into the Movement at its birth is witnessed, due to a lack of generative causality. So too for potential American Episcopalian influences. Rather, there are repeated suggestions that a desire for premodern recovery operates at the heart of the Movement, which has explanatory power for some of the Movement's postmodern character. This desire is highlighted in the hermeneutical approach of the early Evangelical pioneers of renewal, by the Synod report as part of the reason the Movement arose, and in how in Wimber's influential theological system this drove a *Criterion One* experiential emphases in charismatic praxis.

From these discoveries, there are several issues to carry into and inform further lifeworld investigation. Firstly, many of the system manifestations of §2.5.3 have been potentially observed, though not all. More detailed lifeworld investigation is needed to discover if they are actually present or not—the focus of chapters 5–7. Secondly, as predicted, *Criterion One* manifestations are the most strongly seen, and at least in one instance (the Synod Report's analysis), are seen to generate manifestations of another Criterion (*Criterion Two* hermeneutical manifestations) in a catena-like manner. Questions arise as to whether this is seen consistently throughout the Movement's life. Thirdly, there are possible limits to the operation of the *Mutual Origins* model in the Movement, limiting how it can generate postmodern characteristics. Fourthly, consideration of Wimber's received theological system shows how the answers to all the CRQs may be linked in a larger narrative, whereby postmodern characteristics are generated through a *Mutual Origins* reaction that leads back to a recovery of premodern aspects of praxis. Such a narrative can be tested through more detailed lifeworld examination and will indeed be shown to have good explanatory power. Finally, and significantly, little evidence has indicated the existence of *Cultural Catalysis* in the Movement's lifeworld. This is unsurprising, as a historical analysis is not necessarily equipped to answer questions about relationships between ecclesial lifeworlds and wider culture. Further lifeworld investigation needs to be equipped with sociological and anthropological insights to do so—to which the next chapter now turns to develop.

This chapter has borne much fruit, shedding unique light upon four major moments in the Movement's life, therein complementing other studies in wider scholarship illuminating its historical nature. By yielding initial potential answers to this study's CRQs, it has shown the value of both the created transcontextual system for lifeworld investigation, and of a historical approach in this. It has prepared the ground for a detailed study of the Movement through qualitative research methods, while confirming the need within Cartledge's dialectic methodology to first turn to the insights of the social sciences to be equipped to do so.

4

Sociological and Anthropological Insights

SO FAR EVIDENCE HAS been seen through initial historical investigations that the Movement shows some clear postmodern traits, with hints also seen as to whence they originate. However, to go beyond these first surface observations and strike to the heart of the Movement's life and questions of its postmodern nature, a richer and broader level of analysis needs to be brought to it.

To enable this, this chapter returns to the trans-contextual system of this study's dialectical methodology, as well as revisiting some more general questions, bringing findings from its initial explorations into dialogue with social scientific insights into Pentecostal-Charismatic movements, therein further developing the enquiry of the CRQs. Ecclesial practice is often shaped by the social and cultural contexts it is performed in; indeed, the theorized models of CRQ-2 aim to expose some of the links between the two. Hence Cartledge's methodology—as used in this study—suggests a critical dialogue between what has been found in initial lifeworld explorations and social scientific research as the next step after the initial lifeworld explorations of the previous chapter.[1] Here social scientific research is not exhaustively engaged with, but rather, dialogue with two key disciplines, sociology and anthropology, draws out a variety of insights that enables a deeper understanding of what has been found so far, and further equips this study for what is still to be found.

1. See §1.2.3.

The fruit of this is manifold. In development of the *ecclesial postmodernism* system, additional potential manifestations of each of the Analytic Criteria are discovered, broadening the system, and enabling a deepened enquiry into the Movement's postmodern characteristics (CRQ-1). In more general dialogue with social scientific insights, potential answers to the other two CRQs are further contextualized and substantiated. For CRQ-2's enquiry into what models explain the Movement's postmodern characteristics, the context and underlying factors behind both *Mutual Origins* and *Cultural Catalysis* models are revealed—explaining and emphasizing their likely presence in the Movement, with an expansion of *Cultural Catalysis* into two different manners of operation theorized. Similarly, for CRQ-3's enquiry into other important explanative trajectories of movement and influences, the sociological and anthropological impulses behind the discovered desire for a premodern recovery are revealed, likewise explaining and emphasizing its likely presence. Additionally, through a variety of perspectives—especially anthropological ideas of "play"—it is revealed how this premodern recovery desire is potentially linked to a *Mutual Origins* generation of the Movement's postmodern characteristics, a link suggested in the previous chapter's historical explorations.

Combining these findings with those from the previous chapters, a working hypothesis answering all three CRQs is derived, along with a larger narrative that links these answers to explain observations about the Movement's postmodern character considered in chapter 1. This hypothesis forms the basis for the qualitative analysis of the Movement's lifeworld in the second half of this study.

4.1 SOCIOLOGICAL INSIGHTS

Sociological analysis complements the historical approach of the previous chapter—"they provide different dimensions of the same religious manifestation"—the former looking at themes arising from cultural influence and social change, complementing examinations of historical events on the ground.[2] However, important challenges exist to the usage of sociological methods, centering on their intrinsic meta-theory approach, and therein potential ideological biases imported into them. David Martin explains how sociologists often act as courtroom lawyers,

2. Hunt, *History*, 16.

hiding value judgments within the discourse as a result of such a strong approach,[3] something he tries to ameliorate.[4] Milbank criticizes the idea there is a social vantage point from which religion can be analyzed which does not take its own Enlightenment humanist rationalistic starting point into consideration,[5] something others also highlight.[6] Such Foucaultian critiques must be noticed given this study's nature. Percy, commenting on this, laments, "This really won't do when it comes to interpreting the complex and rich nature of neo-Pentecostalism. What is required is a multidisciplinary approach to a multifarious phenomenon."[7] However, this is precisely what is offered in this study: sociological insights are here held together with previous historical and forthcoming anthropological ones, enabling a more nuanced picture—offsetting weaknesses of relying on sociological approaches alone.

4.1.1 The Secularization Thesis and Subsequent Developments

4.1.1.1 The Secularization Thesis

The "Secularization Thesis" has been the touchstone sociological analysis of culture and religion for over a century, recently re-defended in works such as the strong defense of the traditional thesis by Steve Bruce[8] and the nuanced reworking of it by Martin.[9] In simplest form, it postulates that the increasing modernization of society leads to the rejection of religious expression, commitment, and influence in the public domain—precipitating religion's diminished influence and size.[10] Such finds focus in the period of the Movement's birth, and is part of the frustrations noted in §3.1.2.1, the "religious crisis of the Sixties."[11]

---

3. Martin, *Forbidden Revolutions*, 5.
4. Martin, *Future of Christianity*, 26.
5. Milbank, *Theology and Social Theory*, 138–39.
6. Deininger, *Global Pentecostalism*, 8; Dillon, *Handbook*, 6. See also Cartledge, *Testimony in the Spirit*, 6.
7. Percy, "City," 221. The terms "Neo-Pentecostalism" and "charismatic renewal" are sometimes used interchangeably in sociological studies.
8. Bruce, *God Is Dead*.
9. Martin, *On Secularization*.
10. For a discussion of the varieties of Secularization Theory beyond this definition, see Deininger, *Global Pentecostalism*, 13–14.
11. Maiden, *Age of the Spirit*, 16.

Roy Wallis explains that the emergence of new religious phenomena—such as the Movement—are interpreted within this overall thesis of rejection, whereby two possibilities emerge.[12] Firstly, that such movements are manifestations of secularization's effect on traditional religion, causing religion to engage in reclamation work: "The charismatic movement clearly involves an attempt to recover a sense of immediacy, of effective impact, of experiential content in a religious practice which has seen considerable attenuation of such features in recent times."[13] A second possibility is that "secularization stimulates revival through the emergence of sectarian schisms within the tradition, and innovation of new faiths drawing upon sources outside the prevailing traditions."[14] Under CRQ-2's enquiry, both possibilities highlight the sociological context of how *Mutual Origins* impulses might arise, as both are reactions to the effects of cultural modernism. The first—a reclamation of non-modernistic elements of faith (especially *Criterion One* experiential emphases)—is a type of premodern recovery under CRQ-3's analysis, uniting the two. The second possibility would suggest that such emphases are drawn into the Movement at birth from Pentecostalism for similar reasons, as the Church of England sought innovation from outside in adopting charismatic renewal. Martin explains here that charismatic movements are to be seen either a creative restatement of Pentecostalism, or lesser versions of it, in a responsive dialectic decay/compromise with secularization processes ongoing in "the world."[15] However, the argument of §3.1.1 suggests that such a potential relationship between the Movement and Pentecostalism is not strongly corroborated by historical evidence, making Wallis's first suggestion of anti-modern reclamation more explanatorily important.

4.1.1.2 Developments of Secularization Theory

Recent critiques of the secularization thesis mean such possible contextualization of the *Mutual Origins* model must be held lightly. Harvey Cox quips, "Today it is secularity, not spirituality, that may be headed for extinction."[16] Several factors explain why. Pre-eminently, seculariza-

12. Wallis, *Elementary Forms*, 59.
13. Wallis, *Elementary Forms*, 71.
14. Wallis, *Elementary Forms*, 60.
15. Martin, *On Secularization*, 136.
16. Cox, *Fire from Heaven*, xv.

tion ideas ignore "something deep within the human spirit that seeks self-transcending experience and an ultimate grounding for the meaning of life,"[17] meaning "religion has metamorphosed into spirituality."[18] Commenting on the secularization thesis's application to British religion, Jeremy Morris explains that some "have assumed that the core elements of British religion can be construed in such a way as to reflect central aspects of power relations in society"[19]—a manifestation of Feuerbachian religion by which "man becomes acquainted with himself,"[20] denying the possibility of a theocentric understanding of religion. David Holland summarizes a larger tension: "To develop a definition of religion is the essential act of both secularism (from an ideology prescriptively calling for differentiation) and secularization (a historical process of differentiation descriptively captured)."[21]

Partially in reaction to such weaknesses, other theories have been proposed that develop the secularization thesis, which perhaps better contextualize the Movement's observed postmodern characteristics, providing insights into how a *Mutual Origins* model arises from sociological impulses they describe. Two helpful theories to consider here are those of Peter Berger and Charles Taylor, who both also explain religious resurgence in the context of secularization-like processes.

Berger sees religion as a part of the externalization process humans engage in to make sense of reality and find their part in it,[22] pushing beyond relationship with others to the totality of reality.[23] Thus religion creates a "sacred canopy" to process and live reality under, protecting against forces of chaos delegitimizing participation in it. Under this canopy, when confronted with the challenge of modern rational skepticism, people choose what to believe to maintain this protection, and traditional religion adapts to present three options: "deduction, reduction and induction."[24] "Deduction" reasserts traditional beliefs in a modernistically relevant form, contrasting with a "Reduction" of traditional beliefs to forms acceptable to modern criticism. "Induction," creates an emphasis

17. Miller, *Reinventing American Protestantism*, 4.
18. Kay and Dyer, *European Pentecostalism*, 386.
19. Morris, "Secularization," 205.
20. Feuerbach, *Essence of Christianity*, 4.
21. Holland, "On the Volatile," 105.
22. Berger, *Sacred Canopy*, 4.
23. Berger, *Sacred Canopy*, 25.
24. Berger, *Heretical Imperative*, xi.

on experience as the ground of all religious affirmations, with religious tradition capturing past accounts of experience to help process present experiences.[25] One commentator suggests, "Although Berger himself does not explicitly do so, it is more than tempting to put Pentecostalism within this [latter] framework."[26] However, provoked to study the mysterious phenomenon of Pentecostal growth in the twentieth century, Berger later explains, "Much of what goes on in the world today could be called re-enchantment (or counter-secularization). Pentecostalism is a very loud version of this development."[27] Under Berger's analysis, the Movement can be seen either as an expression of "induction" or "re-enchantment." Both can be seen as analogous to Wallis's reclamation possibility, with the "induction" possibility especially laying bare how the centrality of *Criterion One* experiential emphases in the Movement—under a *Mutual Origins* model—leads to premodern recovery, part of a larger narrative initially evidenced in the previous chapter. Framed under Berger's idea of induction, experiences in the Movement, experiences of the Spirit, not understandable through a modernistic frame of understanding that has been found to be wanting, drive a search for premodern understandings that do. Such coheres with the experience-led nature of the Movement.

Taylor's critical adaptation of the secularization thesis argues that religion in the face of modernization has not disappeared, it can be seen by looking in other places in society apart from institutional religion; "cross-pressures" of both belief and unbelief always operate on individuals.[28] Pressures of unbelief come from the advent of the possibility of exclusive deism and humanism, enabling senses of independence and self-achievement; pressures for belief come from a sense of embeddedness in the universe (as opposed to the modernistic development of the "buffered self" transcending it), with a strong sense of God entailed within this. This cross-pressure generates "the nova effect" meaning "more and more third ways are created."[29] In Western society, this has often led to a re-emergence of nineteenth century Romanticism in new guises, "carried down into the 1960s in part through the continuing chain of related counter-cultures,"[30] emphasizing the individual and

---

25. Berger, *Heretical Imperative*, 127.
26. McBain, "Mainline Charismatics," 5.
27. Berger, "Friendly Dissent," 50.
28. Taylor, *Secular Age*, 299.
29. Taylor, *Secular Age*, 302.
30. Taylor, *Secular Age*, 477.

experientially authentic in "the age of authenticity" that has existed since the 1960s.[31] As noted in §3.3.2, such types of Romanticism are perhaps at heart expressivist reactions to modernism, and Taylor describes how they come about on an individual level. Therefore, if General Synod's report is correct in its analysis that the Movement inhabits such reactions, then again it can be seen through Taylor's analysis how an anti-modernistic reaction is foundational to its nature, explaining the sociological generation of *Mutual Origins* impulses in a different sociological frame to Berger's. Additionally, Taylor's description extends Berger's by explaining some of the anti-modern drive in a *Mutual Origins* model on a deeper individual level, that it partially derives from a sense of personal embeddedness in the universe, which cultural movements such as Romanticism and postmodernism give expression to. As will be seen shortly, such personal, universal, senses of being at work in a *Mutual Origins* model finds further description through Cox's idea of "primal" longings, as well as anthropological concepts of "play"—a descriptive thread that elucidates the heart of the *Mutual Origins* model and its connection to CRQ-1 and CRQ-3 answers.

4.1.2 Further Sociological Theories

While the secularization thesis and related sociological theories illuminate a *Mutual Origins* model answer to CRQ-2, consideration of other sociological theories and observations illuminate both it *and* a *Cultural Catalysis* model answer. Importantly, they emphasize the latter's likely presence in the Movement, despite the dearth of evidence for it in the previous chapter. Additional insights from them also provide a wider context for understanding a premodern recovery answer to CRQ-3, and how this might link to the answers of the other CRQs in the larger narrative increasingly described by both evidence and theory.

4.1.2.1 A "Primal" Return

For some sociological commentators, attraction to the experiential nature of Neo-Pentecostal spiritualities—such as of the Movement—speaks both of a reaction against the culmination of modernization felt in Western society and church in the mid-twentieth century, and their promises

---

31. Taylor, *Secular Age*, 473.

to reconnect to premodern spiritualities which satisfy "primal" innate longings for transcendental ontological fulfilment in the face of a society that increasingly cannot offer anything comparable.

This was first theorized in reflection on glossolalia as a connection to the primitive and unutterable non-rational aspects of being, when in church "sacred language has given way to common nomenclature, mystery has been replaced by social concern, while miracles have been mythologized."[32] Killian McDonell explains, "The [charismatic] movement represents a turning back to recapture the original unstructured experience of the meaning of life at a level which, like tongues, is unutterable."[33]

More generally, this idea is how Cox explains the failure of the secularization thesis to predict the upsurge of religion in the twentieth century seen in Pentecostal Spirituality—which he conflates charismatic renewal with. Its success is "because it has spoken to the spiritual emptiness of our time . . . to enter what might be called "primal spirituality," that largely unprocessed nucleus of the psyche in which the unending struggle for sense of purpose and significance goes on."[34] This finds focus in the recovery of "primal speech" (glossolalia), primal piety (dreams, trances, and similar phenomena), and primal hope (a millennial expectation of a better future), explaining why "the re-emergence of this primal spirituality came—perhaps not surprisingly—at just the point in history when both the rationalistic assumptions of modernity and the strategies religions had used to oppose them (or accommodate to them) were all coming unraveled."[35]

Though Cox's triadic analysis of Pentecostalism is rightly accused of reductionism,[36] at least in broad strokes it offers a plausible potential explanation of Pentecostal-Charismatic upsurge amid modernity's impact. Focusing on charismatic renewal, Henry Lederle similarly claims charismatic phenomena are part of "the experiential dimension of normal Christian living which we needed to reclaim after the inroads of materialism,

---

32. Walker, "Pentecostal Power," 105.

33. Killian McDonell, quoted in Sullivan, *Can the Pentecostal Movement*, 5.

34. Cox, *Fire from Heaven*, 81. While Cox comments on anthropological aspects of faith in this analysis, his work here blurs the lines between sociology and anthropology. It is considered here under sociological insights because of its origin in the attempt to explain the failure of a sociological theory, the secularization thesis.

35. Cox, *Fire from Heaven*, 82.

36. Yong, *Discerning the Spirits*, 17–20.

naturalism, and rationalism in the secular era of modernity."[37] It represents an anti-modern movement that occurs because "after three centuries of relegating the nonrational and intuitive aspects of humanity to 'primitive remains' from superstitious times, a new climate has arisen, characterized by a deep hunger for spiritual experience and reality."[38]

On a surface level, such analyses fit the Movement, emphasizing how it can be understood as anti-modern rather than postmodern in its desire to reappropriate *Criterion One* experiential emphases of a premodern/primitive spirituality.[39] Such a process links a premodern recovery answer to CRQ-3 to a here reaffirmed *Mutual Origins* answer to CRQ-2, generating *Criterion One* emphases under CRQ-1's enquiry. As highlighted by McDonell and Cox, *Criterion Two* manifestations such as glossolalia might fit this process well, as well as aspects of Cox's "primal piety" where the mediation of spiritual realities comes through dreams and other means operating with symbology disconnecting signifiers from signified.[40] As will be seen, this larger narrative linking answers to all three CRQs finds further language through anthropological ideas of "play." Additionally, Cox's understanding of the "primal" could be considered an extension of Taylor's understanding of embeddedness, illuminating a psychological aspect to this heart of the *Mutual Origins* model—how one's embeddedness in the universe connects to an innate base longing for purpose and significance within it. How such might specifically relate to modernity to drive a *Mutual Origins* model will likewise also shortly be seen through anthropological ideas of "play."

4.1.2.2 *Cultural Crisis and Deprivation Theories*

As highlighted in §3.1.2.1, in the 1960s, Britain—and generally the whole of the Western world—experienced significant and rapid cultural changes which have been seen as a catalyst for new expressions of religion—especially experientially centered movements such as the Movement. Andrew Walker explains,

37. Lederle, *Theology with Spirit*, 182.
38. Lederle, "Life," 26.
39. Cox leaves the time period of "primitivity" undefined, speaking only of it being ancient enough to be universal. Part of what this study illuminates is the time ranges in the Movement an anti-modern impulse connects to in premodern recovery, helping temporally ground ideas of primitivity.
40. See §2.5.2.

The 1960s was a revolution of experience—sexual and chemical—and in some quarters this revolution was seen as countercultural. The charismatic movement in the churches reflected the idealism, the heightened experience, and the hedonism of this counterculture even though ideologically they were opposed to each other.[41]

This cultural turn had a large effect on the Movement's wider religious context. Seigfried Grossman describes the cultural changes in terms of a "crisis of orientation" because of a disintegration of traditional standards of reference and rapid societal change,[42] which Hunt concurs with.[43] In attempts to find happiness and meaning, people were confronted with a lack of transcendence in life because of a modernistic focus on the immanent which itself was undergoing disintegration. Cohering with Berger's analysis above, lacking "the personal protective power of the Christian faith they have lost,"[44] people sought what was needed in other places and countercultures, as "the demand for immediate, powerful, and deep religious experience . . . could on the whole not be met by the religious bodies" such as rationalistically focused Protestantism.[45] In such contexts, "the charismatic movement offers something which exactly fills the gap,"[46] with "promises of direct experience of God, group experience of the same, and confirmatory signs of the visible working of God."[47]

It is in this climate that proposed sociological deprivation theories can be seen to apply to the Movement which predict a *Cultural Catalysis* answer to CRQ-2. The majority of people involved in the Movement in the mid-twentieth century were from the middle classes of society,[48] despite observations that the outwardly similar Pentecostal "message appealed to the most disenfranchised; those with a little stake in the status quo."[49] Andrew Walker and Luke Bretherton comment that from the outset in Britain, "to be in the renewal in the late 1960s was an altogether broader, more middle-class, therapeutic and 'glad-rags' affair than the

41. Walker, "Thoroughly Modern," 29.
42. Grossmann, *Stewards of God's Grace*, 59.
43. Hunt, *Religion and Everyday Life*, 29.
44. Grossmann, *Stewards of God's Grace*, 60.
45. Bellah, "New Religious," 175.
46. Grossmann, *Stewards of God's Grace*, 64.
47. Grossmann, *Stewards of God's Grace*, 64–68.
48. Mather, "Theology," 48; Steven, "'Worship,'" 15; McLeod, *Religious Crisis*, 138.
49. Cox, *Fire from Heaven*, 106.

old Pentecostalism . . . a gentrified Pentecostalism,"[50] something seen to continue into the 1980s.[51] Sociologists have explained this phenomenon by theorizing that some form of deprivation is felt by those in the middle classes in the context of societal change which is met by the charismatic movement—deprivations other than the material deprivation felt in Pentecostalism's birth.

Cecil Bradfield highlights two possibilities. Firstly, ethical deprivation: a conservative response to changes in the morals of society which perceives discrepancies in society and church to the way things ought to be. Secondly, "psychic" deprivation: where those of religious orientation, perceiving their social and religious world disintegrating, look for alternative meaning systems which encompass the whole of life.[52] This second possibility may be true of attraction to the Movement in its observed combination of a rationally formed worldview from a traditional background infused with an emphasis on experience and emotion. However, ethical deprivation is unlikely, as ethical renewal was never a major emphasis of the Movement, unlike the Keswick Holiness movement and forms of early Pentecostalism which emphasized both subjective experience *and* moral holiness.

Wallis focuses on a type of spiritual deprivation stemming from a protest against prevailing religious institutions that have eschewed experience for dry formalism, perhaps fitting with postmodern moves against institutions more acutely at work in the middle classes than elsewhere. Such a protest was certainly seen in §3.1.2.1 and was commented on by General Synod's report.[53] Wallis explains that those in charismatic renewal

> typically consist of individuals who . . . felt something to be lacking in their spiritual lives, particularly an active experience of God's power working within them and within the church. Involvement in the renewal movement was often motivated by the desire for experience of the power of the Holy Spirit.[54]

Supporting this analysis, Robert Bellah highlights that in the developing experiential-seeking counterculture of the 1960s and beyond, "The

50. Walker, "Recovering," 7.
51. Hunt, "'Doing,'" 88.
52. Bradfield, *Neo-Pentecostalism*, 55.
53. §3.3.2.
54. Wallis, *Elementary Forms*, 36.

more intense religiosity of black and lower-class churches remained largely unavailable to the white middle-class members of the counterculture,"[55] and thus new charismatic churches were especially populated by those of the middle-classes who had nowhere else to go with their longings.

Other relevant forms of deprivation suggested include possible relative economic deprivation, or fear of it; deprivation of traditional community structure in the face of the break-up of societal structure; and specific crises of meaning, moral values, community, identity, and alienation. Hunt gives a helpful overview of these,[56] as well as a critique: what is the evidence that those theorized to feel a type of deprivation do so?[57]

Nonetheless, if forms of deprivation are even partially found in the Movement's sociological context, they are important for CRQ-2's enquiry. Despite not being evidenced significantly in the historical explorations of the Movement in the previous chapter, it is likely that *Cultural Catalysis* would occur when what is felt missing or deprived of is met by existent postmodern characteristics of the Movement. For example, spiritual deprivation met by *Criterion One* experiential emphasis, crises of identity met by *Criterion Three* emphases on personal story, and community deprivation met by *Criterion Four* emphases on community. Valuation and expression of such postmodern characteristics are amplified as they become observed gateways into the Movement—gateways that enlarge as increasingly more people pass through them.

It is important to differentiate here that the elements of wider culture drawn to the Movement in such a model are not postmodern elements, but rather *modernistic* elements, who feel their need for something "more" considering the break-down of modernism around them and are attracted to the postmodern characteristics of the Movement that move them beyond felt modernistic limitations. This is unlike the *Cultural Catalysis* suggested through models of Religious Consumerism.

4.1.2.3 *Religious Consumerism*

A *Cultural Catalysis* answer to CRQ-2 finds further sociological contextualization and support through theories of consumerism, which somewhat overlap with deprivation theories. In such, the appeal of charismatic

---

55. Bellah, "New Religious," 175.
56. Hunt, "Deprivation."
57. Hunt, "Deprivation," 23.

renewal to the middle classes is not linked to a deprivation met by it, but rather to a gain received through it for personal benefit. Of course, one person's felt need can be identical to another's desire above what is necessarily "needed," and the provision for deprivation can be identical to the gain received in consumerism—making distinguishing consumerism and deprivation models difficult. However, sociologically consumerism is linked to the rise of Western consumeristic culture from the 1950s, rather than the disorientating fracturing of society contextualizing deprivation theories. Walker sees this consumeristic turn as intimately linked to the rise of charismatic renewal, explaining,

> It is surely no coincidence that when Pentecostalism was transformed from its working class style to its middle class one we had moved from early to late modernity: an era that with the advent of consumerism in the 1950s saw the demise of aesthetic individualism and the rise of hedonistic individualism.[58]

Elsewhere Hunt sees this as part of the entrance into the *postmodern* age of society,[59] which agrees better with a shift from aesthetic to hedonistic that Walker highlights—a *Criterion One* postmodern shift from the priority of the rational to the experiential and emotional.

The effects of this consumerism upon religion can be understood through Taylor's sociological schema. What swings the individual participant towards one religious expression in the expressively focused "Age of Authenticity" is no longer just what feels most personally comfortable, but also "it must make sense in terms of my spiritual development as I understand it . . . my spiritual path, thus on what insights come to me in the subtler languages that I find meaningful."[60] Various aspects of the Movement can be seen to meet such individualized desires, many of which are postmodern in nature. As early as 1968, McDonnell noted strong resonances between charismatic movements and the secular human potential movement, including a desire for community (*Criterion Four*) and nonverbal forms of communication relying on physical touch (perhaps *Criterion Two*).[61] Meredith McGuire highlights that the (*Criterion One*) emotional appeal of performative inner healing in the charismatic movement may contribute to the "enhancing of the individual's

---

58. Walker, "Thoroughly Modern," 29.
59. Hunt, *Religion and Everyday Life*, 32.
60. Taylor, *Secular Age*, 486.
61. McDonnell, "Holy Spirit."

sense of personal empowerment."[62] In Grace Davie's study of the relative success of both English Cathedral spirituality and the Charismatic Movement in the context of church attendance decline, she concludes their successes hinge on a type of emotional consumerism (*Criterion One*): "It is the experiential or 'feel-good' factor, whether this be expressed in charismatic worship, in the tranquility of cathedral evensong, or a special cathedral occasion."[63] She predicts, "The actively religious in will Europe increasingly work on a market model," gravitating to such places of consumeristic gain.[64]

Religious consumerism, as a thesis, has its critiques. Some do not see anything "new" to it, as people have always made a "rational choice" based on the innate human desire for transcendence and immortality, leading to an attraction to religious systems that either offer high transcendental reward, low personal cost, or optimally both.[65] However, the acultural nature of such rational decision-making must be questioned, and perhaps the most helpful view is to see the rise of cultural consumerism as accelerating this decision-making process, facilitating the rapid rise of new religious movements.

If so, ideas behind religious consumerism contextualize and explain a *Cultural Catalysis* answer to CRQ-2, as postmodern aspects of the Movement attract elements of wider culture operating in consumeristic mode, naturally leading to these characteristics being emphasized—especially in mission to culture. However now, unlike in deprivation theories, *postmodern* elements of wider culture are attracted to the Movement in a seeking of that which resonates with existing (not missing) quantities.

Thus, overall, a *Cultural Catalysis* involving both modernistic elements of wider culture (through meeting felt deprivations), and postmodernistic elements (through meeting consumeristic desire) are two suggested potential manners of its operation. As will be seen, both occur in the Movement.

---

62. McGuire, "Words," 222.
63. Davie, "Is Europe?," 253.
64. Davie, "Is Europe?," 258.
65. Stark and Bainbridge, "Towards."

4.1.3 Specific Sociological Studies

Complementing the above more theoretical approaches, conversation with specific grounded sociological studies offers the promise of bringing a deeper contextual understanding of certain aspects relevant to the CRQs' enquiry. Though there is a relative dearth of such studies, two especially hold pertinent insight.

Firstly, Philip Richter's analysis of TTB sees a Weberian "routinization of charisma,"[66] quenching the Movement's inherent "reaction against modernity" by the 1990s, creating "a religious "midlife crisis,"" meaning the very non-modern aspects of TTB—such as its extreme experiential elements—were actively embraced in their fresh return to the Movement's anti-modernistic heart.[67] Evidence perhaps under CRQ-2's enquiry of how ingrained the Movement's anti-modernistic impulse—as described by the *Mutual Origins* model—is. Additionally, Richter posits that the non-verbal expressions involved in the unusual manifestations of TTB stem from the Movement's interactions with a postmodern society that does not allow the verbalization of transcultural objective truth, leading to a non-language.[68] Here, William Kay similarly notes, "All that is left is a form of communication that is essentially expressive. . . . [T]he Toronto blessing does not indicate spiritual renewal but intellectual exhaustion."[69] If so, a *Criterion Two* disconnection between signifiers and signified, whereby non-verbal physical expressions communicate realities interpretatively, stems from what could be termed postmodern fatigue, and is an alternative to Jaichandran and Madhav's "silence" in the outworking of postmodernism in charismatic movements.[70] As will be seen in chapter 5, Watson offers another option in the adoption of postmodern communicative practices, and important questions arise as to how all three reactions to postmodernism might relate to each other.

Secondly, in a 2006 ethnographic study of St. Michael-le-Belfrey Church, York, Michael Guest studies the church congregation as a living network exposed to the flows of secular modernity, asking, "How do members of the St. Michael's congregation relate such forces to their

---

66. Weber, *From Max Weber*, 262–64.
67. Richter, "'God Is Not a Gentleman!'" 20–23.
68. Richter, "'God Is Not a Gentleman!'" 33–34.
69. Kay, *Apostolic Networks of Britain*, 212.
70. See §2.1.

individual and collective identities as evangelicals?"[71] In important insight, Guest notes it is a strong emphasis on community, and the community of interpretation in particular, that has given the church resiliency in several internal dynamics within this interaction. He notes for example, "Why does subjectivisation within St. Michael's not lead to atomisation and the fragmentation of community? Because subjectivity generates narratives which require *communal* channels of expression in order to secure meaning."[72] In such observations, Guest highlights the formation of strong communities at St. Michael's in a *Criterion Four* manner: communal discernment creates and filters truth in the context of exposure to the outside modern world—aided by interactions with a wider non-Anglican network the church is part of. Additionally, the small groups within the congregation "serve as contexts for the legitimation of shared beliefs"[73] as part of a dynamic interaction with the wider network in which they are embedded, suggesting theorized *Criterion Four* manifestations of *communal interpretation* and *network* creation. As will be seen in chapter 5, such characteristics of St. Michael's first emerged under Watson's leadership, and here their strength over three decades later shows the enduring power of *Criterion Four* postmodern manifestations in its life.

4.2 ANTHROPOLOGICAL INSIGHTS

Complementing sociological insights, anthropological insights further illuminate suggested answers to all three CRQs and highlight how they may be narratively linked. In this, anthropological insights largely rely on ethnographic studies in ground-up analysis of cultures, therein differing from, but complementing, sociological perspectives.[74]

4.2.1 Playful Imagery

The idea of "play" is one used by a variety of disciplines,[75] but perhaps finds its best habitus in the anthropological sphere when describing a cognitive anthropology of Pentecostalism that speaks simultaneously of

71. Guest, *Evangelical Identity*, 18.
72. Guest, *Evangelical Identity*, 196.
73. Guest, *Evangelical Identity*, 195.
74. Morris, *Religion and Anthropology*, 6–11.
75. Burghardt, "Defining," 11.

the individual, the cultural, and the metaphysical. It gives a model and language to express a previously suggested larger narrative that links the answers to all three CRQs.[76]

Though hard to define, André Droogers summarizes play as an application of people's symbolizing capacity to deal simultaneously with two versions of reality—the tension of which might otherwise traumatize. For religion, this is the tension between one's existence and the sacred world impinging on rational reality through human communication of it. Suggestions from Taylor[77] and Cox[78] indicate such a universal tension on the individual level lies at the heart of a *Mutual Origins* model. The idea of "play" helps elucidate this: the act of play in religion creates yet another reality to reduce this tension, which is divine in nature.[79] Wolfgang Vondey further explains, "The execution of play . . . assumes particular forms that can be transmitted, traditioned, and repeated without being thereby assigned to the rationality of ordinary reality" because it creates its rhythm over the nonplay world through the power of collective imagination.[80]

Jean-Jacques Suurmond opines, "The essential contribution of Pentecostal spirituality lies in its playful character,"[81] which is enabled by the dual directive contributions of Word and Spirit, which directs a play that exists between order and chaos. The mistake of the church has been to believe the only alternative to chaos is order; Pentecostal play, most obviously manifested in charismatic manifestations, offers an alternative.[82] This play enables individuals to surpass themselves, casting off the "false self" controlled by order and hierarchy, such as what has been found in the church and other institutions.[83] Here Suurmond sheds further light on the discussion of §4.1.2.1: Pentecostalism enables an anti-modern release of self, allowing experience of a "primal" nature formerly repressed in history. Applying this, a *Mutual Origins* answer to CRQ-2 finds links to a premodern recovery answer to CRQ-3 through the potential of such playful processes occurring in the Movement.

76. See §3.4.1. and §4.1.2.1.
77. §4.1.1.2.
78. §4.1.2.1.
79. Droogers, *Play and Power*, 5.
80. Vondey, *Beyond Pentecostalism*, 174.
81. Suurmond, *Word and Spirit*, 220.
82. Suurmond, *Word and Spirit*, 29.
83. Suurmond, "Church," 252.

Under CRQ-1's enquiry, at least two clear individual postmodern manifestations are seen to be potentially generated in this playful anti-modern return to the more true and perhaps premodern self. In Droogers's observations of play in Pentecostal ritual, a key *Criterion Four* manifestation is seen in its emphasis on spiritual gifts as "the easy access every believer has to the charismatic gifts gives space for individual expressions of belief, not necessarily controlled by the clergy. . . . Since God's gifts of power are free and are available at any time, nobody can claim a privileged position."[84] As previously seen, this emphasis, longed for by Millar and Pytches, was brought into the Movement by Wimber.[85] Margaret Poloma argues the growth of AOG Pentecostalism comes through its ability to offer an "anthropological protest against modernity" by "providing a medium for encountering the supernatural . . . fus[ing] the natural and supernatural, the emotional and rational, the charismatic and institutional in a decidedly postmodern way."[86] If true for the Movement, here "protest" is perhaps a prelude to playful integration whereby such a "fusion" generates its broadened *Criterion One* epistemology which includes emotional as well as rational elements.

Looking ahead, Vondey believes a playful Pentecostalism is the ideal hope of Evangelicalism challenged to have a "Generous" or "Radical" Orthodoxy in the face of postmodernism: a Generous Orthodoxy relying on the tension of the lived-out playful elements of Pentecostal spirituality to overcome traditional dichotomies that are anathema to the postmodern, while simultaneously renewing the center;[87] and a Radical Orthodoxy returning to a premodernism that rejects modernistic dualisms, secularisms, and rationalistic epistemology in favor of an experiential affective religious knowledge.[88] Vondey flags something helpful here: playfulness in Pentecostal spirituality links aspects of it that are congruent with postmodern desire to premodern recovery. Language is given for how the Movement—when inhabiting a similar spirituality—potentially generates a space in which its postmodern characteristics overlap with, and

84. Droogers, *Play and Power*, 97.
85. §3.4.1.1.
86. Poloma, *Assemblies of God*, xix.
87. Vondey, *Beyond Pentecostalism*, 198–99. Vondey understands "Generous Orthodoxy" in the manner of Stanley Grenz's development of Hans Frei's original proposition of it. See Grenz, *Renewing the* Center, 333–59.
88. Vondey, 200–201. Vondey understands a "Radical Orthodoxy" of Anglican and Catholic theologians who opine a return to premodern roots of Christian faith—such as Robert Webber, whose ideas are explored in §7.2.4.

are indeed identical to, premodern characteristics that have been recovered—further substantiating such an answer to CRQ-3.

4.2.2 Cultural Discontinuities

Further anthropological insights help broaden the *ecclesial postmodern system*—a so far unmet aim of this chapter. A key feature seen through anthropological analysis of global Pentecostal-Charismatic Christianity is its ability to create cultural changes wherever it embeds in similar manners, despite dissimilar contexts. A primary facet of this is the generation of radical discontinuities with what has gone before, even "rupture."[89] These discontinuities occur on at least three dimensions: individual, cultural, and eschatological; in some cases, Pentecostalism does not just create them but also lives off them, continually defining itself in antithesis to what has gone before.[90] In the individual dimension, such ruptures facilitate a call to break free from the past, whether institutional associations, habits, or even acquaintances and relationships.[91] Though many of these emphases could be argued as observable in other religious expressions in their all-encompassing claims, the rhetorical appeals to these discontinuities, and the prized place of testimony of them, can be argued to be especially "Pentecostal."[92] Such a rhetorical appeal is a potential manifestation of *Criterion Three*, as this is a call out of a past that emphasizes personal "testimony" which overcomes all other controlling narratives, big or small.

4.2.3 Ritual Life

Despite some insistences within Pentecostal-Charismatic Christianity on its lack of ritual,[93] its ritual life is readily identifiable,[94] a second anthropological insight that helps further broaden the *ecclesial postmodern system*. Anthropological analysis of its two key overlapping components,

---

89. Robbins, "Globalization," 11.
90. Meyer, *Translating the Devil*, 24; Robbins, "Anthropology," 161.
91. Robbins, "Anthropology," 159.
92. See Pfeil, "Imperfect Vessels," 278–99.
93. Lindhardt, "Introduction," 2.
94. Albrecht, *Rites in the Spirit*, 21.

language and embodiment,[95] highlights several insights helpful for the enquiry of the CRQs.

4.2.3.1 Language and Ritual

Csordas explains in ritual performance it is "in rhetoric, that is, in the persuasive means by which a vision is articulated" that "charisma" is rhetorically established and disseminated more widely to transform believer's lives.[96] This is especially seen in the "illocutionary" force of prophetic speech to constitute a "sacred self" giving a strong incitement to "radicalization"—the power of an announced future that fulfils innate desires.[97] This is enabled by the dissociation of symbols from their meanings in language, ultimately expressed in glossolalia, which Csordas sees as both part of the charismatic movement's postmodern quality, and also its premodern quality.[98] This suggests that *Criterion Two* manifestations in spiritual gifts, first theorized in §2.5.3, might find especial expression in *prophetic speech* and *glossolalia* in ecclesial postmodernism; here they are additionally related to a premodern recovery answer to CRQ-3.

Other studies of Pentecostal-Charismatic ritual language highlight further potential system manifestations. In Simon Coleman's ethnographic work, the performative nature of its language is exposed: that in preaching, prophecy and testimony, "the Word is perceived as an independent power rather than a collection of signs in need of socially determined interpretation."[99] Such words both have power in themselves to create tangible instant change, but also sometimes must "be activated to take effect" as they act as a commodity of potentiality, transmitted relationally.[100] This "activation" can be provoked by the original speaker in a ritual manner so that the listener is challenged to submit and receive the word as divine to enable it to have transformative power, meaning that "listeners should themselves perform; partake of the charismatic

---

95. Bialecki, "Affect," 95; Lindhardt, "Introduction," 21.
96. Csordas, *Language, Charisma, and Creativity*, 153. For Csordas, "charisma" has a double meaning of both something related to the charismatic gifts and its more commonly used sense of affective energy.
97. Csordas, *Language, Charisma, and Creativity*, 157–202.
98. Csordas, *Language, Charisma, and Creativity*, 64.
99. Coleman, "Materializing," 168.
100. Coleman, "Materializing," 173–74.

habitus."[101] Such *performative power of language* is clearly a Criterion Two manifestation to be added to the ecclesial postmodernism system, as the language in this act signifies a power beyond what is normally signified by it, disconnecting signifiers from signified.

Similarly, Martin Lindhardt highlights how ritual acts of narrating testimonies of salvation reaffirms shared realities, consolidating membership in Pentecostal-Charismatic communities, and how by their simultaneous personal and stereotypical nature they integrate individual biographies within a shared larger story and worldview, uniting present truth with eternal truth, micronarrative with metanarrative. Thus, such *stereotypical shaping of testimony*, can be regarded as an additional Criterion Three potential ecclesial manifestation.[102]

4.2.3.2 Embodiment of Ritual

Joel Robbins highlights several aspects of embodiment seen in the anthropological literature on Pentecostalism, including the moralization of the body, its ritual training of habitus, and the importance of bodily communication in Pentecostal churches.[103] Such aspects reveal the embodied locus of its epistemology, which locates its Criterion One epistemology; indeed, they are clear potential manifestations of it under CRQ-1's enquiry, as the "body" becomes part of knowing.

Tanya Luhrmann explores how embodiment rituals enable a relationship with God in a manner she calls *metakinesis*, whereby "new believers learn to identify bodily and emotional states as signs of God's presence in their life, identifications that imply quite different learning processes than those entailed by linguistic and cognitive knowledge."[104] Such is a Criterion One move from a purely mind-based rationalistic epistemology,[105] to an embodied experiential one. Substantiating this, Phillip Mellor and Chris Shilling contextualize such shifts within postmodern uncertainty, leading to a re-emphasis, as in the baroque period, upon the body as an indicator of reality. Drawing on Lyotard's work, they explain how in a postmodern climate:

101. Coleman, "Voices," 214.
102. Lindhardt, "Narrating."
103. Robbins, "Anthropology," 165.
104. Luhrmann, "Metakinesis," 519.
105. See §2.2.1.

> A growing sense of uncertainty and fragmentation can play upon the emotions and lead to a resurgence of "irrational" sensuality. . . . [It is] in this context that baroque modern bodies search for phenomena which can be reconsecrated as a sign that humanity still exists.[106]

Michael Wilkinson and Peter Althouse utilize the "Interaction Ritual Theory" of Randall Collins,[107] to analyze some of the embodied emphases of TTB, and in doing so relate the embodied emphasis seen in some of its exotic manifestations with the anthropological concept of play considered above. Interaction Ritual Theory posits, "the center of an interaction ritual is the process in which participants develop a mutual focus of attention and become entrained in each other's bodily micro-rhythms and emotions"[108]—a mechanism enabling a momentarily shared reality, generating solidarity in group membership. This lies at the heart of ritual play in charismatic worship, by which some of the more unusual "manifestations" of TTB can be interpreted as playful activities. Through them, a participant, through ritualized embodiment and language, "not only discovers the divine order of reality but also attends to it by attuning to the whispers and presence of God."[109] As explored in §4.2.1, such playful acts are a means of overcoming the modernistic restrictions of rationalism to recover something previous to it, highlighting through the witness of TTB how a *Criterion One* embodied emphasis is potentially generated through a *Mutual Origins* impulse geared towards premodern recovery—signs again of a larger narrative at work connecting answers to the CRQs.

4.3 CONCLUSION

Engagement with social scientific insights has been highly fruitful, bringing both contextualized understanding to previous observations made under the CRQs' enquiry and suggestions of new system areas to be explored in qualitative lifeworld analysis of the Movement.

For CRQ-1's enquiry, as well as reemphasizing previously described manifestations, various further manifestations of the Analytic Criteria

---

106. Mellor and Shilling, *Re-Forming the Body*, 12.
107. Collins, *Interaction Ritual Chains*.
108. Wilkinson and Althouse, *Catch the Fire*, 72–73.
109. Wilkinson and Althouse, *Catch the Fire*, 79.

have been suggested that are to be incorporated into the ecclesial postmodernism system elucidated in §2.5.3: for *Criterion One*, a epistemological emphasis on the body and embodied emotive ritual; *Criterion Two* manifestations within discontinuities in prophetic language and signs, glossolalia, and in the usage of performative language; *Criterion Three* manifestations in calls to break with previous cultural metanarratives and the ritual stereotypical shaping of testimonies; *Criterion Four* manifestations in emphases on communal interpretation of corporately used spiritual gifts. These additional potential manifestations, added to those suggested previously, create a broader system to bring to qualitative analysis of the Movement's lifeworld.[110]

Sociological and anthropological scholarship suggests no evidence of a *Direct influence* model in answer to CRQ-2. Conversely, they bring understanding to, and provoke expectation of, both *Mutual Origins* and *Cultural Catalysis* models. Sociological metatheories considered to contextualize the Movement's rise suggest a sociological impetus given to it through an anti-modernistic reaction which drives a *Mutual Origins* model. Similar is seen through viewing the Movement through the anthropological idea of "play," together with specific places where this model is indicated, such as in TTB. These insights have especially helped develop an understanding of the underlying potential human participant origins of this anti-modernistic impulse that stems from an embeddedness in the universe (Taylor), correlates to a longing for innate purpose and significance (Cox), and is expressed in playful fashion (Droogers, Vondey). Sociological theories additionally provoke expectation of *Cultural Catalysis* which occurs in two manners in the context of cultural changes in society: deprivation theories suggest catalysis through the Movement's contact with *modernistic* elements of culture and their longings, which the postmodern characteristics of the Movement meet as a salve; ideas of religious consumerism conversely suggest catalysis through contact with *postmodern* elements of culture whose desires are directly met by the Movement's postmodern characteristics.

Finally, continued suggestions that a desire for premodern recovery is key to answering CRQ-3 have been seen in the secularization thesis's suggestions of the reclamation of non-modernistic elements of faith; in ideas of a primal return given by Cox and Lederle; and in the anthropological analysis of a "playful" spirituality which enables a return to a

---

110. The full set of manifestations that describe the larger ecclesial postmodernism system is found in appendix 1.

repressed premodern one. Specific examples of this desire are seen in TTB's embodied emphases and ritual usage of glossolalia and prophecy. Additionally, there have again been repeated suggestions this answer to CRQ-3 links to a *Mutual Origins* answer to CRQ-2 to explain postmodern characteristics of the Movement discerned under CRQ-1's enquiry. This was especially described by Vondey and Lederle's work, bringing explanatory power to suggestions of this larger narrative in chapter 3's consideration of Wimber's ministry.

This study's dialectical methodology has now arrived at the place of re-engagement with the Movement's lifeworld through utilizing detailed qualitative analysis to answer the CRQs. It does so out of initial explorations and reflections being brought into dialogue with results from this chapter to equip its analysis, and out of this it is now able to undertake this analysis with a working hypothesis:

1. CRQ-1: the Movement shows a full range of postmodern characteristics described by the Analytic Criteria, but none to their strongest extent. *Criterion One* manifestations are the most substantially seen and may lead to manifestations of the other criteria, as would be expected in the outworking of a postmodern-like drive internal to the Movement.

2. CRQ-2: a *Direct Influence* model is not substantially seen. However, a *Mutual Origins* model describes the generation of the Movement's above postmodern characteristics, especially the primacy of *Criterion One* ones; yet limitations are perhaps seen on how far it is allowed to go in its anti-modern drive—a drive that explains the prominence of *Criterion One* manifestations in the Movement. This combines with a *Cultural Catalysis* model whereby both modernistic and postmodernistic elements of wider culture catalyze the subsequent growth of such characteristics.

3. CRQ-3: a desire for the recovery of premodern aspects of praxis marks the Movement and is a consequence of a *Mutual Origins* model. Reaction against modernism led the Movement to recover and reemphasize what existed before it, leading to the retrieval of characteristics and practices that, while looking postmodern, are premodern in base identity, with the postmodern and premodern converging in such, as the way forward becomes the way back.

From the above, elements of a larger narrative are hypothesized that explain some of the specific observations of §1.1: the *Cultural Catalysis* of many postmodern-looking premodern characteristics, retrieved through a *Mutual Origins* anti-modern impulse, amplifies their presence in the Movement, making the Movement look postmodern to outside observation. Therefore, the Movement's postmodern label is a misnomer given both the lack of *Direct Influence* discerned and the existence of the above mechanism that explains the Movement's seemingly postmodern nature.

5

Postmodernism and the Early Movement

Now well equipped to do so, this study now enters its most substantive phase of investigation, returning to the lifeworld pole of this study's dialectic methodology to begin an in-depth qualitative analysis and reflection on the Movement which spans the next three chapters. This chapter explores the nature of the early life of the Movement by studying, under the enquiry of the CRQs, the literary corpora of two of its key leaders, Michael Harper and David Watson, adding significantly to previous studies of their work. It explores the presence and relative strength of postmodern characteristics in the early Movement, looks for evidence of the three models—*Direct Influence, Mutual Origins,* and *Cultural Catalysis*—that might describe how these arise, and searches for signs of a premodern recovery impulse that helps further explain them.

In doing so the working hypothesis formulated at the end of the previous chapter is tested and largely verified, with additional detail and nuance added to it. It is verified that the early Movement shows a full range of postmodern characteristics described by the Analytic Criteria, but none to their strongest extent; that *Mutual Origins* and *Cultural Catalysis* models describe dynamics largely responsible for their existence; and that these combine with a premodern recovery impulse driven by the anti-modernism described by the former model to give the early Movement its postmodern character. These findings help frame analysis of the later Movement in the next two subsequent chapters to create a coherent analysis of the Movement's entire lifetime.

5.1 MICHAEL HARPER

Michael Claude Harper (1931–2010) was a pioneering leader within the Movement. Through his directorship of the Fountain Trust, prolific authorship, and numerous ecumenical relationships, throughout the late 1960s to the mid-1990s, Harper's influence on the Movement was paradigmatic. His movement to the Orthodox Church in March 1995 and subsequent ordination within the Antiochian Orthodox Deanery for Great Britain curtailed this influence in the latter part of his life. Yet, as shall be seen, this event clarifies the trajectory of his personal journey and contextualizes a strong desire for premodern recovery that undergirded his previous influence.

5.1.1 CRQ-1: Postmodern Characteristics

Harper's twenty books, numerous editorials and articles in *Renewal* and *Theological Renewal* magazines, and various other articles, paint a picture of the early Movement which manifests clear manifestations of the Analytic Criteria. However, no criteria are manifested in a fully postmodern manner. Manifestations of *Criteria One* and *Three* are the clearest to see, while consideration under *Criterion Four* shows simultaneously some of the Movement's strongest postmodern manifestations and as well as the opposite in manifestation.

5.1.1.1 Criterion One: A Non-Foundational Epistemology

Harper often inhabits a modernistic epistemology. His books are written largely as logical arguments that appeal to the reader's mind, though his testimonial books aim differently. Harper recognizes attacks on such emphases within charismatic renewal, as well as potentially upon his own words. In his critique of modernistically paradigmed theological training in *Let My People Grow* he warns, "It needs to be made clear that these remarks are not a form of anti-intellectualism."[1] However, he balances this with the need to broaden an approach that while not anti-intellectual is not limited to the intellectual. For example, in *These Wonderful Gifts!* he takes pains to emphasize about glossolalia,

> The gift does not downgrade the intellect. . . . But it does recognise that the mind has its own limits. In other words the Spirit is using tongues to restore a balance. He wants to set the Church

---

1. Harper, *These Wonderful Gifts!* 92.

free from being locked into a system of thought which closes the mind to the inspiration of the Holy Spirit.[2]

In such freedom, other epistemological priorities come to the fore and often are *the* prominent way Harper assesses reality. In an early statement in *As At The Beginning*, he explains, "We may be led by the Spirit to do things which on their face value appear unreasonable. But to God, who knows the end from the beginning, there is a reason for such guidance which will eventually be revealed."[3] He is willing for rationalistic orientations to be overridden in the confidence of a superior divine rationality to be manifested in the future.

For Harper, this belief leads to a pragmatic epistemological priority that is often more important than any other, a key postmodern manifestation. In his first book, *Prophecy*, written a year after the Movement's birth, he hopes for his readers, "the lasting excitement which follows the reading of this book is this: the thing works."[4] Throughout his work, he encourages a recovery of NT Christianity because of its fruitfulness.[5] On the Movement's organizational structure, he reflects, "It has developed in a piecemeal fashion, and the American influence has ensured its basically pragmatic approach."[6] Similarly, reflecting on the first edition of *Power For the Body*, he explains his authorial motivation: "The doctrine we had come to grasp and understand, and in which we had experienced ourselves, has been thoroughly tested in practice. In other words—it works."[7] The greatest manifestation of his pragmatic epistemology is seen in defense of Pentecostalism:

> I find it very hard to accept that it is ever possible in any basic sense to produce a magnificent performance which is based on theological error. . . . [H]ow can one have unsound theology

---

2. Harper, *These Wonderful Gifts!* 92.
3. Harper, *As at the Beginning*, 15.
4. Harper, *Prophecy*, 4.
5. Harper, *As at the Beginning*, 14.
6. Harper, *This Is the Day*, 30. See also §3.1.1 on Harper's historiological approach that overemphasizes American influences and §2.3.4 on the American Pragmatic tradition.
7. Harper, *Power for the Body*, 14.

and yet see glorious effects in the lives of people? . . . To put it succinctly, "It works."[8]

In a postmodern manner, Harper is willing to override rationalistic critiques because of pragmatic success which authenticates truth. There are, however, limits to this pragmatism. In his engagement with situational ethics, he strongly disagrees with the idea: "Only the end justifies the means, nothing else."[9] In *Equal and Different* he later charges the Church of England with pragmatism in its acceptance of women's ordination,[10] ironically unaware of his own strong pragmatism, and how this partly drove his previously positive discussion about the viability of such a decision.[11]

Harper's pragmatic epistemology is complemented by a strong experiential one. In *None Can Guess*, Harper opines that the charismatic movement, "Places its chief emphasis on experience."[12] He posits a form of hierarchy, with experiential above rational epistemological approaches, explaining that the 1964 Stoke Poges conference was organized because "we want them [delegates] to experience this [charismatic] life during the conference, even if only for a couple of days. They will then grasp what it is all about far better than if they have heard about it in a talk or read about it in a book."[13] He argues, "Intellect is a secondary element (after experience), it follows after the original experience as an attempt to order and explicate that which has been given."[14] Such a strong experiential emphasis directly explains the temporary demotion of rational epistemological emphases behind experiential ones that received critique and redress noted in the life of the Fountain Trust in §3.2.3. Harper's strong emphasis shaped the whole of the Trust, even if it went against the wider grain of the Movement that held rational and experiential emphases more in parallel.

This experiential priority comes from Scripture. In *Walk in The Spirit*, he quotes Leslie Newbiggin's argument against modern theology's

---

8. Harper, *This Is the Day*, 56.
9. Harper, *Love Affair*, 177.
10. Harper, *Equal and Different*, 142.
11. Harper, *Let My People Grow*, 114.
12. Harper, *None Can Guess*, 80.
13. Harper, *None Can Guess*, 80.
14. Harper, *Love Affair*, 33.

fear of experience, explaining that the NT is free from this fear.[15] In *Glory in the Church*, he explains that Scripture focuses on experience, though also explaining, "the scriptures are also our safeguard to our experiences. They describe in detail both their basis and bounds."[16] This last statement perhaps helps discern Harper's overall approach of refusing to choose between experiential and rational engagement, both need each other, even if the former is more important. Elsewhere he explains, "It is true that it is dangerous to accept a doctrine solely on the grounds of experience. But doctrine without experience is dangerous also."[17] In *You Are My Sons* he equates the two: "What we need for ourselves is a constant *experience* of the promises of God which approximates to their intellectual and theological content."[18] In such comments, perhaps the predicted operative limits of a *Mutual Origins* model that generates such experiential emphases are being discerned by Harper;[19] yet Harper is also somewhat self-unaware of how the witness of his strong experiential emphasis may indeed have led others into the very territory he warns against.

Such limits may also explain why an emotional epistemology is largely unseen in Harper.[20] He rallies against those who react badly to emotions displayed in renewal,[21] but also explains, "It is possible for people to crave for emotional pleasure, which weakens rather than strengthens them, and leads to greater instability than ever."[22] Emotions are an overflow of experience and have no real value in comparison because they do not lead to transformation: "The emotional vibrations may be present also. But if a church and the individuals in it 'experience' the Holy Spirit's power, it will mean that people will be changed."[23]

---

15. Harper, *Walk in the Spirit*, 9.
16. Harper, *Glory in the Church*, 30.
17. Harper, *As at the Beginning*, 101.
18. Harper, *You Are My Sons*, 66.
19. See §5.1.2 below.
20. See §1.1.3.3 for discussion of the difference between experiential and emotional epistemologies in lifeworld analysis. Though many would ascribe emotional emphasis to individualistic modernistic culture, here, and in what follows, I understand the valuing of an emotional epistemology in some aspects of culture as a postmodern turn in the manner postmodernism has been understood in this study. See discussions in Brady, *Emotional Insight*; Ecclestone and Hayes, "Affect."
21. Harper, *As at the Beginning*, 111.
22. Harper, *Love Affair*, 116.
23. Harper, *You Are My Sons*, 85.

Overall, Harper's epistemology exhibits a hierarchical ordering where rational emphases are dethroned. Pragmatic ones hold primacy, with experiential and rational ones vying for second place—the former often winning. Such perhaps helps explain the temporary demotion of rational priorities in the Movement's early life in its experiential ecumenicalism, and why only *external* criticism reversed it.[24] Early leaders such as Harper led the Movement with a radically new epistemological ordering.

A key postmodern mark of Harper's epistemological approach is found in its embodied locus.[25] At times Harper de-emphasizes the body when he sees unhelpful over-emphases, such as in trance-like prophecy,[26] and falling to the floor in baptisms of the Spirit.[27] However, the bodily locus of renewal is rejoiced in when not seen as a dangerous emphasis, such as in those "who have just been baptized in the Spirit whose faces have shone with the literal shekinah glory."[28] Even stronger, in his 1974 works onwards, Harper begins to use terminology that emphasizes the "need for a release of the Spirit . . . his release in us,"[29] which looks like God being able to

> burst forth through every nerve and pore of our bodies. It is to be reflected in our thoughts, our words, our songs, even our physical appearance. We shall have new confidence to lift up our heads. For a growing number of people the lifting up of hands in worship is a token of the fact that God is now in control of our bodies. . . . Renewal is physical as well as spiritual.[30]

This embodiment theme finds greatest expression in his understanding of glossolalia, where the body enables the bypass of the rational:

> The bottleneck is the human mind, which boggles at the wonder and majesty of God, and cannot keep up with the desires which surge up from our innermost being. . . . The gift of tongues is a

---

24. See §§3.2.2–3.2.3.
25. See §4.3.3.2.
26. Harper, *Prophecy*, 28–29.
27. Harper, *Power for the Body*, 13.
28. Harper, *Power for the Body*, 71.
29. Harper, *Glory in the Church*, 18.
30. Harper, *Glory in the Church*, 47.

God-ordained channel or instrument temporarily by-passing or transcending the intellectual processes.[31]

Even more extreme, in the reception of glossolalia, Harper speaks of bodily actualization, not just bypass: "There are always three moves in the baptism in the Holy Spirit. God *always* makes the first move, but will not make his second move (enabling us to speak in tongues) until we have made our move (and begin to speak)."[32] Elsewhere he enjoins practical bodily steps that enable this,[33] and it is hard to deny a clear postmodern embodied emphasis in such instances.

However, despite such postmodern manifestations, epistemological pluralism and relativism are absent in Harper's work, meaning *Criterion One* lacks its fullest set of manifestations. Multiple versions of truth from several types of epistemologies are not held on par together in contradiction, nor subsumed into each other in a relativistic manner. Indeed, against the latter, Harper argues strongly against types of relativism. In his 1979 published lecture *Beauty or Ashes?*—arguing against relativism in sexual ethics in opposition to cultural mores—he derides, "One of the major factors in our modern pseudo-prophecy is the tendency to absolutise what is relative and to relativise what is absolute."[34] Even stronger is his reaction against relativism in his analysis of the acceptance of women's ordination into the Church of England, which he adds to the aforementioned pragmatic charge.[35] *Criterion One* characteristics are clear in Harper's work, yet incomplete in their fullest spread.

5.1.1.2 Criterion Two: Discontinuities Between Signifiers and Signified

In contrast, *Criterion Two* characteristics are relatively absent. For example, in Harper's teaching on prophecy, there is no indication that prophetic signs and utterance leads to a disconnect between them and the reality they indicate. Notably, Harper argues against spiritual or allegorical exegesis of Scripture, explaining, "We need to be aware of certain tendencies, especially when verses are obviously difficult to understand,

---

31. Harper, *Walk in the Spirit*, 22.
32. Harper, *Power for the Body*, 62.
33. Harper, *You Are My Sons*, 83–84.
34. Harper, *Beauty or Ashes?*, 7–9.
35. Harper, *Equal and Different*, 1.

either to spiritualize, demythologize or just miss them out altogether."[36] No doubt, here he is speaking about both Bultmann-esque demythologization and more Pentecostal spiritualization. Though Harper sometimes uses techniques that verge towards the latter, such as in viewing Jesus's baptism in the Spirit as a parallel experience for the Christian believer,[37] his hermeneutic expresses continuity via experience rather than postmodern discontinuity.

Some partial manifestations of *Criterion Two* are seen in Harper's understanding of glossolalia and of performative words. In glossolalia, Harper understands that there is a connection between the words uttered and what is signified, yet "the important thing is not to concentrate on signs or consequences, but on the thing signified. As you come first into the source of all power, and drink as Jesus commands, then rivers will begin to flow."[38] He suggests that that which is signified is the divine reality, but there is a partial disconnect while the words are uninterpreted, so that "it is only when the gift of tongues is coupled with that of interpretation that it edifies the church, when it will be equivalent in value to prophecy."[39] Elsewhere, Harper frames this disconnection in terms of the mind being connected to the signified, and the heart to the signifiers, united yet divided in the body in *both* continuity and discontinuity:

> As we shall see the mind is held and concentrated on the person of Jesus. It is not in a trance or "blank." But it no longer thinks of words. The Holy Spirit through this gift gives us the words to say, and the new language . . . therefore, is able to cope with the overflow from the heart. Speaking in tongues, in other words, is a language of the heart not of the intellect.[40]

Harper also exhibits some postmodern character in his understanding of the performative power of language. In his usage of the name "Jesus" in spiritual warfare, Harper refutes that it is a magical talisman, yet elaborates, "The name of a person in the Bible means the entire person. When, therefore, we talk about the protection of the name of Jesus . . . the name of Jesus means the protective power of His presence."[41] Here, a

36. Harper, *Glory in the Church*, 29.
37. Harper, *Power for the Body*, 30–31.
38. Harper, *Walk in the Spirit*, 23.
39. Harper, *Walk in the Spirit*, 63.
40. Harper, *You Are My Sons*, 71. Such embodiment agrees with Csordas's observations in §4.2.3.1.
41. Harper, *Spiritual Warfare*, 74, 90.

word connects to a reality beyond what would be normally signified in a strictly modernistic understanding. Something similar is seen in words spoken during prayer for healing: "Some years ago I found myself, when praying for sick people, increasingly using the word 'peace'. I would actually speak 'peace' to diseased tissue and infections."[42] Words such as "Jesus" and "peace" here carry a significance beyond their normal meaning in language. However, as in glossolalia, there is still some demonstrable link to what is signified, which in healing is often a future reality not yet present, with continuity and discontinuity held together in tension.[43]

5.1.1.3 Criterion Three: Metanarratives and Micronarratives

Greater evidence is seen of *Criterion Three* postmodern characteristics of Harper's thought, though not to the same level as for *Criterion One* characteristics. Harper repeatedly promotes the power of personal testimony in renewal. In an early work, *Power for the Body of Christ*, he explains his reason for writing was "because of my conviction that the churches were leaving out something very important. I wrote it also because in September 1962 my wife and I had an experience which changed our lives"—which he then explicates.[44] He ends the book with a chapter of individual testimonies of those who have experienced renewal, subtitled, "It happened to me."[45] The emphasis of this early book was to introduce the concept of charismatic renewal to an audience unfamiliar with it, and it is telling that testimonies bookend the means of this. Harper's personal account of charismatic renewal in *None Can Guess*, and his editorship of six renewal testimonies of Anglican Bishops in *Bishops' Move*, indicates how this emphasis on the power of individual testimony continued throughout his writings.[46]

Of even greater power for Harper is the testimony of groups of people and churches: "It is such stories, rather than individual testimonies, which are the best advertisement for miracles which the Holy Spirit can

---

42. Harper, *Jesus the Healer*, 145.

43. It may be argued here that a disconnect between language and reality is inherent to most Christian views of healing because of a worldview that views physical and spiritual realities as mutually intertwined, as for example in Wimber's theological system. See §3.4.1.2.

44. Harper, *Power for the Body*, 10.

45. Harper, *Power for the Body*, 80–84.

46. And also in conferences that he organized. See Maiden, *Age of the Spirit*, 54.

perform."⁴⁷ This is seen in his narration of the story of the Church of the Redeemer, Houston—a book-long exposition of "a success story," which "should be seen in the context of the suffering and sacrifice that has gone with it."⁴⁸ Throughout it, he seeks to provoke the British church as to what might be possible through such communities amid the cultural and ecclesiological crises of the day.

Such testimonies, both individual and communal, are peppered throughout Harper's writings. However, simultaneously he is aware of trends that demote Christian metanarratives in the Movement, likening it to some of the tendencies of Montanism, the "downgrading of history and tradition, and the making of a fresh start with little or no reference to what has gone before."⁴⁹ Noticeably, Harper also often seeks to locate the charismatic movement amid the historical sweep of church history, as a means of legitimation, and also critique.⁵⁰ His overall narrative of renewal itself also has its own metanarrative, rather than simply moving from testimony to testimony: "Christian renewal has an end as well as a beginning. . . . God's will for his people is continuous renewal until the final destination is reached. . . . The coming of Jesus will inaugurate the final renewal."⁵¹

Harper's dual metanarrative and micronarrative emphasis is situated within an awareness of the breakdown of society's metanarratives. He powerfully begins *Glory in the Church* by writing, "This book was begun on New Year's Day, 1974. Time magazine called 1974, 'the first year of the future,' and 1973, 'the last year of the past'"; while suggesting some over-exaggeration, he nonetheless explicates political, economic, and social breakdowns, explains the fact that the church may find herself hitched to this story, and offers an alternative: "The finest hours of the Church have usually been in times of persecution and famine. But our church will need to be renewed in the power of the Holy Spirit if we are to take advantage of this kind of situation."⁵² Harper meets culture's metanarrative breakdown with a solution that does not explicitly call for a break with cultural metanarratives, yet involves a reorientation to a truer narrative, which elsewhere he simply calls "obedience to God

47. Harper, *As at the Beginning*, 70.
48. Harper, *New Way of Living*, 7.
49. Harper, *Equal and Different*, 203.
50. See Harper, *Beauty or Ashes?*, 11; Harper, *Jesus the Healer*, 131–39.
51. Harper, *Glory in the Church*, 76.
52. Harper, *Glory in the Church*, 13–14.

and the coming of his Kingdom on earth,"[53] which progresses historically towards Christ's return.[54] Here, such ideas cohere with §4.2.2's prediction of narrative discontinuities, while not abrogating the importance of metanarratives in general given the truer metanarrative he calls the renewed church to bring to society.

Other potential manifestations of this criterion are unseen. Nowhere is it seen that micronarratives such as testimonies are as important, or more so, than the metanarrative of the Christian faith, or that they are somehow allowed to conflict with it. For Harper testimonies are not stereotypically shaped and are always encapsulated within God's salvation economy, with conflict only occurring when forced into a purely modernistic secular metanarrative instead.[55]

5.1.1.4 Criterion Four: The Importance of Community

Though mostly explained contextually through underlying issues, it is under *Criterion Four* that Harper's most extreme postmodern tendencies, combined with the opposite, are seen. Harper values interpretive communities in the context of renewal. Speaking about "baptism in the Spirit" he explains, "To enjoy the blessing to the full we must be a member of a fellowship, contributing as the spirit leads to the mutual upbuilding of the other members";[56] he also argues, "We also need one another if we are to understand the Bible and interpret it correctly."[57] The Church of the Redeemer Houston pre-eminently showed the importance of such communal discernment for Harper, especially in individual ministry vocations.[58]

Though this emphasis is contextualized in the renewed cultural desire for community, he calls for Christian communities to be birthed primarily because of the potential of ministries that develop within them.[59] He contrasts this priority, present in the charismatic renewal, with a dearth of it in Evangelicalism, meaning, "it seems to be more a movement

---

53. Harper, *Power for the Body*, 23.
54. Harper, *Glory in the Church*, 76.
55. Harper, *Jesus the Healer*, 132.
56. Harper, *Power for the Body*, 76.
57. Harper, *Glory in the Church*, 56.
58. Harper, *New Way of Living*, 72.
59. Harper, *New Way of Living*, 64.

'of the people and for the people' than the evangelical world, and this accounts in part for its world-wide appeal and its rapid growth."[60] Clearly, there is a pragmatism about such communities for Harper, again touching on this postmodern emphasis. However, as seen in §3.2.1, the failure of Harper's vision for new renewal communities to be established suggests voices to the contrary coexisted in the early Movement.

In Harper's view of authority and its structures, the question of postmodern manifestations is more mixed. Theoretically, Harper retains a high view of authority, setting a high bar as to when authority can be abrogated,[61] acknowledging the wider context whereby culture has turned against ideas such as "authority" and "submission."[62] He sees Montanism as a warning to the charismatic movement of getting this wrong,[63] yet in his personal journey in breaking with the Church of England over women's ordination adduces the possibility of the opposite error of unswerving allegiance to errant authority, or at least authority that ceases to be so when theologically heterodox because it no longer coheres with the higher authority of Scripture and church tradition.[64]

When focusing on specific authority holders, a more differentiated picture emerges. Harper is often very critical of rank-and-file clergy, almost explicitly postmodern in his suspicion of their power and priorities, affirming General Synod's 1981 report analysis of "A Reaction Against Clericalism."[65] He speaks of the need for the "emancipation of the laity from the shackles that many churches have put on them,"[66] and it is clear who in these churches have been responsible for this. In the provocatively entitled *Let My People Grow*, likely referencing Pharaoh's enslavement of Israel,[67] he likens ministers to babysitters, to corks in a bottle, and as part of an "elaborate religious system" that imprisons the laity.[68] Harper of course is being deliberately polemical, but he is noticeably postmodern in attitude. Almost directly mirroring Foucault, he explains, "Power has been concentrated in a few hands, and this has produced in the

60. Harper, *This Is the Day*, 36–37.
61. Harper, *You Are My Sons*, 46.
62. Harper, *Let My People Grow*, 153–55.
63. Harper, *Equal and Different*, 203.
64. Harper, *Equal and Different*, 269.
65. See §3.3.2.
66. Harper, *Power for the Body*, 41.
67. Exod 5:1.
68. Harper, *Let My People Grow*, 24–25.

laity generations of sermon tasters and sacramentalists—watching 'the machine' rather than being actively involved in ministry."[69] Though this is perhaps tempered by some more generous descriptions of clergy elsewhere,[70] Harper is clearly anti-authoritarian in his attacks on rank-and-file clergy of his time.

This contrasts with his view on bishops, which is largely positive. In the same book, he laments, "The plain truth of the matter is that there are too few bishops," resulting in a lack of pastoral care of the flock.[71] He has a high regard for the role of bishops and longs for an episcopate that is renewed in the Spirit's power, as per the stories recorded in *Bishops' Move*.[72] Despite sometimes taking pot-shots at the competency of bishops,[73] if normal clergy in charismatic renewal are the "bad guys," bishops are the "good guys." Of course, contextually Harper needed bishops on his side to enable renewal in the Church of England—he was a tactician as well as provocateur. Yet the disparity of views is stark.

As expected from §3.2.1's analysis, Harper's view of authority structures lacks postmodern character, not promoting new structures to replace the old ones on larger scales, while doing so sometimes on smaller scales. On whether those who have experienced charismatic renewal should stay in historic denominations or leave to set up new ones—a question brought into focus by the House Church Movement of the 1970s and 1980s—he is initially open-handed, explaining that divisiveness is not necessarily wrong, yet there is "real danger of every movement in the Church leading to division."[74] He elsewhere explains, "No hard and fast rule can be made which would bind everyone. Each person needs to find out the will of God for himself."[75] Later, however, Harper's view solidifies to be more anti-separative, ironic given his later departure from the Church of England. In the early 1980s, he opines, "God has a *better way*, namely to renew the existing church from within,"[76] lamenting, "We are all too prone to make excuses for our divisions. I believe all divisions

---

69. Harper, *Let My People Grow*, 26.
70. Harper, *Power for the Body*, 73.
71. Harper, *Let My People Grow*, 203.
72. Harper, *Bishops' Move*, 24.
73. Harper, *Spiritual Warfare*, 62–63.
74. Harper, *As at the Beginning*, 113.
75. Harper, *Power for the Body*, 78.
76. Harper, *We May Be One*, 10–11 (emphasis added).

in the body of Christ are sinful."[77] Though he acknowledges the work of God in House Church networks, he explains, "the new wine of the Spirit does not need completely new structures, certainly not new Churches, but renewed people and churches to contain the new movement of God, with structures that are pliable enough to contain the new enthusiasm."[78]

In contrast, on the smaller local parish scale, Harper is more varied. A key lesson he highlights from the story of Redeemer Houston is how "they were all in it together," with no distinction or hierarchy between clergy and laity, or men and women.[79] Though Harper stops short of saying this is how the parish church system should transform, he elsewhere explains, "There is no reason why the leadership of the church cannot be shared among a number of leaders."[80] Harper is less keen on another structural facilitator of renewal, small groups meeting outside of the local church structure, however. Though he praises the meetings of The Full Gospel Men's Fellowship as freeing the laity,[81] he cautions, "The dangers should not be forgotten. This kind of group can become a substitute for a local church, and would, therefore, sap rather than strengthen the church."[82]

Overall, under this criterion there are both strong postmodern tendencies seen, and the opposite, bringing caution to speaking of an overall *Criterion Four* postmodern character. This is strengthened by the absence of other potential postmodern manifestations, such as a suspicion of what is authoritatively received to be true rather than communally discerned—even in Harper's in-depth explication of Redeemer Houston.

5.1.1.5 Conclusions

Examination of Harper's work largely validates the hypothesis formulated at the end of chapter 4—that the Movement shows a full range of postmodern characteristics described by the Analytic Criteria, with none to their strongest extent—and adds some detailed nuancing to it. A helpful conversation partner to exposit this is Bebbington's work, and the

77. Harper, *We May Be One*, 49.
78. Harper, *We May Be One*, 20.
79. Harper, *New Way of Living*, 34.
80. Harper, *Let My People Grow*, 179–80.
81. Harper, *Beauty or Ashes?*, 74.
82. Harper, *Walk in the Spirit*, 74.

above analysis shows how Harper's influence has perhaps been treated by him and others too simplistically, leading to misunderstandings about the Movement by some.[83]

Manifestations of all the criteria are evidenced to some extent, though none in full range. Those that are seen most fully are those of *Criterion One*, followed by *Criterion Three*, with relatively little *Criterion Two* manifestations, and a mixed picture when it comes to *Criterion Four*. Bebbington on the other hand sees things a bit more unambiguously. Quoting Harper he explains, "Insight was often exalted by charismatics against reason,"[84] while here it has been shown under *Criterion One* that reason for Harper was important, yet divine rationality trumped human rationality which meant, yes, sometimes what was seemingly rational took a back seat to God's leading. Pointing to "unintelligible words," Bebbington suggests the Movement adopted the cultural current of the time, while the analysis here under *Criterion Two* suggests a more complex picture that is unconnected to cultural currents. Again, using Harper for support, he posits, "There was an anti-structural bias among the charismatics."[85] Yet analysis here under *Criterion Four* again shows little anti-structural inclination.

Overall, the relative strengths of criterion manifestation can be seen to show an emphasis towards *Criterion One*, affirming predictions of the potential presence of an internal drive akin to a postmodern one generating such manifestations.[86] However, this must be tempered by the fact that none of the *Criterion One* manifestations are necessarily *the* strongest in postmodern tone given Harper's *Criterion Four* radical anti-clericalism. Additionally, variegations in the strength of Harper's postmodern emphases could also be understood to be more contextually driven under his renewal agenda. As an encourager of church-wide charismatic renewal, he primarily targeted changing the way people thought about the practice of faith, so prominences in *Criterion One* characteristics are not surprising. Similarly, testimony of such change was a key means of persuasion in his writings, bringing *Criterion Three* aspects to the fore. The opposers of such change were often local clergy, and so

---

83. See, for example, the recent description by Bray that perpetuates much of Bebbington's original analysis. Bray, *History of Christianity*, 584–85.

84. Bebbington, *Evangelicalism in Modern Britain*, 242.

85. Bebbington, *Evangelicalism in Modern Britain*, 244.

86. §§2.5.3; 4.3.

unsurprisingly certain *Criterion Four* attitudes towards them are given vehement expression.

5.1.2 CRQ-2: Models of Influence

Harper's work confirms hypotheses made about the origins of the Movement's postmodern characteristics. While there is no sense of a *Direct Influence* model present in his work, a *Mutual Origins* model can be identified, and first steps towards *Cultural Catalysis* in both manners of its theorized operation are suggested.

Harper shows a keen awareness of the contours of cultural belief but does not in this suggest its influence on his thinking in a *Direct Influence* manner. Indeed, he stands against it: "The Church is not to ape the world. The Church ought to be both an example to the world and a catalyst to provide changes in society."[87] Specifically he warns,

> We need to remember that we live in an experience-orientated age. . . . People want to feel something, not just to be told . . . [but] we have to look for God's promise, not experiences for their own sake, and set our motivation on the right course.[88]

In *Beauty or Ashes*, Harper diagnoses the reasons why the Western Church is in decline, evidencing the *Mutual Origins* model. Primarily critiqued is a thorough-going modernism in that finds expression in institutionalism, humanism, and rationalism. In words resonant with the context explored in §3.1.2, he opines, "Institutionalism reigns supreme. The 'letter' is more important than the Spirit. . . . Pietism is a dirty word. . . . Man is seen as self-sufficient. . . . A striking example of the decline in spirituality in the Western Churches, is the way in which the Churches have largely ignored the Charismatic Movement."[89] Diagnosing the root of this,

> The name of the disease is humanism . . . which debunked belief in the supernatural, and set the Western Churches in opposition to this element of spirituality which was to surface most effectively and dramatically in the 20th century Pentecostal and Charismatic Movements.[90]

87. Harper, *Let My People Grow*, 32–33.
88. Harper, *Power for the Body*, 23.
89. Harper, *Beauty or Ashes?*, 6–7.
90. Harper, *Beauty or Ashes?*, 11.

Harper sees hope that charismatic renewal could counteract this modernism in the church, yet laments, "There was a time when I believed that the Holy Spirit was going to renew entirely the Churches. I cannot in honesty say that I believe this is going to happen, at least for a very long time. In that sense the disease has a terminal look about it."[91] The end prognosis is, "Reason reigns supreme."[92]

Though there are no suggestions here the Movement formed directly in reaction to such modernism, suggestive evidence for the *Mutual Origins* model is found in how rationalistic influences are seen as antithetical to charismatic priorities, against which they must stand. On renewal's emphasis on experience, he argues,

> We must not shirk the fact that this is an "experience." Something happens to us. We have all grown up in the atmosphere of rationalism. We have received an endless stream of this thinking at school, through the media, and alas, in some of our churches also. So we are not open to things happening which cannot be explained.[93]

Similarly, he highlights rationalistic hindrances to the gift of prophecy and supernatural revelation.[94] Elsewhere, hindrances in the context of spiritual warfare[95] and healing[96] are added. Here, however, a reason to hold lightly the possibility of a *Mutual Origins* model at work in Harper's thought is that he sometimes locates the aforementioned negatives to a time before the Enlightenment. In *Spiritual Warfare*, he blames Aquinas, "who enthroned reason over all else," and the Reformers and Puritans for whom "anything that could not pass the test of reason was probably diabolical."[97] Such statements here expose the range and richness of Harper's desire for premodern recovery of a time before these times—something further explored below.

Though modernism is the primary disease afflicting the church, Harper sees its breakdown in culture as an opportunity for the charismatic church. In reaction to the breakdown of cultural narratives, he

---

91. Harper, *Beauty or Ashes?*, 15.
92. Harper, *Beauty or Ashes?*, 11.
93. Harper, *These Wonderful Gifts!*, 30.
94. Harper, *These Wonderful Gifts!*, 104.
95. Harper, *Jesus the Healer*, 32.
96. Harper, *Jesus the Healer*, 168.
97. Harper, *Spiritual Warfare*, 39.

explains, "Our church will need to be renewed in the power of the Holy Spirit if we are to *take advantage* of this kind of situation."[98] This perhaps is an initial step towards *Cultural Catalysis* of the type explored through deprivation theories in §4.1.2, whereby the Movement's postmodern characteristics appeal to the frustrated longings of *modernistic* elements of wider culture. Similarly, culture's newly awakened desire and emphasis on loving community "presents us today with an *unparalleled opportunity* to show that what man is incapable of doing on his own is possible with the help of God's grace."[99] Here, conversely, might be the first steps towards *Cultural Catalysis* of the type explored through consumerism ideas in §4.1.2.3, whereby a *Criterion Four* mark of the Movement appeals to desires of *postmodern* elements of wider culture. Thus, though there is no direct indicator for a *Cultural Catalysis* model at work, Harper's work suggests the first steps towards both manners of its theorized operation.

5.1.3 CRQ-3: Premodern Recovery

Undergirding Harper's desire for charismatic renewal is a longing to recover what has been lost by the church, stretching back to biblical times, undoing the damaging effects of intervening centuries, resetting the church to the way it should be. His witness affirms that a premodern recovery desire is both a key answer to CRQ-3 and is part of a larger narrative behind the Movement's postmodern characteristics.

Harper comments, "The 'this' of our modern church life is nothing like the 'that' of the apostolic Christianity. Maybe this movement has been sent by God to restore the incongruity."[100] Harper sees this desire as not just his, but also of many others, quoting Billy Graham's desire to take the church back 1900 years, reflecting, "Again and again there has been this desire to return to the shining certainties and primitive simplicity of the age of the apostles."[101] It is especially this time's power that needed recovery, as "there was a time when almost every Christian knew what it meant to have the power which had been promised by our Lord."[102] Primarily this was manifested in two key demonstrations of God's power,

---

98. Harper, *Glory in the Church*, 14 (emphasis added).
99. Harper, *You Are My Sons*, 122 (emphasis added).
100. Harper, *As at the Beginning*, 79.
101. Harper, *As at the Beginning*, 18.
102. Harper, *Spiritual Warfare*, 50.

authenticating the Christian message: the power of signs and wonders and of "the divinely inspired community of a company of people uniting races and cultures in a common love."[103] He explains, "The attractiveness of the gospel to always be marred and spoilt when either of these two elements are missing."[104] Here, two postmodern characteristics, the experience of God at work (*Criterion One*) and renewed community (*Criterion Four*), flow not out of postmodern desire, but a longing for something premodern.

Harper nuances this longing, "If we 'freeze' the Church in the New Testament, then there is much richness of life which we will have to deny, to the detriment of all and the derogation of the Holy Spirit."[105] Additionally, the historic growth of the church was not absent from the Spirit's work, as "from time to time, increasing in frequency, the gifts of the Spirit were reappearing throughout the period from the Reformation to the present day."[106] The trajectory of the Church's growth was of an increasing work of God to recover what it had lost, reflected in people's desire to "live again 'as at the beginning.'"[107]

The depth of Harper's desire for premodernism finds ultimate expression in his departure from the Church of England for the Antiochian Orthodox Church in 1995. Articles and lectures published on the *Father Michael Harper Foundation* website highlight his later view that the Orthodox Church was the fulfilment of a lifelong desire. In initial encounters with it, he reflects, "I was increasingly captivated by the whole approach of Orthodoxy to Christianity. I found a fullness of faith and doctrine which I had never seen or experienced before. It was all there, nothing was missing."[108] Earlier in his life, Harper explained the reason for this, that comparing the Eastern with the Western church, "the former has allowed much more scope for the Holy Spirit and His more direct ways of inspiration, whereas the latter has emphasised reason and logic."[109] He believed the Eastern Orthodox church had never been enslaved by modernity and had stayed truer to a more premodern form of Christianity

---

103. Harper, *New Way of Living*, 121.
104. Harper, *New Way of Living*, 122.
105. Harper, *Let My People Grow*, 163.
106. Harper, *As at the Beginning*, 19.
107. Harper, *As at the Beginning*, 22.
108. Harper, "Orthodox Way."
109. Harper, *As at the Beginning*, 18.

which Harper longed for throughout his career.¹¹⁰ Neither had the Orthodox Church ever succumbed to postmodernity. In a sequel homage to C. S. Lewis's *The Screwtape Letters*, Screwtape lambasts and delights in the Western church's pursuit of modernity. Yet turning to the Orthodox church: "They don't claim to be 'post-modern.' They are not even modern. We have never been so foolish as to try to be modern ourselves, for we know it would be our undoing. So this is a hopeless tactic with these awful Orthodox people."¹¹¹ Elsewhere Harper explains, "Sometimes I am asked if the Orthodox Church is post-modern, and I have to reply that it is not yet "modern," for it never passed through the traumatic events of the Reformation and the Enlightenment. Thus its thinking is different."¹¹²

The Orthodox church offers Harper a third way that allows a recovery of an ancient unsullied Christianity which does not tread the path of modernity or postmodernity. This latter hope is the biggest precipitating cause for Harper's move to Antiochian Orthodoxy specifically. In his later work exploring the theological basis of such a move in *The True Light*,¹¹³ his analysis of the Church of England explores three "buzzwords" identifiable as postmodern traits that have infected it: "Pluralism," "Relativism," and "Subjectivism," which has led to "The Death of Truth."¹¹⁴ In direct contrast, he commends, "The traits so self-evident [of original Eastern Orthodoxy], according to the records of the New Testament and other early Christian literature, *are still observable in Antiochian Orthodox Churches now*."¹¹⁵ Antiochian Orthodoxy is specifically to be chosen from among Orthodox traditions because it comes closest to recapturing primitive Christianity, appealing to both Evangelicals and Charismatics because it includes emphases of Scripture and the work of the Spirit therein.¹¹⁶

Harper's Antiochian move leaves unanswered questions. Harper likely overstates the charismatic nature of the Orthodox Church in

---

110. Harper, *As at the Beginning*, 18.

111. Harper, "Screwtape Returns," 1.

112. Harper, "Orthodox Contribution," 4.

113. Later republished under the title *A Faith Fulfilled*—the new title is suggestive of this analysis. See Harper, *Faith Fulfilled*.

114. Harper, *True Light*, 11–20. Here Harper perhaps offers a skewed analysis due to his strong emotional reaction to the vote of General Synod to ordain women that helped impel his leaving the Church of England.

115. Harper, *True Light*, 58.

116. Harper, *True Light*, 143–80.

self-justification for his move, and the move might be seen as an abandonment of the renewal emphasis that he championed for so long.[117] Nevertheless, Harper's "third way" should be interpreted as the culmination of a life of seeking to recover that which is free from the effects of modernity, and latterly uninfected by postmodernity, rather than just a specific reaction to state of the Church of England in the early 1990s. The move is again a pragmatic one, to a church whose "Living Tradition" brings a range of centuries encompassed by premodernism into the present in a previously unseen manner in the Western church.[118] If such a personal journey can be said at all to have influenced the Movement, or reflected currents within it—and both are feasible—further evidence is seen that many seemingly postmodern characteristics of the Movement are better read as part of a narrative of *premodern* recovery.

5.2 DAVID WATSON

David Christopher Knight Watson (1933–84), like Harper, was an influential leader in the early Movement, though in a differing manner. There is no doubting his significance; Hocken in 2002 explains he was the "renewal leader with perhaps the greatest spiritual impact on Britain to date."[119] Yet despite this, little has been written about him,[120] which this chapter helps remedy.

An important component of his influence was his leadership of St. Michael-le-Belfrey Church, York, until just before his death, which for many modelled and mapped the future of the Movement in the local church.[121] Collins, reflecting on his time as vicar of HTB, explained, "I can't imagine how I could have got on without David doing what he did in York. He had a profound influence. . . . I do believe that the beacon of light that he lit at Saint Michael's York really enabled the whole movement of the Spirit to survive, and that has had a profound influence all over the

---

117. Cf. Cartledge, *Encountering the Spirit*, 50.

118. See discussion in Williams, *Looking East in Winter*, 158–84.

119. Hocken, "David Watson."

120. Lord, *Transforming Renewal*, 14. Lord's work and Watson's biography are the only substantive published pieces of analysis on Watson, alongside a shorter analysis by Matthew Porter. See Saunders and Sansom, *David Watson*; Porter, *David Watson*.

121. For example, St. Michael's "Renewal Weeks" regularly invited in visiting clergy to learn from the church. See Watson, *You Are My God*, 172–78.

place."[122] For Evangelicals, Watson "gave permission for the next generation of church leaders to build charismatic evangelical churches."[123]

Watson had different priorities to Harper: the latter a leader who sought to enable charismatic renewal across the nation, the former a church leader whose priority was not renewal but evangelism, explaining in *I Believe in the Church*, "For many years now, I found this to be God's primary calling."[124] This focus translated to influence upon the Movement because he understood the needed power for it: "Unless renewal proceeds evangelism, the credibility gap between what the church preaches and what the church is, will be too wide to be bridged," causing him to ask, "How, then, can renewal come to the church today?"[125] Watson's evangelistic imperative translated into an agenda for charismatic renewal, and he deftly integrated the two.

Watson authored works of lasting influence. His sometime publisher Edward England comments that they were to "bless a wider market than those of any British evangelical author."[126] Analysis of them supports and refines insights seen in analysis of Harper's work under the CRQs' enquiry.

5.2.1 CRQ-1: Postmodern Characteristics

5.2.1.1 *Criterion One: A Non-Foundational Epistemology*

Watson's epistemology, like Harper's, is not a clearly systemized aspect of his thought. However, unlike Harper's, it evidences greater levels of integration whereby it does not display an epistemological hierarchy, but rather a holistic parallelism. Some clear postmodern characteristics are seen—especially a missional pluralism—which are likely to have had strong effect on the wider Movement.

Like Harper, Watson often models a modernistic epistemology focused on rational argumentation. Most of his works are carefully constructed pieces of either logical evangelistic appeal or discipleship instruction. He again recognizes the tendency within charismatic renewal

---

122. Quoted in Porter, *David Watson*, 3.
123. Porter, *David Watson*, 3. For more on the influence of St. Michael-le-Belfrey, see Guest, *Evangelical Identity*, 57–58.
124. Watson, *Believe in the Church*, 17.
125. Watson, *Believe in the Church*, 18.
126. England, *David Watson*, 154.

against the intellectual approach, explaining in *I Believe in Evangelism*, "Dependence on the Holy Spirit does not mean being anti-intellectual."[127] He lambasts in *One in the Spirit*, "A super-spiritual, anti-intellectual laziness when it comes to preparing talks and sermons."[128] Indeed, Watson is aware of the dangers of this from the popularity of Eastern mysticism of his time—in *Discipleship* warning of, "*Anti-intellectualism* . . . where there can be a dangerous stress on experience and rejection of mind," explaining, "Some of the more extreme expressions of the charismatic movement have fallen into this danger."[129]

Despite these strong warnings, Watson's epistemology seeks to go beyond rationalism to embrace other priorities. In *Through the Year with David Watson*, he explains,

> Many people fail to realise there are different kinds of knowing. There's mathematical knowledge, based on reasoning, scientific knowledge, based on testing hypotheses, and there's personal knowledge. If you try to explain personal knowledge in either mathematical or scientific terms, the result is ludicrous.[130]

Throughout his corpus Watson models a holism, for example explaining in charismatic understandings of worship, "We worship the Father in Spirit as well as in truth. Not Spirit alone, for that could be purely emotional, nor truth alone, for that could be purely intellectual. But 'all that is within me' should bless his holy name."[131] In this more integrated view, there is no epistemological priority that is evidenced above another. Indeed, Harper's pragmatic epistemology, primary for him, is noticeably absent from Watson's writings, only really appearing when focusing on successful methods of evangelism.[132]

Of greater emphasis are experiential and emotional means of knowledge, wherein Watson emphasizes their importance, while warning against overemphasis. He explains that experience is essential to the Christian faith:

> Truth that is not experienced is no better than error, and maybe fully as dangerous. The scribes who sat in Moses' seat were not

127. Watson, *Believe in Evangelism*, 176.
128. Watson, *One in the Spirit*, 85–86.
129. Watson, *Discipleship*, 145–46 (emphasis in original).
130. Watson and Watson, *Through the Year*, 237.
131. Watson, *One in the Spirit*, 111.
132. Watson, *Believe in the Church*, 224.

the victims of error; they were the victims of their failure to experience the truth they taught. . . . [T]heir rationalism had become an arrogant stumbling block to a knowledge of God.[133]

In *Live a New Life*, Watson explains that experience is the hallmark of Christian conversion that convinces,[134] and elsewhere explains that the main alternative to "convincing personal experience" in the church's worship is the choice of the recitation of "a meaningless creed in a dreary service."[135] This is not what the world looks for in Watson's opinion, and without experience "our words, however true (as propositional statements), will strike others as pious platitudes."[136]

However, like Harper, Watson is aware that the experiential cannot safely be split from the rational: "Rely on subjective experiences and you will be up and down like a yo-yo; but depend on the objective facts of God's promises, and you have a basic stability."[137] Proof for Watson of this was the Jesus Movement, which, by paralleling similar experiential cultures, created some "appalling casualties."[138] In darker tones, culture's experiential mood gives rise to the potential of counterfeits in churches that overemphasize experience,[139] and Watson explains in *Hidden Warfare*, "The devil can tie us up in knots by urging us to seek a certain type of experience that we have read or heard about."[140] Such warnings perhaps describe a discerned limit to the anti-modern generation of this postmodern characteristic seen in historical explorations of the Movement in chapter 3. They also witness to Watson's resonance with the previously evidenced trend to hold rational and experiential epistemological emphases in parallel within the Movement, rather than promoting the latter over the former.[141]

Similar is seen in Watson's view of emotional knowledge: it is important, to be combined with other types, yet dangerous when overemphasized. He holds it in greater esteem than Harper, testifying in *My God is Real*, "Christianity does not leave the emotions untouched. The only

133. Watson, *Discipleship*, 143.
134. Watson, *Live a New Life*, 48.
135. Watson, *Discipleship*, 95.
136. Watson, *Believe in Evangelism*, 76.
137. Watson, *Live a New Life*, 19.
138. Watson, *Believe in Evangelism*, 69.
139. Watson and Watson, *Through the Year*, 164.
140. Watson, *Hidden Warfare*, 133–34.
141. See §3.2.3 and §3.4.2.

thing which has no emotions is a dead body, and if your faith is without emotion it is a dead faith."[142] Elsewhere he testifies about a well-remembered communion service at Canterbury Cathedral: "A very moving experience, our emotions were quite naturally involved in our worship and praise!"[143]—emotion here a natural expression of experience, evidence again of his integrated holism. Ever the evangelist, this engendering of emotions in worship is needed to "communicate very powerfully to what is often called a 'feelings generation.'"[144] Nevertheless, Watson balances this with warning: "To by-pass the mind altogether and whip up the emotions is something I am as much against as anyone else."[145] This was especially brought home to Watson when dealing with the "Shepherding Movement" in the later stages of his ministry, discovering that its roots lay in Bob Mumford's attempts to combat in charismatic renewal how "in the past we taught people to act as they 'felt led.' The result in many places was chaos."[146] For Watson the whole situation highlighted the dangers of an over-emotional faith in renewal circles.

Even more than Harper, in a postmodern manner the locus of Watson's epistemology was to be newly found in the body as well as mind: "Too often the churches pictured by stiff motionless bodies which, by their unbending formality, do not speak of the God of action and the spirit of movement. We need to understand the culture of today."[147] In *You Are My God* he explains this failure's root:

> Much Western Christianity ignores the body, suppresses the emotions and concentrates almost exclusively upon the mind. God wants our bodies to be the dwelling-place of the Holy Spirit, and it is by presenting our bodies to God that we offer him spiritual worship.[148]

Elsewhere Watson equates this error with the gnostic heresy,[149] and highlights that Old Testament (OT) theology kept the body as central

---

142. Watson, *My God Is Real*, 83.
143. Watson and Watson, *Through the Year*, 118.
144. Watson, *Believe in the Church*, 41.
145. Watson, *My God Is Real*, 83.
146. Watson, *Discipleship*, 74–75.
147. Watson, *Believe in the Church*, 224.
148. Watson, *You Are My God*, 133.
149. Watson and Watson, *Through the Year*, 323.

in worship in contrast.[150] Combining these threads, Watson's embodied emphasis exhibits an anti-modernism, spurred by culture, driving him to a postmodern emphasis, yet looking towards the premodern in the OT witness. A microcosm of this study's hypothesized larger narrative in certain ways.

Watson, in most regards, is not an epistemological relativist or pluralist. However, in his missional practice of reconciliation, another picture emerges. In attempts to square the circle of church unity and truth, he affirms that for the church the "one outstanding and essential mark is faithfulness to the gospel of Jesus Christ," since it is "a pillar and bulwark of truth."[151] This narrative of truth, focused on the cross, is the unifying force for the different denominations.[152] However, referencing the pluralistic picture of the elephant and the courtiers, he calls for a realization: "Is it not likely that different churches may see very clearly certain aspects of God's truth while apparently being blind in others?"[153] Watson commends dropping the idea that some are "right" or "wrong," lamenting that globally the church has needed "liberation" from the Western preoccupation with theological questions therein. Through this the witness of true unity may arise, achieved by the work of the Spirit.[154] Here Watson says unity is based in truth, but then simultaneously that it is based in the work of the Spirit who unites us to overcome different understandings of the truth. While this pluralism is not generated from different truths found in different forms of epistemology being united (as theorized in §2.5.2), it is a missional pluralism which is generated by a generous epistemology that emphasizes subjectivity, and thus has some postmodern character to it.

The practical expression of this approach is repeatedly outworked in his city-wide missions which had the three-fold aim of "reconciliation, renewal and evangelism."[155] His reconciliation work in Ireland had a lasting legacy for the local Irish church,[156] and this pragmatically orientated missional pluralism, and perhaps even pragmatic relativism, due to such effectiveness, likely had huge influence within the

150. Watson, *Believe in Evangelism*, 160–62.
151. Watson, *Believe in the Church*, 334; cf. 1 Tim 3:15.
152. Watson, *Believe in the Church*, 338, 342.
153. Watson, *Believe in the Church*, 344.
154. Watson, *Believe in Evangelism*, 346–47.
155. Watson, *You Are My God*, 184.
156. See Saunders and Sansom, *David Watson*, 184–91.

Movement—especially for hundreds of leaders who came to Watson to study his missional techniques.[157]

5.2.1.2 Criterion Two: Discontinuities Between Signifiers and Signified

Watson's work exhibits manifestations of the second Analytic criterion in an overlapping manner with Harper's, yet with some much stronger additional postmodern tendencies manifested, especially in evangelistic communication. Like Harper, Watson has little space for spiritual or allegorical hermeneutics. In response to the splitting of "rhēma" from "logos" words of Scripture arising in some charismatic circles (including at St. Michael's),[158] Watson vehemently explains there is no justification from the Greek NT text that "*logos* is taken to refer to the whole teaching of the objective word of God in the scriptures that is always true, whereas *rhēma* is much more the particular word that God is now speaking."[159] Since the words are used interchangeably and synonymously, he has no truck with splitting NT texts from their original meaning into "erroneous private interpretation."[160] Additionally, and unlike Harper, Watson's view of glossolalia bends more towards the modern rather than postmodern: "'Tongues' are not irrational, but trans-rational, or supra-rational, God is not limited to human rational thought, important though that is," and this is because they are the communication of one's spirit with God who is spirit in words that are representational of content even if not understood by others.[161]

Watson is more postmodern in his understanding of prophetic and performative words—as seen with Harper. In prophecy, he explains that human words may be disconnected from God's, as "we should not be surprised if the prophetic utterances are in the speaker's own words and thought-forms, reflecting his or her own burdens, since God uses us as human beings, with all our human outlooks and experiences, to convey his word."[162] He also sees the power of words to signify more than just their

---

157. Maiden, *Age of the Spirit*, 156.
158. Watson, *You Are My God*, 167.
159. Watson, *Discipleship*, 152.
160. Watson and Watson, *Through the Year*, 184.
161. Watson, "David Watson," 90.
162. Watson and Watson, *Through the Year*, 160.

communicative context to enable spiritual power. Again, he emphasizes the use of Jesus's name in spiritual warfare,[163] and explains the power of speaking about fear and failure as having the power to keep in bondage to such things.[164] Arguably in such there is correspondence between physical, spoken, and spiritual realities, with divine mystery as to how they manifest through each other. However, there are also moments of clear disconnection as well, seen pre-eminently in Watson's testimony in *Fear No Evil*, where he entertains the idea that at the root of his terminal cancer was a revelation that it was a "suffering from a deep wound caused by the strife of tongues"[165]—critical words causing the cancer, yet with no discernible connection between the two adduced.

The greatest level of *Criterion Two* postmodern manifestation seen in Watson's work is found in his usage of postmodern communication theory in evangelism. From the previous mapping of the *ecclesial postmodern* system this is an unpredicted manifestation of *Criterion Two*, and the dialectic methodology of this study allows this to be integrated into the system for ongoing lifeworld analysis—showing some of the strength of Cartledge's methodology when it is applied in a truly dialectic manner such that system and lifeworld are brought into conversation in a way that the latter can inform the former.[166]

Watson adopted Marshall McLuhan's thesis that "the medium is the message," meaning "the presentation and context of the messages [of the Christian faith] are of considerable importance for today's world"[167]—a call to the church to "give urgent attention to its methods of communication."[168] In such what is signified is not necessarily linked to normal signifiers, but rather the medium of communication itself becomes part of the signifier. Matthew Porter's research suggests that Watson's development of McLuhan's insights directed him towards postmodern expressions of evangelism. In this, Graham Cray—colleague and later successor of Watson's in York—explains that Watson was aware "we were not into anything that was dominantly post-modern before the 1980s. But clearly the writing was on the wall," and that reading the signs of the times Watson's communication method reflected "the need to be visual

163. Watson, *Hidden Warfare*, 127.
164. Watson, *Hidden Warfare*, 120.
165. Watson, *Fear No Evil*, 149.
166. See discussion in §2.5.1.
167. Watson, *Believe in the Church*, 120; cf. McLuhan, *Understanding Media*, 1–18.
168. Watson, *Believe in the Church*, 224.

and not just verbal; the need for experience; the breaking away from a purely linear, rational way of thinking."[169] Porter additionally suggests this was motivated by Watson's familiarity with Hans Rookmaaker's *Modern Art and the Death of a Culture*,[170] which described the great cultural revolutions afoot at the end of the Enlightenment period of history, as well as the influence of young people who surrounded Watson's ministry at York and introduced him to new cultural expressions.[171] The translation of these influences into his evangelistic techniques led Michael Green to express, "He was totally post-modern before post-modernism—very much into story. He was into the creative arts, drama, dance, music; he was into every member ministry."[172] Porter's work suggests that Watson modelled a culturally postmodern communicative technique, based on a communication theory that itself has strong postmodern aspects,[173] which is likely to have had significant effect on the wider Movement through adoption by other churches who looked to St. Michael's as a model.

Watson's practice of this represents an alternative response to the postmodern breakdown of linkage between signifiers and signified analyzed under this criterion. In §2.5.1 Jaichandran and Madhav suggested that this would lead to an emphasis on silence and in §4.1.3 Richter noted that part of TTB's unusual manifestations was perhaps an attempt to process a postmodern silencing of verbal language. Watson models another way: in this disconnection an emphasis on the communication of signifiers *as* what is signified relinks them. If Watson instinctually understood this, he shows how adept he was at intuiting the cultural mood and responding in novel reconceptualizations—something further seen in evidence for a *Cultural Catalysis* model below.

5.2.1.3 Criterion Three: Metanarratives and Micronarratives

In contrast to the clear manifestations of postmodern character seen under the first two criteria, what is seen in Watson's work under the third criterion is more complex. Watson prioritized the Christian metanarrative; as seen in the discussion of his reconciliation ministry, he

---

169. Quoted in Porter, *David Watson*, 9–10.
170. See Rookmaaker, *Modern Art*.
171. Porter, *David Watson*, 10; Porter, "Missiological Influence," 33.
172. Quoted in Porter, "Missiological Influence," 33.
173. See Guardiani, "Postmodernity."

emphasized the importance of the Christian gospel as the compelling vision not just for unity but for all elements of faith, and this is largely how he was able to overcome the differences in traditions—uniting differing narratives into a single metanarrative, both actively de-emphasizing micronarratives yet simultaneously speaking highly of certain learnings to be had from within them.[174] Similarly, in a transcription of talks that Watson gave in his university student missions, he addresses the question "Conversion—escape from Reality?"[175] Tellingly, his answer is no; rather, the larger Christian story gives a new means of viewing and engaging with the wider world. No calls to come out of culture, as suggested in §4.2.2, are found in Watson.

Watson saw the great power of personal testimony in evangelism, a key micronarrative of faith: "Many a person has found Christ through the testimony of a Christian, however inexperienced that Christian might be."[176] At various points in his most evangelistic material, *Jesus: Then and Now*, he references short summaries of people's lives to authenticate their input into the topic matter at hand. In his prayer chapter, he includes prayers from named children referenced by age and global location to authenticate the power of their simplicity.[177] In this, Watson shows an adept ability to present the gospel metanarrative by using personal narratives as authentication, puncturing the Christian metanarrative with micronarratives to connect with contextual culture. Yet fascinatingly, nowhere does he teach this as a model of evangelism, even in his didactic works dedicated to it. This could theoretically be due to his overriding concern with a clear response to the metanarrative of the Christian gospel beyond subjective testimony. However, such would not explain a similar lack of teaching about testimony's usefulness in post-conversion discipleship, which starkly contrasts with what he modelled in his ministerial autobiography,[178] his posthumously published account of his struggle with cancer,[179] and other places such as his account of his prayer life.[180] Whatever underlies the complexities of his usage of micronarratives, nonetheless, as with Harper, nowhere is fullest postmodern expression

174. Watson, *Believe in the Church*, 344.
175. Watson, *My God Is Real*, 78–87.
176. Watson, *Live a New Life*, 48.
177. Watson and Jenkins, *Jesus*, 61–62, 68, 83.
178. Watson, *You Are My God*.
179. Watson, *Fear No Evil*.
180. Watson, "David Watson," 85–95.

found either in a valuing of micronarratives to an equal or greater measure to metanarratives of faith, or in appeals to cultural discontinuities, or in stereotypical shaping of testimony.

5.2.1.4 Criterion Four: The Importance of Community

Watson's understanding of community and authority parallels Harper's. Like Harper, he believed in the power of radical Christian community, modelling it in his vicarage, and inspiring the growth of other expressions of communal living and discipleship such as "The Mustard Seed" in York.[181] He thus modelled a deeper active practice of community than Harper, likely having a greater impact on the Movement as a result. Such communities shared resources and lived in a clear sense of communal accountability making them look quite postmodern in a cultural sense. Watson's passion for community was driven by the sadness that "one of the greatest weaknesses of today, especially among evangelicals, is individualism. . . . It is the quality, depth and unity of a Christian fellowship as a whole that is of paramount importance"[182]—believing in the power of community to overcome modernistic individualism in the church, pointing towards a *Mutual Origins* model.

In postmodern resonance, such communities bear important interpretive insights. Watson explains that in the study of Scripture, "I can see how powerfully God can communicate with individuals in a group setting. It is not just the non-readers who need to rediscover the importance of Christian community."[183] He prioritizes community "for learning basic lessons concerning the body of Christ,"[184] commenting that "guidance is often corporate; it is not a private affair,"[185] and suggesting that effectiveness in ministry is dependent on community.[186] However, there is no sense in Watson's writings that such emphases veered into stronger postmodern attitudes where communal discernment becomes more important than what is received from wider tradition and church teaching.

---

181. Watson, *You Are My God*, 114–26, 142–49. See also Saunders and Sansom, *David Watson*, 151–60.

182. Watson, *One in the Spirit*, 107.

183. Watson, *Believe in Evangelism*, 123.

184. Watson, *Believe in Evangelism*, 164.

185. Watson, *Believe in Evangelism*, 179.

186. Watson, *Believe in the Church*, 72.

Watson's view of authority and its structures parallels Harper's as well. Like Harper, he generally holds a high view of authority; there is "no excuse for rebellion, inward or outward, silent or vocal."[187] Bishops are important as holders of authority;[188] like Harper he enjoins the need for a renewed episcopate to enable God's intention for it to be fulfilled.[189] Watson's view of the clergy takes on similar, though softer, tones to Harper's. He critiques local clergy as inhibitors of church growth, using the same language from Michael Ortiz that they are "the bottleneck of the church" such that there "is an acute shortage of gifts and ministries in most churches."[190] This is especially true of charismatic renewal, where "many clergy ministers are cautious and suspicious," leading to it often shifting to home-based "renewal fellowships" instead.[191] Such may be why Watson argues that lay people should be able to baptize and celebrate holy communion, not just because it was biblical but also necessitated by the stifling effect of clergy.[192]

Again, like Harper, Watson shows clear non-postmodern attitudes that oppose the promotion of new structures on a larger scale, combined with a tendency to the opposite on the local scale. On the larger scale, Watson's clear focus is on unity, believing that division is indefensible when over minor doctrinal issues.[193] Like Harper, he strongly believes in the charismatic renewal of historical denominations and laments those leaving to join new independent churches.[194] Watson, however, was not one to maintain the status quo uncritically. There was genuine frustration for many Christians about how they were being governed "from the top" in Watson's opinion.[195] His writings constantly call for change, arguing, "The old order of the established an organised church, relying on its structures and traditions instead of the renewing of the Spirit of God, will not do,"[196] especially as such an order simply becomes self-perpetuating

---

187. Watson, *Believe in the Church*, 151.
188. Watson, *Believe in the Church*, 275.
189. Watson, *Believe in the Church*, 276.
190. Watson, *Believe in Evangelism*, 129.
191. Watson, *Discipleship*, 69.
192. Watson, *Believe in the Church*, 250–51.
193. Watson, *Hidden Warfare*, 96–97.
194. Watson, *You Are My God*, 110.
195. Watson, *Discipleship*, 68.
196. Watson, *Hidden Warfare*, 25.

and worldly,[197] and ultimately, as explained in *In Search of God*, lives as if God was dead.[198] Though Watson carefully discourages "a spirit of independence or anarchy on the part of the local church towards the wider church,"[199] he reacted badly to the dry institutional formalism seen to contextualize the Movement's birth.[200]

Watson comments that he worked hard to keep St. Michael's Anglican, though an investigative report by the Archbishop's Council on Evangelism in 1977 suggests some "un-Anglican experimenting,"[201] an example of which was the creation of an alternative Anglican parish structure. In October 1970, in cooperation with the Bishop of Selby, six men were commissioned to serve as church "elders" on a one-year basis,[202] who then oversaw several leaders of house groups.[203] This office of elder was a distinctly un-Anglican one, and Watson explains, "In July 1972 we went one stage further, and one of the elders, Peter Hodgson, was commissioned as a full time lay pastor."[204] Watson's desire to create alternative local structures, if not motivated by postmodern impetus, certainly might appear so in the context of frustrations with the wider church.

Porter suggests that this postmodern characteristic of Watson's ecclesiology may have come to a fuller expression in his later move to London, had it not been cut short by his death. Here Watson may have sought to create a teaching seminary and church for young people in London, Anne Watson later commenting that they "went round umpteen buildings"[205] to find the right location. Porter theorizes that if this were to have come about "there would have been a major clash between him and the diocesan authorities, for the parish system in the Church of England does not allow clergy to start a new church wherever they wish."[206] While ultimately hypothetical, the episode highlights that towards the end of his

---

197. Watson, *Hidden Warfare*, 25.

198. Watson, *In Search of God*, 29. Watson quotes Samuel Beckett's "Waiting for Godot."

199. Watson, *Believe in the Church*, 111.

200. §§3.1.2.1; 3.3.2.

201. Saunders and Sansom, *David Watson*, 242.

202. Watson, *You Are My God*, 151, 153.

203. Watson, *Discipleship*, 92.

204. Watson, *You Are My God*, 151, 153.

205. Porter, "Missiological Influence," 69.

206. Porter, *David Watson*, 21–22.

life, Watson exhibited temptations, if not actions, that looked increasingly anti-institutional and postmodern in nature. Of course, such a scenario would have foreshadowed cross-parish church planting and grafting that occurred later in the Movement, but as will be seen in §6.1.4, this was done in partnership with diocesan authorities, not opposition.

5.2.1.5 Conclusions

Conclusions made through examining Harper's work largely hold for Watson's, yet with some noticeable exceptions. Bringing what is seen into conversation with other scholarship on Watson, scarce as it is, helps augment a wider understanding of his thought here.

Under *Criterion One*, Watson has a more integrated epistemological view of reality than Harper, which supports Andrew Lord's analysis that for Watson it was "as whole people" we are created to relate to others and God.[207] Lord's understanding of this being set in the context of human bodily weakness may go some way to explain why resultantly his emphasis on embodiment goes beyond Harper's. However, Lord's assessment that Watson had a more engaged approach to theology than some in the Movement finds some challenge in his epistemologically pluralistic approach to reconciliation that subsumed theological truth differences under a call for unity, muting potentially creative theological conversations fueled by such differences—as Lord's work itself seeks to do in bringing Watson and Thomas Merton into conversation.[208] Under *Criterion Two*, Watson looks decidedly more postmodern than Harper in his usage of postmodern communication. If lines of influence upon the early Movement are traced out from this, as Porter does, the weakness of this postmodern approach is highlighted in how it opened the gates to more extreme and ultimately dangerous forms of expression in its midlife, most notoriously the late 1980s and early 1990s "9 O'clock Service" at St. Thomas's Church, Sheffield.[209] Roland Howard narrates how at St. Thomas's the label "postmodern"—seen to be missionally effective in postmodern communicative practices—was easily and uncritically transferred to other practices, including legitimating abusive control of

---

207. Lord, *Transforming Renewal*, 56.
208. Lord, *Transforming Renewal*, 46.
209. Porter, *David Watson*, 16.

female attire.[210] Watson's overriding heart was for the church to reach postmodern culture, and as a result Watson perhaps instinctively leapt into postmodern waters without concern for a theological framework for its expression, which when emulated by those without his strong theological moorings led in very different directions. His contemporary Michael Green was later at pains to reflect on postmodern evangelism deeply, and later work by missiologists such as David Bosch elucidates the deeper framework which Watson's approach needed to be married with to avoid possible later corruption in the Movement.[211]

Criterion Three characteristics in Watson's work are exhibited in a complex manifestation, which contrasts with these being some of the clearest expressions of postmodern character in Harper's work. This agrees with Lord's analysis that for Watson renewal "focuses on the reality of God,"[212] which is held in tension with "the reality of sin and suffering" so that individuals, communities, denominations, and the world might be transformed.[213] It is perhaps this very tension that leads to complexity here, with priority in his teaching geared toward the metanarrative of God's reality, yet modelling a micronarrative approach to meet a second reality, enabling a conversation journey that births renewal.[214] Under *Criterion Four*, potential postmodern characteristics are clearly exhibited, including a greater emphasis on communal discernment and a softer form of Harper's anti-clericalism. While the hypothetical church planting situation Porter investigates must be viewed with caution, its likelihood also suggests a potential display of this criterion by Watson in an underlying anti-institutional attitude.

Overall, as with Harper, *Criterion One* characteristics are some of the strongest in Watson's thought, affirming predictions of an internal postmodern-like drive within the Movement. However, though his epistemology is perhaps more strongly postmodern than Harper's due to signs of pluralism, *Criterion Two* postmodern communication methods are arguably the strongest postmodern characteristic of Watson's thought, again adding slight pause to this observation.

---

210. Howard, *Rise and Fall*, 27, 69.
211. Green, *Adventure of Faith*, 149–72; Bosch, *Transforming Mission*, 357–71.
212. Lord, *Transforming Renewal*, 35.
213. Lord, *Transforming Renewal*, 20.
214. Lord, *Transforming Renewal*, 81.

5.2.2 CRQ-2: Models of Influence

In Watson's work, contrasting Harper's, there are hints of a *Direct Influence* model at work. Simultaneously, there is less sense of a *Mutual Origins* model, while a *Cultural Catalysis* model is more strongly evidenced in how Watson responded to the breakdown of modernistic culture and the emphases of postmodern culture in evangelism.

Like Harper, Watson shows strong awareness of the cultural paradigms of his time, and perhaps more so was able to point to transitions that preluded the changing of the dominant modernistic narrative towards postmodernism, showing awareness of the philosophical thought of Buber,[215] Sartre,[216] Kant,[217] and referencing existentialist philosophy[218]—yet with no sense that they informed his thinking and practice in a *Direct Influence* manner. Rather they helped him situate it. Significantly, however, the above-explored effect of postmodern communication theory on Watson's later ministry suggests some later shaping by postmodern ideals, which fits under this model's paradigm.

Watson was keenly aware of the cultural crisis of modernity. Resonating with Lyotard's analysis, he sees culture as frustrated about the failure of the narrative of the "irresistible progress of mankind," about the promise of technology, and about hopes for jobs and studies.[219] He is concurrently aware, "in almost every area of life the traditional concepts of authority are being challenged, and the church is no exception."[220] Watson highlights culture's resultant search for reality, "revealed in sexual license, experiments with drugs, and the persistent search for an "*ultimate*" experience."[221] In *Is Anyone There?*, he agrees with Pinnock's assessment that the dawning realization was that "[the modern] age is grossly overrated"[222]—throughout his writings seeking to use this insight to point beyond it. However, for Watson, the solution was not a

---

215. Watson, *One in the Spirit*, 44.
216. Watson, *In Search of God*, 32.
217. Watson, *Fear No Evil*, 75.
218. Watson, *Believe in Evangelism*, 21; Watson, *Hidden Warfare*, 29.
219. Watson, *In Search of God*, 25–29.
220. Watson, *Believe in the Church*, 261.
221. Watson, *My God Is Real*, 10.
222. Watson, *Is Anyone There?*, 15.

postmodern direction of travel, but Jesus: "If nothing else, Jesus is supremely relevant to all these basic needs."[223]

In this context Watson repeatedly espoused anti-modern attitudes, the first step in a *Mutual Origins* model. Generally, he was critical of Enlightenment rationalism, explaining in *Start a New Life* that it was unfit for assessment in areas where it "is hard to prove these things, but it is not hard to know their reality,"[224] including God. The "'rational-optimist' philosophy," was pre-eminently shattered through the reality of WW2, and the modernistic metanarrative approach found wanting in the light of harsh personal reality.[225] However, unlike Harper, he did see some merits to the "age of reason," as in the church it led to "fresh theological thinking, and renewed examination of the reality and credibility of Christian claims, and also a further surge of missionary movements throughout the world."[226]

Watson's general outlook critiqued the fruits of modernism in the Church, lamenting, "We Christians have been affected more than we realized by the scientific materialistic outlook of this age," which especially manifested in a lack of belief in divine healing.[227] Significantly, he laments the effect of his rationalistic worldview on his belief in God's healing power in the light of cancer,[228] no doubt influenced by Wimber's aforementioned influence.[229] Yet, unlike Harper, other than his belief in the power of community to counter modernistic individualism in the church,[230] there is scant evidence that charismatic priorities were to be actively sought in a reaction to modernism in a full *Mutual Origins* manner. Rather, they are issues that are of "particular significance in view of our past neglect of the Holy Spirit,"[231] pointing more to his premodern recovery desire.

Instead, for Watson, the clearest evidence of a model seen in response to CRQ-2 is of *Cultural Catalysis*, and in both theorized manners of its operation—catalyzation by modernistic and postmodernistic

223. Watson and Jenkins, *Jesus*, 1.
224. Watson, *Start a New Life*, 8.
225. Watson, *My God Is Real*, 26.
226. Watson, *Believe in the Church*, 32.
227. Watson and Watson, *Through the Year*, 314.
228. Watson, *Fear No Evil*, 74.
229. Watson, *Fear No Evil*, 79. See §3.1.4.2.
230. §5.2.1.1.
231. Watson, *One in the Spirit*, 14.

elements of wider culture. This is unsurprising considering Watson's evangelistic emphasis—he believed that charismatic Christianity met the cultural need of the time as a point of missional contact. Resonating with the deprivation models of §4.1.2.2, potential catalyzation occurs through reaching the longings of modernistic cultural elements. He explains contextually, "We are entering into the last quarter of this 20th century with both profound consciousnesses of the utter futility of life without God, and at the same time an altogether new hunger and thirst for spiritual reality."[232] Catalyzation of various postmodern characteristics of the Movement occurs through an appeal to this modernistic crisis. In Watson's emphasis on the community he explains, "In an age of isolation, the joy of really belonging to God and to have been a part of his people throughout the world . . . is one of the most relevant features of the Christian message of good news";[233] in his emphasis on non-traditional forms of communication, he similarly argues, "In an age when people are satiated with words, various art forms can be immensely effective, at least in the first stages of communication."[234] Postmodern qualities clearly being amplified due to cultural resonance here.

As well as meeting crises of modernity in culture, culture's postmodern elements draw out postmodern characteristics in Watson's practice in the predicted second manner of catalysis. As seen previously, Watson's embodiment emphasis speaks of the need to escape "stiff motionless bodies" partly because "we need to understand the culture of today";[235] a cultural appreciation of physical embodiment, especially likely in postmodern cultural elements, generates a catalytic emphasis on this characteristic. The clearest witness of this second mode of *Cultural Catalysis* is seen in Watson's appeal to a feelings culture:

> [God is] creating colour and movement in worship once again, with dance, mime, drama, visual arts and spiritual gifts being rediscovered, all of which can communicate very powerfully to what is often called a "feelings generation." People today need to feel God's presence and sense his reality before they are able to listen to his words.[236]

232. Watson, *Believe in the Church*, 37.
233. Watson, *Believe in the Church*, 76.
234. Watson, *Believe in Evangelism*, 141; see also Watson, *Believe in the Church*, 199–224.
235. Watson, *Believe in the Church*, 224.
236. Watson, *Believe in the Church*, 41.

The outworking of this in charismatic worship styles, though tempered with a balancing need for more modernistic imperatives,[237] no doubt amplified the importance of the emotional aspects of Watson's missional praxis, with subsequent impact on churches across the Movement.

Watson seeks to meet the consumeristic desires of postmodern elements of culture in missional outreach, as predicted in §4.1.2.3. Thus, while Harper initially exhibits the first steps to both hypothesized manners of *Cultural Catalysis* in the Movement, Watson exhibits them more fully: the Movement's existent postmodern characteristics being catalyzed in growth by missional outreach to both the felt negative deficiencies of modernistic cultural elements *and* the positive desires of postmodern ones.

5.2.3 CRQ-3: Premodern Recovery

Watson, like Harper, evidences a desire to recover a Christianity from older times, yet not to the same level of personal effect, nor overriding pragmatism. Lord comments that for Watson, "renewal was about the restoration of the church to its original state."[238] In his early ministry, the witness of past revivals led him to a fresh study of the book of Acts, and it was there, not the revivals themselves, he found the paradigm he longed for.[239] This is unlike Harper, who had a richer view of church history and the recovery of its life from throughout its earlier expressions. It could be argued that his infamous statement about the Reformation as a "tragedy" points to a desire to recover a church before it, rather than specifically NT Christianity. However, this would miss contextual nuance: his comment expressed his desire for unity, which was hindered by Reformation emphases, rather than a desire to return to a better state of church before it. This desire for unity is rooted in NT description and longings, affirmed by the councils of the Early Church.[240]

The only place where Watson appears to explicitly support the value of recovering elements from the Church's history beyond the Early Church comes not from his own work, but in his forward to the British first edition of Richard Foster's *A Celebration of Discipline*. Critiquing

---

237. Watson, *Believe in the Church*, 329; Watson, *Believe in Evangelism*, 65.
238. Lord, *Transforming Renewal*, 29.
239. Watson, *You Are My God*, 50.
240. Watson, *Believe in the Church*, 331.

modern culture, he explains, "We have forgotten how to be still, trapped as we are in the vortex of modern life," to which he points to the witness of "the history of the Church" as providing a remedy, commending Foster's work if "the Church is to rediscover its lost spirituality," and "the great treasuries of the devotional life from St. John of the Cross to Evelyn Underhill."[241] Watson highlights how helpful he finds Foster's recovery impulse, yet a lack of argument for such wider recovery in his own work suggests it was a secondary desire drawn out in writing a forward to Foster's work, and, in contrast to Harper, not worth actively pursuing given the overriding need to recover the life of the Early Church.

In this, Watson sees the earliest Church as the "ideal state" of Christianity, which subsequently "was seen to be mixed with impurities."[242] Charismatic Christianity seeks to recover the power of this ideal state:

> The Acts of the Apostles records an astonishing growth rate. . . . What were the reasons . . . and what is missing when the ineffectiveness and irrelevance of the church is all too apparent? . . . The manifest power of God that was demonstrated so fruitfully in the New Testament church was, of course, the power of the Holy Spirit.[243]

This outworks in several charismatic emphases, including the need to be baptized with the Spirit,[244] the call to community,[245] the return to Early Church leadership,[246] and the recovery of the church's extended family,[247] all to reanimate dry and dead institutionalism.[248]

More than Harper, Watson nuances this with a dose of reality. Rather than a narrative of simple degradation, he sees a "constant ebb and flow of spiritual life within the church all down the years."[249] Perhaps with the House Church Movement in mind, he is aware of the danger that a desire to "get back to the New Testament church could lead to the rigid imposition of certain structures which related to history and culture

---

241. Watson, Foreword.
242. Watson, *Believe in the Church*, 23.
243. Watson, *Believe in Evangelism*, 168–69.
244. Watson, *Hidden Warfare*, 133.
245. Watson, *Live a New Life*, 40.
246. Watson, *Believe in the Church*, 249.
247. Watson, *Believe in the Church*, 85.
248. Watson, *Believe in the Church*, 18.
249. Watson, *Believe in the Church*, 20.

of the day, but which could be irrelevant for an entirely different setting in the latter part of the 20th century."[250] He similarly warns about uncritically returning to New Testament means of communication.[251]

Clearly, Watson's Evangelical ethos causes him to look to the New Testament Church. However, there is evidence that the breakdown of modernistic culture also helped precipitate this in an anti-modern trajectory. He explains, "Today the climate is astonishingly similar to that facing the early church. . . . And therefore, similar means for communicating the word of God are highly relevant."[252] Watson comments, "Every significant renewal by the Spirit of God has brought back to the church something lost since the days of the early church. Yet these renewals have often been preceded by times of particular crisis."[253] As seen in the previous section, the implied crisis perhaps in view is modernism's breakdown in culture. If so, Watson again, alongside Harper, shows how some postmodern characteristics of the Movement may be driven by a reaction to modernism in a desire to return to premodern means. Such may be amplified by the catalytic effect of culture, clearly seen in Watson's work, which causes them to be amplified in magnitude. The hypothesized larger narrative of §4.3 finds continued substantiation.

5.3 CONCLUSION

This chapter has shown how this study's ongoing contentions find support and expansion through the examination of the early Movement by analysis of Harper and Watson's written corpora. In doing so it has also significantly contributed to existing scholarship on both figures, extending and at times challenging it.

Under CRQ-1's enquiry, the early Movement exhibits various postmodern characteristics, and herein this chapter has proved the power and fruitfulness of using the derived *ecclesial postmodernism* system to analyze the Movement's lifeworld. Here, there are many similarities between Watson and Harper, yet also some differences: Harper's more postmodern pragmatic emphasis and rabid anti-clericalism; Watson's more postmodern pluralistic emphases and usage of postmodern communication

---

250. Watson, *Believe in the Church*, 270.
251. Watson, *Believe in Evangelism*, 140.
252. Watson, *Believe in Evangelism*, 53.
253. Watson, *Believe in the Church*, 22.

techniques. For both, the strength of *Criterion One* characteristics can tentatively be viewed to be greater than for others, suggesting the possible outworking of an internal postmodern-like drive within the Movement.

The hypothesized dynamics behind these characteristics are verified under CRQ-2's enquiry. Relatively little is seen of a *Direct Influence* model apart from in Watson's postmodern communicative practices. For Harper, a *Mutual Origins* model is somewhat observable, with at least an anti-modern inclination seen in Watson's view of the power of community, tentatively suggesting the internal drive identified under CRQ-1's enquiry above is of an anti-modern reaction. However, its predicted operative limits are hard to discern, evidence only perhaps being shown of them in awareness of when charismatic emphases lead too far from modernistic moorings, as in emotionalism. Examining evidence for *Cultural Catalysis*, both hypothesized manners of it are seen (catalysis by modernistic and postmodernistic cultural elements)—tentatively in Harper's work and in clearer manifestation in Watson's.

Under CRQ-3's enquiry, both show a clear personal and theological motivation towards premodern recovery which can be tied to a reaction to modernism in the church, a motivation which also indicates that some seen postmodern characteristics are reclamations of premodern ones. Placed in combination with evidence for *Cultural Catalysis*, this helps confirm the hypothesized larger narrative of the generation of these characteristics. For Watson, this recovery is tightly focused on the NT Church; for Harper, this focus was later broadened via a focus on the Orthodox church, which he saw preserved primitive Christianity's nature before the unhelpful influences of the Reformation, modernism, and postmodernism.

Given Harper's influential leadership of the Fountain Trust, and Watson's equally influential modelling ministry in York, answers to the CRQs discerned in analysis of their work are likely true for the early Movement more generally, especially as they were both leaders influencing it and participants themselves mapping its nature. Their influence means that the same types of answers to the CRQs are to be expected across the later Movement, which was so shaped by their ministries. However, it is of interest to discern which of their more unique emphases are transmitted to the later Movement. Is Watson's usage of postmodern communicative theory later seen? Or Harper's broader and richer desire for premodern recovery? Relatedly, are new postmodern characteristics seen that were not present in their witness—and what was the means of their generation? Answering such questions will help complete the detailed picture of the Movement's postmodern character begun in this chapter's analysis of the early Movement.

6

Postmodernism and the Later Movement (I)

Postmodern Characteristics

BUILDING ON THE PREVIOUS chapter's analysis of the early Movement, the next two chapters analyze its later life through an examination of the thought of key leaders within it, continuing this study's substantive qualitative research phase of investigation. This is performed through analysis of interviews with a selection of leaders which enables the thus far discovered answers to the study's CRQs to be strengthened, critiqued, and expanded. Though their written corpora are important, interviews afford the ability to specifically investigate the CRQs in a richer manner, with interview questions and answers directly targeting the CRQs' enquiries.[1]

An overall narrative linking the answers of the CRQs has been repeatedly indicated in this study so far. Hence, while this chapter primarily focuses on responses to questions under CRQ-1's enquiry—the Movement's postmodern characteristics—areas under CRQs-2 and 3 are highlighted and explored when appropriate to the discussion. The next chapter then completes the analysis by focusing on CRQs-2 and 3's enquiry through analyzing responses to specific questions targeting them.

What is found is that just as in the lifeworld of the early Movement a range of manifestations of the Analytic Criteria occur, though a complete set is not seen under any criterion. *Criterion One* manifestations are most prominent and new manifestations of the other criteria are seen as well.

---

1. See methodological reflections in §1.3.

Analysis of these tentatively indicate hypothesized answers to CRQs-2 and 3—which explain underlying responsible dynamics—continue to be confirmed, as well as an overall narrative linking the Movement's postmodern characteristics, setting the ground for a more in-depth analysis of these answers in the next chapter.

6.1 THE INTERVIEWS

Nine leaders were interviewed between September 2021 and March 2022:

David MacInnes after serving his curacy at St. Mark's Gillingham under John Collins (1957–61), experienced charismatic renewal while serving a second curacy at St. Helen's Bishopsgate in London (1961–67).[2] He was regularly part of the activities of the Fountain Trust upon its establishment and took up a position as Canon Precentor at Birmingham Cathedral (1967–78) and Diocesan Missioner in the Diocese of Birmingham (1979–87). Subsequently, he served as Rector of St. Aldates Church, Oxford, from 1987 until his retirement in 2002.[3]

David Pytches served curacies in Oxford and Southwark,[4] before volunteering for service in Chile with the South American Missionary Society in 1959. He came into charismatic renewal through the testimony of his wife Mary in 1969.[5] In 1970 he was made a suffragan bishop and in 1972 became Bishop of Chile, Bolivia, and Peru. In 1977 he returned to England as vicar of St. Andrew's Church, Chorleywood, which became a major center for charismatic renewal, especially through the visits of John Wimber in the 1980s.[6] In 1989 he started the New Wine summer conferences to help other churches come into renewal, which he led until his retirement in 1996, having seen it grow to attract over twenty thousand people yearly.[7] David died in November 2023.

Mary Pytches was married to David and was instrumental to the reception and leadership of charismatic renewal in Britain, serving alongside him in his leadership of St. Andrew's Chorleywood and New Wine.[8]

---

2. See §3.1.
3. Church of England, *Crockford's Clerical Directory*, 568.
4. Church of England, *Crockford's Clerical Directory*, 727.
5. Hocken, "David Pytches."
6. See §3.4.
7. Harcourt, *Greater Things*, 27–67.
8. Harcourt, *Greater Things*, 1–26.

She is the author of several books focusing on charismatic renewal, counselling, and discipleship,[9] and has been seen in her own right as an influential figurehead within the Charismatic Movement in Britain.[10]

Sandy Millar spent most of his ordained ministry at HTB where he served as curate under John Collins (1976–85), before becoming vicar until his retirement in 2005, whereupon he was made an Honorary Assistant Bishop in the Anglican Church of Uganda. With David Pytches, he was integral to enabling the new phase of renewal brought by John Wimber into Britain, as well as subsequently the "Toronto Blessing."[11] With Nicky Gumbel, he enabled the redesigned Alpha Course to be propagated across the church worldwide,[12] and oversaw the planting and revitalization of several churches from HTB.[13]

Graham Cray served as curate at St. Mark's Church, Gillingham (1971–75), before becoming an Area Youth Coordinator for the Church Pastoral Aid Society (1975–78). He subsequently became curate at St. Michael-le-Belfrey Church, York (1978–82), effectively acting as vicar, enabling David Watson to be released into more national ministry,[14] and then officially succeeding Watson as vicar (1982–92). He was subsequently appointed as Principal of Ridley Hall, Cambridge (1992–2001) and then consecrated as Bishop of Maidstone (2001–9). He then served as the Archbishops' Missioner to Fresh Expressions until his retirement in 2014.[15] He has written and taught extensively on issues of culture, postmodernity, and mission.

Charlie Cleverly served as Rector of St. Aldates Church, Oxford (2002–21) after succeeding David MacInnes. Before this, he was vicar of Belleville Reformed Church in Paris (1989–2002), where he hosted John Wimber in an ecumenical ministry trip to France.[16] Previous to this he was a curate and church planter in the Diocese of Chelmsford (1982–89).[17] He is a popular author and speaker in charismatic circles.

---

9. Pytches, *There Is Still More*, 157.

10. Dixon, *Signs of Revival*, 60.

11. See §3.4.

12. Atherstone, *Repackaging Christianity*.

13. Church of England, *Crockford's Clerical Directory*, 606; Atherstone, *Repackaging Christianity*, 40.

14. Saunders and Sansom, *David Watson*, 146.

15. Church of England, *Crockford's Clerical Directory*, 203.

16. Atherstone, "John Wimber's European Impact," 236.

17. Church of England, *Crockford's Clerical Directory*, 171.

Alison Morgan was ordained in 1996,[18] and is the author of several books on the Christian Faith. Also a recognized Dante scholar, from 2004–16 she was an associate of ReSource, writing and teaching on charismatic renewal both nationally and globally.[19] ReSource is an Anglican renewal and missions agency founded in 2004, which has its roots in Anglican Renewal Ministries (ARM) founded in 1981;[20] ARM is often located in the line of succession in encouraging renewal in Anglican churches after the closure of the Fountain Trust in 1980.[21]

Nicky Gumbel served as curate at HTB (1986–2005) under Sandy Millar.[22] During this time, he rewrote the Alpha Course to become an evangelistic course and led its large uptake across the national and global church.[23] The course consists of a series of weekly meetings and a Spirit-focused weekend, set in the context of food and discussion in small "table" groups, whereupon talks on the basics of the Christian faith are given. Gumbel succeeded Millar as vicar of HTB (2005–22) and oversaw the expansion of the church's ministry to include a church-planting network latterly enabled by the Church Revitalisation Trust.[24]

Christian Selvaratnam was formerly a pastor and church planter with the Newfrontiers network of churches, before being ordained as one of the Church of England's first Pioneer Ministers in 2008 to plant a church out of St. Michael-le-Belfrey Church, York.[25] This later became known as G2, which he led until 2021.[26] Simultaneously he held roles on the staff team at St. Michael's, as well as at Alpha International as National Director (2014–17) and Director of Networks (2018–19). He joined St. Hild College in 2019, where he currently serves as Dean of Church Planting.[27]

These leaders represent a variety of contexts, yet with some continuity with those of Harper and Watson's, enabling larger narratives to be discerned. The range of interviewees enables further adoption of the twin

18. Church of England, *Crockford's Clerical Directory*, 619.
19. Morgan, *Wild Gospel*, 1.
20. ReSource, "History, Vision, and Values."
21. Anderson, *Introduction to Pentecostalism*, 170.
22. Church of England, *Crockford's Clerical Directory*, 365.
23. Atherstone, *Repackaging Christianity*, 43.
24. Lings and Perkin, *Dynasty or Diversity?*; Atherstone, *Repackaging Christianity*, 230.
25. Church of England, *Crockford's Clerical Directory*, 798.
26. Selvaratnam, *Craft of Church Planting*, 14.
27. St. Hild College, "Christian Selvaratnam."

contextual approaches of analysis taken in the previous chapter. They enable a concentration on three key local places of charismatic renewal—St. Aldates, Oxford (MacInnes, Cleverly), St. Michael-le-Belfrey, York (Cray, Selvaratnam), and HTB (Millar, Gumbel)—continuing the perspective gained by looking at influential local churches in the Movement begun with David Watson. Simultaneously, corresponding more with Harper's network-orientated leadership, three key networks of charismatic renewal are also explored through these interviews: New Wine (Mary and David Pytches), Resource (Morgan) and HTB's wider church planting network (Millar, Gumbel).

6.2 CRQ-1: POSTMODERN CHARACTERISTICS

6.2.1 Criterion One: A Non-Foundational Epistemology

Like Harper and Watson, the interviewees communicate a strong emphasis on rationalistic epistemologies, while seeking to move beyond them both in critiques of epistemologies dominated by rationalism and in desires to incorporate other epistemological forms. There is some trajectory of development from Harper and Watson, such that the articulation of this is stronger in the later Movement, though not uniformly across all interviewees. Here Morgan, Millar, and Gumbel especially stand out.

All the interviewees responded to primary and follow-up questions by giving reasons for their opinion that often hinged on reference to themes of Scripture (especially Millar), or logical inference from wider analyses that others have made (especially Cray). Many of the interviewees are authors of books that show similar emphasis in their central theses. It can be confidently said that all the interviewees have high regard for the life of the mind, and that rational analysis is integral to their understanding of charismatic renewal.

However, this is potentially dangerous if left as the end word on knowing God. An example is seen in MacInnes's dealings with criticism about the effects of TTB at St. Aldates. He explains that "people in Oxford are honing their critical faculties to an extreme degree," which led to a strong reaction against the seemingly non-rational physical manifestations and decisions he made in his leadership during the time. He recounts an event where he showed a willingness to engage systematically with a multi-point written critique made by a mathematics lecturer at Oxford University who was part of his congregation, showing a regard for the need for rational engagement. Yet he concluded from such instances that the critical faculties in reaction to renewal "can be very good or it can be very destructive," and the key issue was the call to "not lay down your critical faculties, but to lay down criticism." He saw a negative aspect to over-rationalistically orientated responses, which he challenged to make space for the reception of the work of God. This emphasis perhaps enabled his successor Cleverly to inherit a church which "has a huge spectrum of ways of determining what is of God and what isn't"—of which critical rational analysis was just one.

Millar exemplifies an even stronger reaction against rationalism. Though he opines "We need to train ourselves to ask" sequential questions to analyze whether a charismatic phenomenon is from God, he simultaneously laments, "Our modern mind suffers from a passion for analyzing everything, putting everything into some sort of box that we understand that makes it more and more under our control." Millar's responses highlight two examples of how this view outworked in his leading of renewal. Firstly, he views glossolalia a way of prayer that joins in with God's activity and puts a hand up to the statement "I don't need to understand," which God is actively looking to "use." Secondly, through learning developed in growing the Alpha Course, his ecclesiology changed such that he believed doctrinal espousal ought no longer to control whether one belonged to a church community, but that "you belong before you believe."[28] Similar sentiments from Gumbel and Selvaratnam infer that though the Alpha Course retains a strongly rationalistic core in its didactic talk content, it also contains more postmodern emphases of learning through small group structures and sharing of food together, which compete with its importance.[29]

In such movements away from an exclusively rationalistic epistemology, interviewees explained the need for a more holistic one. Cray comments, "The renewal movement at its best . . . has treated human beings as whole beings with body, mind and spirit, and that the Christian faith engages all of those and the Holy Spirit engages all of that." Millar gives the analogy of love: "I don't know how you express love without an

28. In this context, an often-used inversion of Davie's observation of religious attitudes in Britain towards the end of the twentieth century built upon the work of others she credits. This inversion's first usage is hard to trace but is likely first seen in print in work by Rick Richardson. See Davie, "Believing"; Richardson, *Reimagining Evangelism*, 16.

29. See Hunt, *Alpha Enterprise*, 58–60, 64; Heard, "Re-Evangelising Britain?," 129–56.

element of emotion," opining that the cognitive and emotional belong together in a relationship with God. Cleverly speaks of how in his discernment of God's leading he seeks to "reconcile" and "synthesize" extremes in ways of knowing, using a "mixture of logic . . . mixed in with the Word of God . . . and then just the sort of heart thumping conviction that this is the thing. This is the Lord." Elements of this more holistic set of epistemologies cannot be seen to have a clear hierarchy as was present in Harper's work. Watson's parallelism is more observable, though, as shall be seen, Gumbel takes on Harper's mantle in prioritizing the pragmatic.

Experiential epistemological emphases continue to be at the heart of the Movement for those interviewed, yet in a manner that continues to hold it in parallel with more rational emphases, rather than above them in priority. Morgan comments on the joy of people "who have suddenly become very excited by the fact that God is actually working through them," witnessing to a faith that is not experientially second-hand. Cray explains that in the global spread of renewal, there has been "a real continuity or regaining of the Spirit's experience of empowerment, permission of the gifts of the Spirit, of certain understandings of worship and so on." However, he laments that this has led to a diversity in the wider Movement, with some "whose sense of identity is based almost entirely on intense experiences." This is of course what both Watson and Harper sought to mitigate, and yet it would appear in the flow of the Movement with only partial success. As has been noted, ironically the witness of Harper's earlier strong experiential emphasis, among others, may be partly why. However, another explanation might include the previously seen experiential emphases in surrounding culture, amplifying them in the Movement beyond what was seen to be healthy as a result—*Cultural Catalysis*. If so, predicted limits of the *Mutual Origins* model that generated experiential emphases are perhaps overcome by *Cultural Catalysis* at work, as the external pressure of culture that valued such emphases overcomes internal forces that saw danger in their overemphasis. Similar may also be true for emotional emphases considered below.

The positive fruits of experiential emphases are seen in their power to witness the Christian faith to others. MacInnes commends the power of vulnerability in relating personal testimony in Christian discipleship, which "is very disarming" for those struggling with their faith, and "takes away the intellectual argument of it"—referring to the defeat of rationally conceived objections to ongoing Christian faith; what is seen to be true for others effects personal belief. Evangelism in the Movement is similarly enabled by an experiential emphasis. Millar explains part of Alpha's success was that participants received "an experience of a village that they see loving one another." Selvaratnam concurs and adds that this experience is complemented by the power of the direct experience of the Holy Spirit on the Alpha weekend away, "the charismatic personal experience was a significant standout for most people." Such experiential emphases complement other above observations of it, affirming that the later Movement's overall epistemology has a significant experiential element. Additionally, as previously highlighted, these insights hint that a *Cultural Catalysis* model is at work here, whereupon at least for some experience is seen as valuable for the increasingly experiential culture that the church found itself amid in the later stages of the Movement.

In this, Cleverly shows some hints that the understanding of the type of experience sought in the Movement undergoes some development in its later life. He lambasts some charismatic churches that are only a "positive church" in their portrayals of reality, perhaps examples of disruptive narratives explored in §4.2.2. Instead, Cleverly calls for those who "understand about suffering, and that the deep work of the Holy Spirit is to console us in our suffering," which meets some of the deepest questions young people have in culture today. Experience here is still at the Movement's heart, yet develops greater richness in hitherto unseen emphases as the Movement outworks its life through reflective leaders such as Cleverly.

In contrast to the experiential, emotional epistemological priorities in the Movement are largely muted in the response of the interviewees, and little development has taken place beyond Watson's view: emotional elements of renewal are to be expected, embraced, not actively sought, and safeguarded against excess. Mary Pytches, talking about the inner healing practices that she helped bring into the Movement's life, explained that to heal in any emotional sort of way, "there's got to be feelings." However, simultaneously, she recognizes that in the times of renewal at St. Andrew's Chorleywood "some of it was emotionalism" mixed in with the "real stuff" of God's work, a somewhat negative fallout from the capacity of renewal to touch human emotions. Similarly, Morgan speaks of those on the "extreme end of the charismatic movement" who are led to seek emotional engagement as a priority, leading to "pastoral complexities" when feelings do not match realities, such as in physical healing.

Various means are employed to guard against unhealthy emotionalism. To guard against a "splurging of emotion" in the usage of testimony,

MacInnes sought to encourage people to think through their testimony and submit it to others so that it could be reshaped away from such possibilities,[30] something like the shaping of testimony suggested in §4.2.3.1, yet not a stereotypical one to fit a larger narrative. Similarly, David Pytches sought to enable people to start new initiatives in the context of what they "felt" in the throes of charismatic renewal but said "do it for three months, [and] we'll meet every month and talk about [it] and see how you're going." This strong consistent guarding against emotionalism, seen both in the earlier and later Movement, no doubt arises from the Movement's more rational modernistic emphases in interaction with its postmodern ones, perhaps combined with an awareness of the potential amplifying influence of wider cultural contexts that overvalued emotional emphases; *Cultural Catalysis* guarded against—though not always successfully.

Strong pragmatic priorities in the later Movement are seen to abound in the responses of some of the interviewees. In a philosophical sense that tends towards explicit postmodernism, Morgan explains the question must be, "Does it work? Because a philosophy has to work. . . . [I]t has to make sense of life as you experience it." However, the specific instances of pragmatism unite more as a type of outworking of a combination of Harper's clear pragmatic priorities in combination with Watson's missional focus, a missional pragmatic emphasis, rather than a philosophically motivated one. Cray laments that the Movement only in its later stages was able to gradually "discover . . . the missionary calling of the church," opining, "renewal without mission is self-indulgence, renewal is for mission." Renewal's telos for Cray is not about anything but its ability to empower mission, a developed continuation of his predecessor Watson's ethos at St. Michael-le-Belfrey. Others such as Millar concur, recounting how his wife was empowered with new evangelistic zeal through personal renewal, telling him that wherever he ministered, "you will tell them won't you—it makes a difference, it really makes a difference!" Cray does question whether this missionary focus of charismatic renewal was more a rediscovery of its Evangelical roots which had historically prioritized it, but nonetheless the pragmatic ability to reach those with no faith that renewal enabled came to the fore in the Movement's later life.

---

30. This touches on Cartledge's later rescripting approach and may be representative of a wider praxis in the Movement. See Cartledge, *Testimony in the Spirit*.

This missional pragmatism is seen in greatest measure in the ministry of Gumbel and the Alpha Course. In his responses, Gumbel exhibits levels of pragmatism for the sake of mission that surpasses even Harper's. He explains that he is only happy to be called a "Charismatic" if he can also be labelled with other descriptions simultaneously, such as "Catholic," "Orthodox," and "Liberal." He wants "all the labels or none ... because labels enable people to dismiss you, you know they pigeonhole you, and we're trying with Alpha to work with everybody." Though "the ministry of the Holy Spirit [is] right at the heart of the course," giving it a charismatic distinctive, he wants Alpha to be adopted by all denominations, and so is pragmatic about what he labels himself as.

Pragmatism for the same reason shapes the taught content of the Alpha Course. Gumbel explains that Alpha's teaching "is completely compatible with the teaching of every kind" of church and denomination, apart from one that "insists you have to speak in tongues to be filled with the Spirit." Gumbel explains he made "tiny changes" to Alpha's content to enable this, but Selvaratnam comments that this was much larger, and that early in Alpha's development teaching on the two Anglican Sacraments was removed because "he [Gumbel] perceived that Holy Communion and Baptism were the two issues that divided denominations that he would not be able to resolve, and so he just took those things out of Alpha."[31] Given how Alpha became part of the standard life of churches within the later Movement,[32] this high level of pragmatism witnesses a Movement happy to devalue some basic aspects of the Christian faith and tradition for pragmatic reasons, receiving Gumbel's lead in this.[33] Noticeably here, Gumbel suggests there is a set core of teaching agreed by all denominations (though one could question if this is true and if Alpha exposits it if so),[34] showing a nuanced modernistic approach in Alpha combined with more postmodern expression, postmodernism synergistically coexisting with modernism, as predicted in §2.5.1.

---

31. This solves the contradiction in Atherstone's account of Alpha that alternates between saying that Holy Communion was both excluded and included in its taught material. Atherstone, *Repackaging Christianity*, 148, 167.

32. Hunt, *Alpha Enterprise*, 18.

33. Atherstone notes how similarly its divisive historically orthodox teaching around homosexuality was gradually removed from Alpha supporting material over the period between 1994 and 2013, highlighting a longevity to this impetus. Atherstone, *Repackaging Christianity*, 181–86. See further discussion in §8.2.3.2.

34. There was theological concern at such a premise from various quarters when first formulated. See Atherstone, *Repackaging Christianity*, 148–49.

Not all are happy with the levels of pragmatism in the Movement. Morgan—in the same breath as supporting a pragmatic outlook—critiques that when it becomes the sole outlook, "the danger comes that [one] loses what is true, and it all becomes fluffy." Cleverly again critiques charismatic culture in churches within the Movement, whose pragmatic emphases lead to "received or imitated behavior rather than actual encounter with God," lamenting "a generation that's grown up in that kind of environment." He explains, "I think that sometimes so-called charismatic churches are very pragmatic because they are not very experienced at knowing a real work of the Holy Spirit . . . there can be a kind of 'we know this works, so let's do it even if it's not.'" Cleverly calls out the hollowness of this; however, he and Morgan likely inhabit a minority of critical voices given the weight of pragmatic missional emphasis transmitted and accepted through the fruitful ministries of Gumbel and others.

Cray gives a reason why this pragmatic emphasis perhaps gained theological traction in the Movement, explaining, "I think there is in the church, generally, a much better understanding . . . of engaging culture where it is, call it inculturation, call it contextualization. So as a missiologist, that's where my mind goes, and it goes there about ecclesiology." Indeed, elsewhere Cray's contextualization model of mission explains, "There must be no substantial cultural gap between the two cultures [church and surrounding society's], other than a moral one," changing approaches to communication such that "the 'forms' form content,"[35] akin to Watson's previously seen postmodern impulse. Theologians in the later Movement such as Cray, or at least interpretations of their thought, could be seen to give a culture-driven theological agenda towards the pragmatic expressions of church seen in Gumbel and others, illuminating how a *Cultural Catalysis* model arises from such ideas.[36]

The locus of the later Movement's broadened epistemology continues to encompass a fresh emphasis on embodiment. The level of this emphasis is generally more than that of Watson's, yet the postmodern extremes of Harper's ideas of bodily actualization are not seen. Mary Pytches recalls that in renewal in Chorleywood "there was a lot of physicality" with people shaking and falling to the floor, which combines with her testimony of walking laps around the deck of a ship "feeling like she

---

35. Cray, "Methods," 14–15; cf. Cray, "On Not Knowing."

36. Cray here assumes little cultural gap in his model of contextualization, in disagreement with some. The question of how different models of contextualization relate to the *Cultural Catalysis* model is explored further in §7.1.3.

was going to explode" when she first experienced it. This bodily emphasis became such a part of the ritual life of worship in the later Movement that MacInnes could evaluate the fading of charismatic renewal when he began at St. Aldates through the small number who would physically "come up for prayer" at the end of a service.

Overlapping reasons are given as to why this bodily emphasis occurs: "It's really an expression of what's going on on the inside" (MacInnes); "There are people who temperamentally express themselves in that way" (Millar); "Your whole being is being affected by the Spirit of God" (Mary Pytches). Nevertheless, it was sometimes less genuine, occurring "because everyone else is doing it" (MacInnes), and even for "self-aggrandizement" (Millar). Morgan speaks of "a recovery of [physical demonstrations of worship] because it's more holistic" than modernistically controlled non-emotional worship. Cray diagnoses the cultural impulse behind such expressions: "It's a whole load of white rationalists discovering they've got bodies." Similarly, Cleverly comments, "We are embodied people . . . and the church sometimes forgets that." Morgan, Cray, and Cleverly here all highlight an anti-modern impulse, pointing to a *Mutual Origins* model at work behind this embodied emphasis. However, no postmodern bodily actualization is seen—unlike as in Harper's work. The closest to this is Cleverley's belief that usage of the body is "an attempt to indicate by your physical attitude your openness to the God of the universe."

Like Harper, most interviewees exhibit little sense of either epistemologically orientated pluralism or relativism that acts as a framework to hold together different and sometimes non-complementary truths derived from several types of epistemologies within a bodily locus— something that would be expected as a postmodern characteristic in the strongest manifestation of *Criterion One*. However, there is an ongoing strain of missional pluralism, perhaps deriving from Watson's influence. In a measured manner, Selvaratnam speaks of his missional ethos here as being "conservative in theology—I'm not looking to [re]think who Jesus is in a new way—I believe the Evangelical approach, but my practice is Liberal," such that how this is expressed is completely "up for grabs" in creatively contextualizing the faith for missional purposes. Much stronger is the missional pluralism seen in the context of HTB and the Alpha Course. Though both Millar and Gumbel make statements that emphasize the need for clear singular truths to be upheld,[37] both also witness a certain level of pluralism for the sake of mission through Alpha. Millar comments that part of Alpha's success was how in its post-talk discussion groups, "we thought we put up our point for twenty minutes, [so] they should be allowed to put their point [across]," implying that Alpha hinged on environments of multiple and sometimes competing truths being espoused.

Gumbel's praxis explicitly exhibits pluralism. He explains that it is wrong to say, "Evangelicals are the only ones [right] or the Catholics," because, "you lose the perspective of the Orthodox, the Pentecostals, and it's only when you have the whole church, that you actually get the truth, because none of us have the truth, Jesus is the truth." This is not likely due to an inherently postmodern outlook, but rather again a missional pragmatism such that "there is nothing in Alpha that is contrary to the teaching in the Catholic church, or Orthodox church, or the Pentecostal church." Gumbel's embracive pluralism is specifically directed towards Alpha's adoption by the wider church, gaining postmodern character in ignoring contradiction between the great traditions, sublimating them to lowest common denominator theology. Yet underlying this is a more modernistic impulse rooted in his Evangelical background that prioritizes individual gospel salvation. Again, postmodern and modern characteristics combine in dynamic synthesis.

This pragmatic embrace of multiple Christian traditions, a hallmark of Gumbel's approach, may have helped bring about a desire for a type of premodern recovery in the later Movement through him, as hypothesized in response to CRQ-3's enquiry. For example, the preacher to the papal household, Raniero Cantalamessa, is quoted three times in a written version of the Alpha talks,[38] and was invited to speak at the 2015 Alpha Leadership Conference,[39] as other Catholic figures have been at other Alpha Leadership Conferences.[40] In his address at the 2015 Conference, Cantalamessa exposited the thoughts of premodern theologians such as Anselm, Aquinas, and at length Augustine, explicitly commending a recovery impulse: "We need to go back to the time of the Apostles: they faced a pre-Christian world, and we are facing a largely post-Christian world," yet with tactful nuance warning against "ignoring the great

37. See also Atherstone, *Repackaging Christianity*, 58–59.
38. Gumbel, *Questions of Life*, 40, 45, 234.
39. HTB Church, "Leadership Conference."
40. Byassee, *Northern Lights*, 84.

theological and spiritual enrichment that came from the Reformation or desiring to go back to the time before it."[41] While continuing to espouse ideas that fit with a more Evangelical orientation focused on the recovery of NT Christianity,[42] it can be theorized publicly platformed examples, such as Cantalamessa, engender a desire among segments of the later Movement influenced by Alpha to also rediscover and recover older traditions of theology.[43]

In summary, under the question of manifestations of this first criterion, there is much continuity with Harper and Watson's thought earlier in the Movement. A holistic epistemology is seen which critiques rationalism and embraces both experiential and emotional aspects of knowledge, with safeguards against excess. The bodily locus of this epistemology is newly emphasized, though not quite to the same level of postmodern manifestation as with Harper. However, it is the development of Watson's missional pragmatism and pluralism—witnessed to by Gumbel, Millar, and the Alpha Course more generally—which suggests the greatest level of *Criterion One* postmodernism in the later Movement.

6.2.2 Criterion Two: Discontinuities Between Signifiers and Signified

Analysis of *Criterion Two* manifestations in the later Movement highlights some notable progressions from the early Movement. There is a weakening of some manifestations, such as in the practice of prophecy and glossolalia, yet conversely a marked increase of postmodern character through widening hermeneutical approaches to Scripture. Of notable importance, there is a relative paucity in uptake of Watson's emphasis on postmodern communicative methods, perhaps indicating here that the Movement's modernistic characteristics were strong enough to resist more overtly postmodern methods and imports.

When interviewees were asked about their understanding of prophecy, little is seen to indicate discontinuities between signifiers and signified, yet with some important exceptions. Generally, any symbolic nature of prophetic "words" given helps the recipient understand what

---

41. The full text of his address is recorded in Catholic Herald, "Papal Preacher."
42. See §3.1.5.
43. On the breadth of this incorporation of wider traditions see Atherstone, *Repackaging Christianity*, 168–69.

God is saying, rather than rupturing a given reality to bring them into something disconnected from it. For Mary Pytches it is because some people are "very pictorial" while some are "much more verbal" that God accommodates himself to both. For Cleverly it is because we are "embodied people who are helped to understand things by images," assuming more of a universality and reflecting inhabitation of a holistic epistemology seen above. It was noted in §5.2.1.2 that Watson saw in prophecy some potential for disconnection between "the speaker's own words and thought forms" and God's, with prophetic content reflecting more the speaker's internal reality, which God takes up to speak his words. While this idea was not replicated among interviewees, two other potential developments towards postmodern discontinuity are observable. Firstly, Cleverly notes that given God's creative nature, a "banal" prophecy is distinguished "from a true one" through the question "Is there a stark quality and originality of the image if they are used in what is communicated? If I find it boring, I feel it's probably not from God." Cleverly expects some type of discontinuity between what might normally be heard outside of prophetic practice and what is heard within it, though falls short of desiring a complete discontinuity, as signified and signified are still linked within this. Morgan highlights a clearer discontinuity when she describes occasions where the giver of a prophecy has communicated, through imagery, a reality that they did not comprehend, yet the recipient did. She says, "I think that can be immensely powerful because the person that you're praying for doesn't know why you've said that . . . or how you knew." A discontinuity of understanding between the giver and receiver of prophecy highlights some disconnect between their two realities, yet prophecy is still grounded in this understanding in the action of the divine that unites the two for his purpose. Signifier and signified are still linked but held by different agents.

The action of such prophecy is not to create realities in a performative manner, as both Harper and Watson showed some potential desire for, but rather to call people into a reality that is "prepared by God" (Cray), giving vital courage to do so because in it he "gives you a conviction that this is what he wants to do" (David Pytches). Here Morgan does wonder whether God's desired reality would happen when a prophetic word about it is withheld, leaving it an open question rather than directly connecting the two in a performative manner. Morgan does warn occasionally such words do have an unhelpful different type of performative power to create realities not of God's direction when "it [has] been wishful thinking or it's been a subconscious desire to not exactly manipulate, but to give people the confidence to move in a certain direction . . . that is not in fact dictated by God."

Ritual language is not observed to be performative in a postmodern nature either. David Pytches, who authored the well-known handbook on charismatic practice *Come Holy Spirit*, laments the titular phrase being used by those "very often not meaning it," implying he believed its power was the expression of something deeper that effected change—not the words themselves. Similarly, Cray expresses, "My current irritation is the extremely vague use of the word 'prophetic,'" lamenting the "buzz" it engenders without substance. Seligman et al. highlight some potential deeper undercurrents here, suggesting that ritual describes reality "as if" compared to a reform movement's sincerity of seeking to describe reality "as it really is,"[44] often in response to the latter as empty and hypocritical.[45] Not only do renewal movements "tend to be tamed over time with new creations of ritual,"[46] but such rituals, can act as "language in which the medium is very much the message," acting as "external signs for an internal state that may not be present," in a manner that is not understood by Enlightenment formed sensibilities of more direct analogy.[47] Though agreeing that constant repetition can end up "denying the ontological character of the new," it does this in "favor of what is beyond time 'being brought into the present.'"[48] Thus, the truths behind the seemingly empty ritualized expressions in the later Movement, if contextualized as a reform movement of a *Mutual Origins* reaction to modernistic forms of church and theology, may indeed have been "performative" in another manner, in a postmodern manner bringing about the realities they describe into the participant's life in a more passive manner than realized by Cray and Pytches.

Paralleling some of the above, a relative lack of postmodern character is seen in interviewee's understanding of glossolalia. Interviewees are united in seeing it as not irrational, but in agreement with Watson,[49] it is "trans-rational" or "supra-rational" such that there is a rationality to

---

44. Seligman et al., *Ritual and Its Consequences*, 8.
45. Seligman et al., *Ritual and Its Consequences*, 103.
46. Seligman et al., *Ritual and Its Consequences*, 104.
47. Seligman et al., *Ritual and Its Consequences*, 113.
48. Seligman et al., *Ritual and Its Consequences*, 123.
49. §5.2.1.2.

it, yet one that cannot necessarily be explained in its expression.[50] Millar highlights that Paul in Scripture explains that there are "three things happening when I pray in tongues to God"—building oneself up, praising, or praying in intercession God's prayers. He believes that we "take that by faith" that something rational is occurring, one of these three, and that in glossolalia God is looking for someone "who's willing to pray without insisting on understanding exactly what I'm trying to do" as his activity is much bigger than can be understood. Others interviewed also agreed about the mysterious but rational activity occurring through glossolalia, with Cleverly suggesting that "spiritual warfare" sometimes is fought in its employment from his experience.[51]

§5.1.1.2 described how Harper theorized a bodily discontinuity in the experience of glossolalia, whereby the signified resided in the mind while the signifier was expressed in the heart through the tongue. However, interviewees seem to disagree, speaking here not of a discontinuity, but more a type of parallelism, happily living with the potentially bi-partite anthropology of action this might lead to because of its biblical basis.[52] For Morgan this is a continuous parallelism: "It's not really so much a bypassing my mind because my mind is also praying and worshiping. It's just that the part of it which speaks is doing something else at the same time." By faith she sees two streams of prayer occurring simultaneously from different parts of her body. For others such as David Pytches and Millar, the parallelism is more sequential, whereby when the mind has run out of ways to pray (Pytches) or express love for God (Millar), glossolalia enables one to continue. For Millar, this was an ironic experience. Having been rigorously trained as a barrister to be articulate, he encountered an inability to express love, a barrier that glossolalia broke through—something which could almost describe as a breakthrough into a more *post*modern articulation from a refined modernistic ability. Mary Pytches sees cross-influence in this parallelism, explaining, "as you pray in tongues, you get more insight or more understanding of something," yet without explaining why the mind is affected by such bodily activity. Here, as explored in §4.1.2.1, an anti-modern/postmodern "primal" glossolalia—located in the body rather than mind—is glimpsed, yet not simply as a direct split between body and mind.

50. David Pytches uses the term "transrational" in Pytches, *Come Holy Spirit*, 105.
51. See similar views in Smith, "Church Militant," 98.
52. 1 Cor 14:14–15 seems to indicate such parallelistic splitting between mind and spirit, both praying independent of each other.

Significantly under this criterion, unlike Harper and Watson, interviewees expressed a range of appreciation for, and usage of, spiritual and allegorical exegesis, the heaviest indicator of this criterion's presence in the later Movement. At the lower end of the range, Mary Pytches testifies that in charismatic renewal Scripture "came alive" with a greater sense of experience of it, and "a lot more application" of it to life through the Spirit's work. Importantly, she speaks of this in terms of the differing experiences of "logos" and "rhēma" words, showing that Watson's compelling arguments against this splitting did not completely win the day in the Movement's lifeworld. In the usage of such "rhēma" words, scriptural exegesis links with prophetic utterance, such that a "now" word from Scripture is a prophetic word.[53] In a different fashion Cray speaks of "the sacramentality of scripture" whereby there are depths beyond its literal level that are not just "we jump into allegory because we don't know what to make of the text." He explains that Craig Keener's recent work, *Spirit Hermeneutics*, has been his guide in this, enabling him to have a richer view than plain literal meaning, while not "totally being at home with too allegorical a reading."

However, in opposition to this view, and on a much stronger end of the spectrum, lie Millar, Cleverly, and Morgan's views. From the viewpoint of a specialist in medieval literature, Morgan explains that the Movement has seen a recovery of "the basic distinction between the literal interpretation and the spiritual interpretation—allegorical, as I used to call it, whereby one can experience God speaking through a passage in a way not connected to its original meaning but speaking personally using it." She challenges, "Is God confined to a specific interpretation of Scripture? No, I don't think so!" Cleverly explicitly models allegorical interpretation of scripture in his commentary on the Song of Songs published in 2015.[54] He explains that in it, "I was often digging up or uncovering, or removing the rubble from the church fathers and from . . . people of previous centuries who had great insights, which chimed with mine." He thereby does not claim that the Holy Spirit brought fresh revelation of hidden meanings of the text, yet also explains that he was writing "responding to the Holy Spirit." Tellingly, he quips, "Could someone who wasn't charismatic write a commentary on the Song of Songs? Obviously, they could, but it probably would not be an allegorical commentary." This opinion

---

53. See Cartledge, "Charismatic Prophecy," 90.
54. Cleverly, *Song of Songs*.

is not justified given the number of allegorical interpretations of the Song of Songs written before the rise of the charismatic movement in the twentieth century[55] and those written by non-charismatic Catholic commentators today.[56] Nevertheless, something that emerges importantly here is that Cleverly and Morgan exhibit an impulse towards premodern recovery in their usage of allegorical exegesis.

Millar argues that, looking at Paul's unconventional allegorical exegesis in Galatians, what authenticated it was that "it's linked to the whole of his life. His approach his teaching, his attitudes, his love," and arguing that "in terms of what the Spirit does, that's how we test it. Is there, more love, more joy, more peace, more deference, more kindness or self-control?" Differing from Cleverly and Morgan's approach, he argues for allegorical exegesis rooted not in past practice or hermeneutical understanding, but rather in its present effects, another pragmatically driven emphasis.

Thus, for at least these three leaders, allegorical exegesis that partially splits the meaning of Scripture from its originally received meaning is to be embraced and recovered, evidencing a hermeneutical splitting of signifiers and signified, which was previously argued against in the earlier Movement. Whence did this come from? Perhaps a later *Mutual Origins* generation of this characteristic can be discerned by comparing this trend to the work of Henri de Lubac and similar Catholic Neo-Scholastic scholars also engaged in the retrieval of older methods of allegorical exegesis in the twentieth century. Quoting Nietzsche's *Ecce Homo*, du Lubac explains his impetus comes from understanding, "'rationality at any costs' is 'a dangerous force that saps life.' We know that mere abstract principles are no substitute for a *mystique*. . . . We will no longer tolerate a divorce between knowledge and life."[57] Joseph Komonchak explains this as "de Lubac's attempt to recover the world of symbolism in which Christian thought revealed before the 'Christian rationalism' of medieval scholasticism and his effort to relegitimize the spiritual interpretation of the Scriptures alongside their literal interpretation."[58] If there are parallels here of the later desire in the Movement to recover more premodern allegorical means of exegesis through a *Mutual Origins* reaction against

---

55. See overview in Tanner, "History."
56. For example, Pennington, *Song of Songs*.
57. Lubac, *Drama of Atheist Humanism*, 85.
58. Komonchak, "Theology," 600.

rationalistic hermeneutics, this would lie within the hypothesized larger narrative explaining the Movement's postmodern character.

This strong manifestation of *Criterion Two* sits in contrast to what might have been expected to be the strongest manifestation based on the Movement's early life, an embrace of postmodern communicative techniques in the creative arts, drama, and dance, which Watson modelled in his influential leadership. Cray does hint that at St. Michael-le-Belfrey he continued to create "a home where creative people could be creative without having to defend themselves." Gumbel testifies to the usage of video in Alpha that constantly had to be updated with changing culture, perhaps an expression of non-traditional communication—though not explicitly postmodern. Here Morgan does argue non-verbal means of communication such as dance have been "very helpful because it would take your mind off the tangible and the static and the fixed." However, despite this, other interviewees did not express a desire or prioritization of such means of communication. It might be theorized that some of the Movement's ongoing more modernistic nature could not receive the level of the novel postmodern emphasis in Watson's model wholesale and that such communicative means therefore remain peripheral and occasional at best.

Overall, the progression of postmodern characteristics under this criterion from the early to later Movement is not one of straightforward development. Though development can be seen in the growth of spiritual and allegorical hermeneutics, manifestations of which are strongly postmodern in character, this is the only case. In prophetic communication, ritual and performative language, and glossolalia, there is little development, and indeed in some cases less postmodern character. Indeed, the relative absence of postmodern communicative means may highlight how strong ongoing modernistic characteristics of the Movement overtly resisted some postmodern influences in the Movement's development.

6.2.3 Criterion Three: Metanarratives and Micronarratives

In the later Movement the importance of micronarratives is again emphasized, with equivalent and sometimes greater valuation in comparison to the early Movement. However, micronarratives are again not seen to be as important as metanarratives of the Christian faith, nor is there any hint of deliberate rupture with wider culture in their usage. Thus, the later Movement again shows incomplete postmodern character under this criterion.

Interviewees are clear that the usage of personal testimony in the Movement is important. David Pytches summarizes that in his ministry "I think I just constantly told stories"—stories of encounters with God by the Holy Spirit—lamenting, "I think there is not nearly enough of it [now]," pointing to the model of how Jesus used stories for corroboration of this emphasis. One might question whether Pytches did "just tell stories" given the nature of the didactic content of his preaching and books, but interestingly this is his generalization looking back. Similarly, MacInnes looking back explains that testimony in the Movement has been "very significant" and a key part of the bigger work of renewal and its import into Anglican worship.[59] Testimony was "one of the ways of breaking into what otherwise was formal and didn't seem to leave much room for the Spirit."

Assorted reasons are given as to why personal testimony was found to have such power, all hinging on the importance of experience. For Morgan, because renewal was about "charismatic experience or direct experience of the work of the Spirit in your life," experiential testimony "authenticated" and made "more powerful" such experiences. Similarly, MacInnes explains that the exposure of "your inner self" in personal testimony "takes away the intellectual argument" within faith struggles, and challenges "what ought to be happening to me." Cleverly, in even stronger postmodern orientation, explains that one needs a personal testimony to see fruitfulness in ministry, giving the example of a musical worship leader who, "when she's singing, she's not just singing about ideas, she's singing about her own story."

This experientially driven shift is understood primarily as a theological expansion by interviewees, rather than due to any postmodern import. Mary Pytches explains that whereas in previous conservative Evangelical tradition, she had been taught the value of the personal testimony of initial salvation, in renewal this expanded to testimony about the ongoing work of God. Morgan concurs: "My testimony becomes not how I became a Christian, or not *only* how I became a Christian, but what God is doing in my life now. So, I should be able to give you a testimony from last week, not from 1983." Cray explains, "If you end up with a theology of encounter, then your testimony becomes how you

---

59. An analysis supported in Cartledge, *Testimony*.

have encountered God in your daily life recently . . . and it becomes a much more living thing." Such explicates the seen link between testimony and *Criterion One* experiential emphases highlighted in General Synod's 1981 report[60]—the Movement's expanded epistemology enables other more postmodern expressions in its lifeworld as would be expected in the outworking of an internal postmodern-like drive.[61]

Though this theological expansion is the primary force behind what is observed, interviewees also speak of cultural factors, witnessing to a hypothesized manner of *Cultural Catalysis* at work. Cray explains that evangelism used to be about turning the stories of "the Gospels into truth as they had been written in Paul's letters," but from 1960 onwards, "if you're going to use Paul's letters, you've got to find them in story form, because people engage with stories. And now that's, that's partly about the culture change." Morgan explains,

> We live in a culture that's all about story in a way, and my story and my journey and my experience and my truth, and if I don't have an actual story that affects my whole life . . . then maybe I don't seem authentic, and I've not really got anything that's going to impact anybody else.

Here, an emphasis on micronarratives in culture, especially likely in postmodern cultural elements, creates a resonant emphasis in the Movement's lifeworld in a *Cultural Catalysis* fashion. As an example of this in action, Selvaratnam explains that in Alpha the sharing of personal viewpoints and hearing of others in short testimony form was perhaps more important than "the talk"—though the talks themselves proliferate with testimonies as well.[62]

However, the fullest of postmodern manifestation is not seen here—that such micronarratives are deemed as important as metanarratives of faith, or more so. Millar explains that on Alpha courses, they desired to correct any overemphasis on personal testimony by always asking the question "What differences has Jesus made to you?" that "brings us right back to the big story, the Redeemer of the world," allowing the climax of faith to be the larger story of Christian salvation centered on Jesus. Cleverly likewise in preaching warns, "Testimony should come after the speaking [of the big story of the gospel and salvation] or if it comes

60. §3.3.2.
61. See §2.5.3.
62. Brian, "Alpha Course," 69.

before, it should then lead to this the bigger story." However, for Morgan there is no easy delineation: "My story is part of the bigger story; my life is part of our shared life. . . . [Testimony] draws me as an individual into an ongoing story or enables me to tell an ongoing story." Some more postmodern character is again seen in Morgan's viewpoint, who, though often a unique voice among the interviewees, is representative of at least some in the later Movement.

As in Harper and Watson's thought, corporate micronarratives are also seen to be important, yet not above the larger metanarratives of faith that they are embedded in. Cray recalls a mapping exercise that he conducted with the congregation at St. Michael-le-Belfrey of God's particular story for them and where it would go next. Morgan recalls a similar emphasis in ReSource whereby their team sought to "help churches discern their own calling and mission in the context of their own communities." MacInnes relates how the personal testimonies of experience at St. Aldates became part of the corporate narrative of the effects of TTB. However, in all these, there is no sense these corporate narratives replace larger more universal narratives of faith. Rather they are its contextual expressions.

Furthermore, no evidence is seen of micronarratives that are related to discontinuities and ruptures with wider culture that such testimonies are a narrative of an anti-modern or postmodern impetus, nor of appeals to the fracturing of cultural narratives like Harper makes. Nor are the testimonies seen to be stereotypically formed to fit a larger metanarrative which would demarcate them as especially postmodern in character as previously suggested.

Hence, in summary, though some postmodern emphases on micronarratives are seen, as with the early Movement the later Movement is neither fully nor strongly postmodern under *Criterion Three*. Personal testimony is of crucial importance as authentication, amplification, and fruitful expression of charismatic experience. However, this stems from a theological expansion that narrates a theology of continuous encounter, and care is taken to ensure such micronarratives do not replace the primary importance of metanarratives of faith. Similar corporate narratives are largely contextual expressions of macronarratives rather than replacements, and potential marks of stronger postmodernisms under this criterion are again absent.

As noted, reflecting on the consistent place of testimonies in the later Movement, David Pytches's comment that he "just told stories" because it was Jesus's model is a questionable reflection. However, it indicates that at least part of what is at work here is more premodern recovery, as identified under CRQ-3's enquiry. Like Watson being inspired by stories of past revivals (§5.2.3), and the effect of stories of the East African revivals (§3.1.2.1), stories in the Movement communicate exciting premodern realities made present, personal, and possible today.

6.2.4 Criterion Four: The Importance of Community

Analysis of the early Movement under the last criterion highlighted some of its strongest postmodern characteristics. However, the later Movement exhibits much less *Criterion Four* postmodern character, especially in formerly espoused views of anti-clericalism.

The later Movement continues to emphasize the necessity, place, and power of community. Morgan opines that for the whole church, "The charismatic movement has been a catalyst in making us increasingly aware of that need to depend upon one another and to be a community." Interviewees gave examples of this in action. Mary Pytches explains that New Wine was setup "because we wanted the churches to know what the leaders already were experiencing" in charismatic renewal, and they saw that this larger community buy-in to renewal was essential to seeing it spread. This is unlike what was seen with the Fountain Trust, which primarily targeted leaders to the same end, speaking perhaps to an increased awareness of the importance of community in renewal. Conversely, on the smaller scale, MacInnes notes in a period of cessation of ministries at St. Aldates following the impact of TTB, people "largely got very restless" for the resumption of smaller fellowship groups, so ingrained was the importance of such smaller communities in the life of the church.

Some interviewees gave theological reasons for this emphasis. Morgan explains that in the Movement, "the focus on 1 Corinthians 12 has taught us that we are part of the body of Christ, not members only as individuals, but that we form a community, and we need to rely on each other to bring gifts that we haven't got." Millar concurs, speaking of the community "the Spirit brings into existence which . . . is supposed to be a community of exercising those [spiritual] gifts." Such resonates with the valuing of community by Harper because of ministries grown in them by the Spirit—a continuing impetus in the Movement's timeline.

However, another reason for this emphasis is also seen, resonating more with Harper's understanding of the pragmatic winsomeness of such communities. Millar also speaks of the attractional power to those outside church of "a community that loves one another like the early church." Gumbel explains that this emphasis led his development of Alpha towards focusing on the small groups at its heart, responding to surveys done after every course that fed back how much they were valued above all. Here some signs of *Cultural Catalysis* through the Movement's contact with postmodern cultural elements which value community—one of its two predicted manners of operation—can be potentially seen. A development from Harper who insisted that no cultural import was at work in his vision for community at the heart of renewal.

Cray sees the effect of surrounding culture to be more negative for the life of communities in the Movement, however. He viewed the demise of the extended households, setup under Watson and others' ministries, as partly due to the "corrosive" effects of "powerful individualizing consumer forces," which "made real corporate mutual love . . . more difficult to sustain." Resultantly, "the deeply mutual corporate sense of belonging that was the fruit of renewal at one time, is rarer to find now." If true, it could be concluded that while postmodern elements of culture encourage certain elements of this community emphasis in the later Movement, the converse influences of strong modernistic elements of culture also mitigated against them. However, this view from Cray must be nuanced through comparison with Guest's previously cited study of St. Michael-le-Belfrey in 2006.[63] Guest views the resilience of the church against the powers of cultural modernity as being *enabled* by the strength of internal communities at York, partly contradicting Cray's view, as for him it was the demise of the quality of such community's lives that showed a lack of resilience against modern culture's power. Cray may still be right in the general sense, however, and indeed community emphases at St. Michael's probably fared better than many other places in the Movement over the long term because of Watson's strong initial vision for community life.

The interpretative importance of such communities is seen in the interviewee's responses, but not to the degree of a postmodern emphasis which promotes community interpretation above what is received from institution and tradition. Interpretation is mainly focused on the revelatory gifts of the Spirit, such as the importance of community to discern

---

63. Guest, *Evangelical Identity*. Cf. §4.1.3.

the truthfulness and application of prophetic utterance. Clear structures enabling communal discernment are spoken of by the interviewees. Cray explains how in York he "put processes in" whereby what was heard from God in mid-week small groups could be passed on to those "in the oversight of the church" due to the impracticality of doing this in a large Sunday congregation—enabling all to hear and discern. Morgan agrees on the priority of this every person possibility, explaining how "we need leaders who have got the courage to depend on voices from within the congregation when a lot of the congregation isn't actually renewed by the Spirit and may not even have a clear understanding of a personal commitment to God." Here MacInnes partially disagrees with Morgan's generosity, explaining the need for a right "group [for] understanding to see whether the thing is bonkers or if it's actually right" because "there was a lot of nonsense" generated in experiences of renewal. MacInnes models this in his dealing with events following the impact of TTB at St. Aldates in 1994–95, speaking of seeking the discernment of the prophetic words he received first with the church staff team, then the church's parochial church council (PCC), before seeking the whole church's feedback. Morgan and MacInnes represent two ends of a spectrum between postmodernistic and modernistic leanings here, though in more modernistic emphasis both concur on the need for ultimate decisions from communal discernment to reside with church leaders.

Little postmodern character is seen in views of authority and its structures in the later Movement, and importantly less so than the strong manifestations in Harper and Watson's work. Like them, interviewees had high regard for the concept of positional authority, perhaps no more so than Gumbel, who explained that the model he looked to was Jesus, whose "authority came from being under his Father's authority"; no matter how bad government through the Church of England is, Gumbel is committed to lead under authority within it. However, this view stands in contrast perhaps with his understanding of the place of authority in mission, whereby Alpha sought to deliberately downplay the concept of authority to appeal to a postmodern culture suspicious of it, while simultaneously never saying anything against it explicitly.[64] Selvaratnam explains that in Alpha, "the best run small groups are ones where the guests feel that they are in charge" and that group leaders are actively trained not to answer questions. Given how Gumbel shaped Alpha, one feels there is

64. Atherstone, *Repackaging Christianity*, 146–47; Gumbel, *Telling Others*, 114.

a disparity here: authority is highly regarded in the church at one level, but in the witness of the church this is muted for the sake of reaching a more postmodern culture—a pragmatic missional postmodernism seen again in Gumbel's ministry. Questions arise about what happens when those who come into churches such as HTB through Alpha meet more modernistic views of authority in its main life and tensions that might occur as a result. Research undertaken by Steve Aisthorpe indicates that this type of tension may lead some to leave such churches through a mixture of "cumulative disaffection" and "final straws" when authority is unexpectedly exerted.[65]

Interviewees similarly hold high regard for specific authority holders. Like Harper and Watson, they have a high view of episcopal leadership, and two of those interviewed—Cray and Millar—were consecrated as bishops after leading charismatic churches, showing the openness of those in the Movement to episcopal authority.[66] Indeed, Millar lambasts that the Church of England is an episcopal organization and those disliking this "shouldn't join the Church of England—you'd better go." This high regard is not simply idealistic for Gumbel, who explains that in church planting he always sought to work under the authority of the Bishop of London. At one point when asked by the Bishop of London not to plant, "I had one phone call, and I pulled out because I'm under authority."

Surprisingly, a lack of critique of normal clergy in the Church of England is seen in interview responses, despite Harper and Watson's earlier strongly critiques of them as inhibitors of renewal and enslavers of the laity. Though Morgan speaks of some feeling of this when she went through the discernment process for ordination in 1996, hers is the only testimony, and nowhere as strong as Harper and Watson espoused. If earlier critiques were at all formed by a postmodern impetus or the effects of a postmodern cultural environment, this was short-lived, perhaps because of residual strong modernistic views of authority that ran alongside the critiques. Such may have combined with MacInnes and Cray's supposition that renewal had spread across the clergy of the Church of England by the later stages of the Movement, meaning it became harder to criticize clergy as authority figures who impeded renewal as many were charismatics themselves.

65. Aisthorpe, *Invisible Church*, 69–74.

66. Additionally, David Pytches was already a bishop while leading St. Andrew's, Chorleywood and New Wine.

Commenting on authority structures, Cleverly laments the lack of engagement of charismatics with the synodical structures of the Church of England; yet this is not due to a postmodern attitude of rebellion, rather a "short-sighted" concentration on the immediate work of the Spirit rather than the larger picture. Complementing this, interviewees especially highlight two case examples, New Wine and church planting in the Movement, which show that attitudes to the larger structures are deficit of postmodern attitudes of rejection of authority structures, as was found earlier with the Fountain Trust.[67]

According to his wife Mary, New Wine originated as a largely Anglican network due to its leadership by David Pytches, a clear Anglican. This in turn meant through relational connections "all the leaders that they would invite onto the leadership team were Anglicans," and this has remained largely the case. From Pytches's wider account of its organic and slightly haphazard growth, one surmises that it was not set up as an alternative Anglican structure on purpose, even if the result may have felt so. Cleverly concurs: "It's not a political body, it's a renewal thing," though for some, "it can be such a sort of bubble world within itself that those involved in it haven't got time to do anything else," and may indeed perhaps constitute an alternative Anglican structure. In a less critical view, Mary Pytches views New Wine as actually helping charismatics, lay and ordained, to stay in the Church of England rather than reject it: "New Wine helped them stick it out"—its events acting as an oasis of renewal amid perceived larger Anglican aridity.

Rejection of Anglican structures cannot be seen for church planting in the later Movement either. In early church planting out of St. Andrew's Chorleywood, an overflow of the Pytches's experience in South America, Mary Pytches expresses how the authorities "did not like it" because the parochial system did not yet allow for such possibilities. Though this was not a deliberate rejection of Anglican structures per se, it could be viewed at least as an ignoring of them, which as seen could have also been a possibility with Watson's approach.[68] However, later in the Movement practitioners sought to be fully compliant with local Anglican structures and rules. Gumbel explains that even though it slowed the process of church planting, as one in the Church of England "you can't be a part of an organization and then ignore its customs and rules," and the long-term fruitful

---

67. §3.2.1.

68. While also seeking to win it over; see Pytches and Skinner, *New Wineskins*.

approach was to work with diocesan systems in church planting. This was also true for Selvaratnam's experience of planting G2 out of St. Michael-le-Belfrey. Despite a decided lack of support and encouragement from diocesan structures apart from his bishop, he explains how they abided by the conditions of the local parish priest in the parish they planted into to not advertise their presence, nor for anyone but him to celebrate communion until Selvaratnam was ordained priest. High regard for Anglican authority structures is seen even amid difficult relationships with them. Selvaratnam reflects here on Ralph Winter's missiological structures of sodalities and modalities,[69] and explains how both are needed—the larger structure and from that a task-driven dynamic team on mission. He does not reject one in favor of the other in a postmodern fashion but sees a need for the two to coexist.

On local church levels of structures, Watson's experimental reconstituting of the church with a new wider leadership team was adopted by many larger churches in the later Movement. Yet other possible postmodern trends towards new local structures were mitigated against. For example, MacInnes explained how at St. Aldates he worked hard to bring in a group of worshipers who had set up an alternative and more charismatic service back into the main body of the church, avoiding painful fracturing into sub-communities. Morgan witnesses to how in the church that she primarily ministered in, rather than replace the PCC in its leadership function she observed attempts to bring those touched by renewal into the PCC, again seeking maintenance and usage of existing structures.

Overall, on both larger and smaller scales, charismatics took the *via media* route recommended by Cartledge in his study of possible tensions between charismatics and the Church of England, such that for the new, Spirit-inspired tasks renewal brought, he concluded that "insofar as institutional structures enable and facilitate such purpose, then Charismatics must be prepared to hold onto them."[70] A pragmatic approach, as appreciated in §6.2.1, but beyond that not a postmodern one. Such an attitude is in keeping with a later Movement that at times shows some marks of postmodern character under this criterion, but overall is deficit in them. The Movement's continued emphasis on community as both of theological and interpretive importance shows some postmodern character; yet

---

69. See Winter, "Two Structures."
70. Cartledge, "New Via Media," 283.

a now largely muted critique of authority holders and continued desire to work within larger institutional structures, as well as alongside them through new structures, witnesses strongly to the opposite.

6.3 CONCLUSION

This chapter has continued to prove the fruitfulness of using the derived *ecclesial postmodernism* system to analyze the Movement's lifeworld. Having analyzed both the early and later Movement, it is now possible to answer CRQ-1 with greater completeness. What is found agrees with initial hypotheses. It is inaccurate to simplistically describe the Movement's *nature* as postmodern in the way postmodernism has been defined in this study; at no point in its lifeworld history does it exhibit any of the Analytic's criterion in fullest extent. However, that which is seen does give it postmodern *character*. Throughout its history the strongest postmodern characteristics consistently observable are those of *Criterion One*, yet simultaneously other strong postmodernisms are seen, such as Watson's postmodern communicative techniques and Cleverly's allegorical exegesis (both *Criterion Two)*, and Watson and Harper's fierce anticlericalism (*Criterion Four*). The consistency of the strength of *Criterion One* characteristics in both periods adds evidence to the supposition that an outworking of an internal postmodern-like drive within the Movement generates its postmodern characteristics, which, as shall be seen, is indeed the anti-modernistic one described by a *Mutual Origins* model.

It is revealing to note that throughout the temporal length of the Movement, key postmodern characteristics are consistently seen, as well as unseen. Under *Criterion One*, seen throughout are expressions of a broadened non-foundation epistemology, partially found in embodied locus, combined with strong missional pragmatism and pluralism. In these last two characteristics, Watson's legacy is not only taken up but then furthered by leaders such as Cray, Millar, and Gumbel. However, relativism is not seen throughout the Movement's life with similar consistency. Under *Criterion Two*, there are some consistent understandings of prophetic signs, glossolalia, and performative language that display postmodern characteristics, though in a mixed and variable manner in exactly how and to what extent signifiers and signified are split. Under *Criterion Three*, there are constant postmodern characteristics seen in emphases on personal testimony and its power, yet without a loss of the primary importance of larger Christian metanarrative. Sharp discontinuities promoted against wider culture are consistently unseen. Under *Criterion Four*, there is a consistent emphasis on communities and their interpretative function, as well as a desire to change structures on the local level, yet throughout a high valuing of larger structures.

However, perhaps what is even more revealing are the moments of change from the early to later stages of the Movement. Only one strong postmodern characteristic is "gained" in the later stages of the Movement, that of an appreciation for spiritual and allegorical exegesis. Another that could be said to be gained is that of an anti-authority emphasis in Alpha's small groups, yet, as has been seen, this is in juxtaposition with other higher views of authority held by the relevant interviewees. In contrast, there are more postmodern characteristics that are "lost" or lessened in manifestation. For example, the performative nature of language is seen with less force than in both Harper's and Watson's examples, and Watson's strong emphasis on the application of postmodern communication theory is muted and not detectable for most interviewees. Notably, there is a complete loss of anti-authority views towards local clergy that was so strongly seen in Watson and Harper. Overall, there are more instances of loss than gain in postmodern characteristics over the lifespan of the Movement, though one can argue that the increased strength of missional pluralism and pragmatism might help offset this in terms of speaking about the Movement's overall postmodern character. Nevertheless, one cannot describe a simple spread of postmodernism in and through the Movement over time in increasing manifestation. Rather, as expected, such postmodern characteristics must be rooted in other dynamics at work.

This helpfully brings this study to its next stage. Throughout this chapter's analysis, there have been continued suggestions of key responses to CRQs-2 and 3 which explain observations of the Movement's postmodern character better than viewing it as inherently postmodern in nature. Namely that such characteristics are constituted by a reaction against modernism (a *Mutual Origins* model), with characteristics catalyzed by interaction with wider culture (a *Cultural Catalysis* model). Additionally, potential evidence of a key component of the larger hypothesized narrative that links the outworking of a *Mutual Origins* model to a desire to recover premodern forms of praxis—that an *anti-modern* reaction led to some postmodern characteristics being generated that were *premodern* retrievals—has been seen in the discussion of allegorical and spiritual exegesis. The next chapter explores these ideas through analysis of answers to questions targeted at CRQs-2 and 3 to complete this study's analysis.

Before leaving this part of the analysis, it is informative to look at its results from another dimension, that of local development. It was noted in the selection of interviewees that three key places of charismatic renewal can be located: St. Aldates Church, Oxford, St. Michael-le-Belfrey Church, York, and HTB. What can be said about the postmodern question in local contexts? The clearest answer is continuation and progression, whereby many postmodern characteristics stayed over time and were developed. It was noted that in Oxford, the battles that MacInnes fought to overcome rationalism in the university city context allowed the growth of a wider range of epistemological understandings under Cleverly. In York, characteristics such as Watson's holistic epistemological approach and strong missional pragmatism continued to inform the life at St. Michael's under Cray—later developed with greater theological understanding by him. The next chapter will show how further downstream in York, Selvaratnam's G2 shows the marks of a church seeking to formulate itself to pragmatically fit culture as most fully possible. The strongest sense of continuation and development is clearly at HTB, no doubt due to the strong overlap of Millar and Gumbel's leadership. Through the development of Alpha, Gumbel shares and takes on Millar's impulse towards missional pluralism and pragmatism, developing it to new heights in Alpha's global reach. It is only in York where one can see the opposite trend at work as well, the relative loss of postmodern characteristics: the ebbing of Watson's anti-clericalism and emphasis on postmodern communication. However, these characteristics are less prominent across the lifeworld of the later Movement generally, suggesting that modernistic characteristics inherited from its birthing background inhibited the propagation of these more overt postmodern characteristics, despite Watson's considerable and wide influence.

By in large the picture is of the growth and development of observed postmodern characteristics in local centers. This in turn suggests that these larger renewal centers held internal cultures strongly over prolonged periods, and that it is unsurprising if their long-term witness within the informal and formal charismatic networks they were part of helped encourage the retention and adoption of postmodern characteristics across the Movement as key influences within it. In cited interview responses Cleverly, Cray, and Millar all explicitly exhibit moments of criticism of the Movement's lifeworld, showing that this was not an accidental retention and propagation, but a critically thought-through one. The dynamics behind observable postmodern characteristics explored in the next chapter are likely to have found stable homes to be outworked in these and other such renewal centers in the Movement.

7

Postmodernism and the Later Movement (II)

Models and Trajectories

IN THE PREVIOUS CHAPTER, the postmodern characteristics of the later Movement were explored in response to CRQ-1's enquiry through analysis of interviews of nine leaders within it. Completing this study's qualitative investigation of the Movement, this chapter now analyzes these same interviews under the enquiry of CRQs-2 and 3, exploring the dynamics behind these characteristics' generation and growth, enabling a rich set of conclusions to be found about the Movement's postmodern character.

What is seen builds on what was found for the early Movement, adding important developmental description. Again, the Movement's postmodern characteristics are largely unlikely to be a result of a *Direct Influence* of postmodern thought upon the Movement. Rather, key is the ongoing working of both a *Mutual Origins* model describing the generation of postmodern characteristics in reaction to contextual modernism, which is subsequently encouraged in growth by a *Cultural Catalysis* interaction with culture. Importantly, *Cultural Catalysis* is evidenced to a wider extent in the later Movement, which enables two distinct modes of its operation (active and passive) to be discerned.

As in the earlier Movement, a primary trajectory of movement within a *Mutual Origins* dynamic is towards a recovery of Christian faith and expressions of church life that are premodern in nature, and how this operates is described. Again, this is primarily focused on the New

Testament church, yet in the later Movement a broader and richer recovery of other periods of the Western Church occurs. Consideration of parallel movements in the twentieth century helps affirm that understanding this recovery impulse is crucial to explaining the Movement's postmodern characteristics by showing how premodern and postmodern themes overlap and become indistinguishable.

7.1 CRQ-2: MODELS OF INFLUENCE

7.1.1 Direct Influence

In continuity with previous analyses, there is a relative paucity of evidence to support the supposition of a *Direct Influence* model at work in the later Movement. Interviewees' understandings of postmodernism range from "No idea!" (David Pytches) to more detailed assessments (Cray, Morgan). Numerous interviewees offer their versions of what it is, often hesitantly: "Self-relational, all about us" (Millar); "Ego-centric . . . about my truths and not the Truth" (Mary Pytches); from a postmodern literary angle, "Those kinds of disconnected events that don't seem to be part of life, [and] have not got an organizing philosophy" (Cleverly). Selvaratnam speaks of the post-postmodern culture that he ministers to, which takes on some postmodern moorings such as a "less institutional" and "community emphasis." Gumbel speaks about it being "a shift in the culture . . . a shift in attitude to truth . . . a shift in attitudes to experience," yet contextualized in the important realization that "there are parts of culture that are premodern, there are parts that are modern, and there are parts that are postmodern." Unsurprisingly astute observations given Gumbel's missional pragmatism which involves tactical outreach to changing cultural currents.

Equally unsurprising, Cray, who has written on missional engagement to postmodern culture,[1] delineates philosophical postmodernism—"Derrida, Foucault, Lyotard, et cetera"—from it as a "sociological phenomenon" described by commentators such as David Lyon and Zygmunt Bauman's "liquid modernity,"[2] preferring to focus on the latter phenomenon as the key means of the former having "bite." With similar levels of awareness, Morgan, who speaks of her active research into

---

1. Cray, *Postmodern Culture*.
2. Bauman, *Liquid Modernity*; Lyon, *Postmodernity*.

postmodern culture, defines it "in comparison to modernism," whereby, "the postmodern approach is more intuitive, brings the emotional dimension back into things . . . releasing of a [modernistic] straight-jacket . . . without necessarily discarding what had gone before." However, in interview Cray and Morgan do not explore any changed praxis explicitly based on postmodern insights (though their engagement with them may well still shape some of it less directly), suggesting little evidence of a *Direct Influence* model at work in the later Movement via its leader's conscious engagement with postmodern ideas. For Cray, this is said aware of, and despite, Andrew Davison and Alison Milbank's critique of the Anglican report *Mission-Shaped Church*[3]—which Cray chaired the writing of—a critique that levels accusations of postmodern importation.[4] This study perhaps helps correct such a critique, giving nuanced language to how something can look postmodern without being so. Evidence will be seen below as to how Cray inhabits a *Mutual Origins* model such that his praxis may stem from yes, anti-modern, but not postmodern desires.

The unlikelihood of a *Direct Influence* model is substantiated by the spectrum of views as to whether postmodernism is to be rejected or embraced flowing from interviewees' understanding of it. For some, like Harper's instincts towards cultural influences,[5] rejection is clear: Millar opines, "The sooner that [self-relationism] is recognized and countered, the better"; Mary Pytches laments, "The lack of truth is what concerns me . . . that you can't speak reality." However, most view it as neither a potentially good nor bad influence per se, but simply something to be recognized as "present" in culture (Gumbel), such that one "has to engage with the society where it finds itself" (Cray). Only Morgan acts as a strong outlier, speaking of the value of postmodernism's presence in culture, describing herself as "being a sort of child that straddles modernism and postmodernism" in her formation, leading her to ask questions of her faith like, "Does it work? . . . What does my faith do for me other than be true because I'm not really looking for something that stops with that—I'm looking for a way of living my life." The charismatic movement meets these more postmodern desires for Morgan.

From both the low levels of understanding of what postmodernism is and the lack of positive responses to its value, a paucity of evidence is found for a *Direct Influence* model at work in the later Movement,

3. Cray, *Mission-Shaped Church*.
4. Davison and Milbank, *For the Parish*, 100–102, 117–18.
5. §5.1.2.

agreeing with assessments made of its earlier life through the work of Harper and Watson. However, Morgan's depth of knowledge and shaping by postmodern ideas offers a word of caution, indicating that for some smaller sections of the later Movement postmodern ideas do indeed inform charismatic praxis. This, combined with the witness of Watson's adoption of postmodern communication methods in the 1970s and 1980s, indicates that though observed postmodern characteristics of the Movement are unlikely to be due to its formation through the *Direct Influence* of formal philosophical postmodernism, as it grew it showed some openness to more culturally transmitted postmodern ideas, such as in Watson's case, with perhaps a minority of practitioners such as Morgan additionally receiving more explicitly philosophical postmodernism into their praxis later in the Movement's life.

7.1.2 Mutual Origins

Chapter 5 observed how Watson was critical of the fruit of the Enlightenment and modernism in the church, and how Harper further suggested that charismatic renewal was the great hope to counteract this problem, providing initial evidence for a *Mutual Origins* model at work in the early Movement. The previous chapter highlighted some postmodern characteristics in the later Movement that may be seen to develop through this model's anti-modernistic dynamic, namely an emphasis on embodiment (Morgan, Cray, Cleverly), allegorical exegesis (Millar, Morgan, Cleverly), and possibly in at least one understanding of glossolalia (Millar). Probing interviewees about specific areas concerning this model confirms its clear presence throughout the Movement's timeline—whereby a shared negative assessment of modernism motivated innovative approaches. Such an anti-modernistic drive internal to the Movement is therefore likely what was identified in the previous chapter as the responsible postmodern-like drive behind the consistent strength of *Criterion One* characteristics; as previously argued, the former type of drive is contained within the latter from analysis of the historical origins of postmodernism, and thus helps explain much of the postmodern character of characteristics generated out of an anti-modern impulse.

The negative aspects of modernism in the church were seen to be a generative cause of charismatic renewal for many. Morgan bluntly opines that for renewal, "we can only make sense of it by realizing that in modernism we lost it," causing a search for that which was lost due to it, and an "embracing of what God is spontaneously doing now." Cleverly locates the renewal movement in the context of a God who "is perpetually pouring water on thirsty land and perpetually looking for times and places to renew the church," and Mary Pytches is clear that she and others in the church had "got a bit stagnant . . . stuck in our focus on knowledge," which renewal broke into. MacInnes highlights how changes in the surrounding culture enabled the church to expect "something fresh," which for Millar in his experience of renewal especially was for "mainly tired clergy . . . what was needed was a fresh touch of the Spirit, fresh encouragement, fresh power, fresh understanding of the church was meant to look like and its place in the community." Water metaphors abound, and responses collectively suggest the same reactions to a "dry" modernistic church as seen in §3.1.2.1.

Charismatic renewal is additionally seen to bring freedom from the same frustrations with an inherited Evangelicalism controlled by modernism explored in §3.1.2.2. David Pytches notes how he was influenced by Evangelicals such as John Stott, Jim Packer, and Alec Motyer, yet he was left even now in old age "wanting more and more of God" which leads to personal renewal, enabling one to "see God in a completely different way." This is not brand-new revelation—rather what was known previously is made vividly new through the experience of the Spirit. His wife Mary similarly opines that renewal sprung from a place "very focused on Bible knowledge, and doctrinally sound," yet missed the experience of God. Cray goes as far as to speak of praising the effects of postmodernism, which "took a bulldozer over the arrogant epistemology of the Enlightenment," helping expose an Evangelicalism "defending Christian truth and Scripture on the basis . . . [of] an Enlightenment foundation that has been found severely wanting."

MacInnes again suggests the historical reasons for such "wanting" foundations—that it was "because Evangelicals were struggling to regain a position within a church and [were assessed] as lacking in any kind of intelligence"; as "modernism took center stage" it led to some such as Stott to go "back to Scripture to acquire some kind of intellectual justification." This sought-after justification was seen as needed to enable Evangelicals to play on the same intellectual playing field as more modernistic liberal scholarship.[6] This ongoing impulse, added to moves

---

6. See §3.1.2.2.

of "escaping from the rather woolly Keswick teaching about second blessing," meant that in Trinitarian terms "experience was centered around the Father and the Son," and the Holy Spirit "didn't feature as part of our experience." Renewal came in the context of "a certain dryness, we were focusing on how you could be sure about the exact justification of Scripture and how that could be justified and so on, and there was a loss of the inner heart experience and the devotional side." As previously seen, it is debatable whether MacInnes in his analysis of Evangelical history is correct. However, what is of importance is that this was the controlling narrative MacInnes led in charismatic renewal from, and influenced a whole generation of subsequent charismatic leaders out of, in an *ongoing* manner—not just at the Movement's birth: the narrative of charismatic renewal as a recovery of a lost experiential emphasis within modernistic rationalistic Evangelicalism.

In addition to those postmodern characteristics of the later Movement seen in the previous chapter to derive from a *Mutual Origins* model at work, further characteristics are observed by interviewees when directly questioned about modernism's effects. Millar comments that some of the unusual aspects of the "Toronto stuff" was "God confounding the so-called wisdom of the wise with the foolishness of God"[7]—confrontation of preoccupations with intelligibility and reasonableness. The fact that Millar sees this as an ongoing need, with the events he reflects on found in the 1990s, exposes a longevity of the anti-modernistic impulse at the Movement's heart that goes beyond its early life. Morgan similarly witnesses to this in her experience of prayer, reflecting that previously she had been taught to pray from Scripture, reading it through a hermeneutical lens whereby she was to seek "the truth, a command, and a promise." However, she reflects, "Sometimes I couldn't find the truth, a command, or promise, so I then failed." The critical move, related to her new approach to Scripture in the context of renewal,[8] was "if I allow the gospel just to speak to me in the way it wants, I always found that I was coming away with something which couldn't necessarily be boxed into that which was true, tangible, or applicable." She explains that this was part of a larger theological movement of "being released from systematic theology and a purely rational approach to faith." Perhaps subtly detectable

---

7. Cf. 1 Cor 1:25; 3:19.
8. See §6.1.

here in Morgan is the outworking of an individual tension that playfully leads to a new freer reality, as described in §4.2.1.

Interviewees, however, offered some caveats to these anti-modernistic impulses in renewal. Morgan also sees the positives in modernism of scientific progress, and in the ecclesial sphere a "rigorous engagement of Scripture, new ways of looking analytically . . . [meaning] we mustn't ever throw away the achievements of a previous generation of Christians." Here, Cleverly argues that if in the work of the Spirit in renewal's practical outworking "a call went in the opposite direction of everything I've been doing, especially for the church. . . . I would probably think . . . it may not be the Holy Spirit." Synthesizing these viewpoints, the reaction and travel away from modernism in the Movement is perhaps not as discontinuous as the strength of the above negative opinions about modernism, and subsequent desire for something new or recovered, might suggest. It is more likely, as previous chapters have indicated, modernistic emphases continue to be embraced in central aspects of the Movement; just as seen within postmodernism in its philosophical roots, modernistic and anti-modernistic impulses are held together in tension in the Movement's life. Here however, as noted in §6.2.1, earlier warnings against an overemphasis on both *Criterion One* experiential and emotional epistemological manifestations, rooted in the Movement's more modernistic heritage and impulses that prescribed limits for the *Mutual Origins* generations of them, seem to have failed by the time of the later Movement in some quarters. This overcoming of modernistic elements by postmodernistic ones in the admixture of the two may well be due to the powerful effect of *Cultural Catalysis* in the later Movement, which emphasized and grew the latter over the warnings of the former.

7.1.3 Cultural Catalysis

Unlike the previous two models, *Cultural Catalysis* does not purport to explain the origins of the Movement's postmodern characteristics seen in answering CRQ-1. Rather it focuses on the later growth of these characteristics. It asks if the Movement's interaction with its complex cultural surroundings cause these postmodern characteristics to especially grow in prominence, perhaps such that outside observers, such as those examined in §1.1, mistakenly see some type of *Direct Influence* model at work: postmodern elements of this surrounding culture resonated so clearly with what developed within the Movement that some form of genesis relationship between the two is assumed.

In the previous chapter signs of *Cultural Catalysis* were seen in analysis of various postmodern manifestations within the later Movement: potentially in the failure within the Movement to stop extreme experientialism and emotionalism; in evangelistic usage of testimony; in Alpha's emphasis on the experience of the Holy Spirit and community; and potentially contextualizing Gumbel's missional pragmatism more generally. This builds upon what was discovered in the early Movement: Harper evidenced initial stepping-stone indications of *Cultural Catalysis*, while Watson exhibited substantial manifestations of it.

Responses to questions specifically targeted upon this model in the later Movement reveal it to be strongly present as a key means through which postmodern characteristics are encouraged to grow from nascence in the above-described *Mutual Origins* model. As predicted in chapter 4, and then evidenced in chapter 5, this catalysis occurs through the Movement's postmodern characteristics appealing to both postmodernistic and modernistic elements of wider culture, meeting the desires of the former and the crises of the latter. In the later Movement, the extent of Catalysis is more evident and widespread than in the earlier; as the Movement grew, so did its contact with culture, especially through missional outreach, increasing the levels of *Cultural Catalysis* within it.

Two categories of response can be discerned from responses that indicate the outworking of the *Cultural Catalysis* model in the later Movement, suggesting two subtly different modes of the model's operation. Firstly, a *passive* mode, where perceived cultural resonances with the Movement's postmodern characteristics makes it likely that these characteristics were allowed to continue to grow from initial genesis, because of their value to meet outside culture where it was in mission. This is despite the clear ongoing modernistic emphases in the Movement which would potentially cause the opposite attitude. Secondly, *active* emphases on such postmodern characteristics to reach culture in mission, to connect to places of resonance, therein causing such characteristics to be emphasized and amplified. In a sense, the first mode acts as a restraint to digging up the postmodern characteristics growing in the field because they are identified as useful rather than being weeds, while the second mode acts to pour fertilizer on them causing them to grow further. Both models are congruent with the postmodern missional pragmatism seen in §6.1.1, as it is the pragmatic usefulness of some postmodern characteristics that cause them to be emphasized.

Evidence of the passive mode is seen in comments on the timely similarities between characteristics of the Movement and *postmodern* elements of culture—one of its two predicted manners of its operation. To repeat Morgan's comments,

> [Charismatic renewal] has made it possible to reach out to people who don't start out life with the question of "What is truth?" but start with "How do I make sense of my life?" . . . [and] "Is there any other kind of experience which will help me go somewhere?" . . . and the charismatic movement says yes, there is this other doorway.

Similarly, Millar points to experience of the Holy Spirit on Alpha as culturally resonant, and in such a context that postmodernism is "good," as it values such experience and is drawn to it. In different emphasis, Cleverly points to pragmatic elements of culture: "What people want is something that works . . . [not] on a kind of narrative level of historical truth"—proceeding to speak about how the city council in Oxford came not only to appreciate but rely on St. Aldates because of its work among the homeless as an example of this, commenting, "The Holy Spirit is on the side of the poor." A fascinating comment tying together a so far unseen aspect of charismatic renewal (social justice), and cultural pragmatism.

In this passive mode, *Cultural Catalysis* by the needs of *modernistic* elements of culture is again highlighted, the other of its two predicted manners of operation. Cray observes in a general sense how he was part of "a movement trying to follow the Holy Spirit to engage with where our culture was vulnerable, but hopefully having some roots that went deeper [than culture's]." For Gumbel, this is more of a void than a vulnerability—a void of spirituality due to cultural secularism, which he has seen fail over his time leading Alpha, exampled by the diminishment of "New Atheists" in its small groups who once were always present. Concurring with previously explored deprivation theories,[9] he highlights "a culture that is lacking a spirituality is hungry for meaning, for purpose, to know that they're loved, for belonging—all those things which they find on Alpha."

In a second, *active*, mode of catalysis, Selvaratnam comments that in his church planting outreach, "Our initial engagement with people was

---

9. §4.1.2.2.

often consumeristic," seeking to reach consumeristic aspects of culture, so that, for example, on the church's website, "there is an initial transactional element where [it] needs to sort of say, 'this is a place you might like.... You might connect with the content.... [Y]ou owe it to yourself to check it out.'" Where this consumerism overlaps with a desire for postmodern emphases in what is desired to be "consumed" it can easily be seen how such a church is drawn to emphasize them. Similar tones are found in Gumbel's repetition of Wimber's aphorism—"The meat is on the street"—and how meeting people where they are ought to control the nature of lived-out faith. Both Gumbel and Millar highlight how constant developmental reactions to the post-course comments of Alpha guests facilitated this at HTB. Given Gumbel's comments about "the hidden gift we've received *from* Alpha"[10] and that HTB has a "big open door, which is young people coming in through Alpha," this means it is not hard to see that this approach likely subsequently shapes the wider later Movement through HTB and its networked churches. Though this might be rightly seen as an ongoing gift of a means of cultural emphases being brought into the Movement, it might also be challenged due to a manner of importing them which does not have an in-built means of weighing their theological value or implications. An open door is established without discernment mechanisms in place.[11]

Various postmodern characteristics within the Movement are emphasized in such active catalytic interfaces with culture, thereby encouraging their further growth. MacInnes broadly speaks of an emphasis on "freer" times of worship due to this dynamic, but others are much more specific: a deliberate focus on personal testimony and story (Cray), missionally pragmatic drives such as environmental action geared towards a culture that wants to see the church do something (Cleverly), shifts from emphasis on the authority of the Bible to experience of the Spirit in outreach (Gumbel). Selvaratnam gives a good case example of appealing to an anti-institutional culture in choosing to plant a church in a non-church building because older church buildings generate "a set of feelings about a building like that." In all these examples, the catalytic encouragement of postmodern characteristics is clear, even if not to those at the time.

---

10. Emphasis mine.
11. See §8.2.2.2 on potential discernment mechanisms.

Morgan and Cray take an even stronger step in this direction by indicating an active reception of, not just emphasis on, postmodern emphases from culture—through a missional interface where postmodern emphases in culture are to be actively embraced. Importantly, such reception feeds into the Movement's existing postmodern characteristics, and so is not generative of them in a *Direct Influence* manner. However, the strength of the explicit adoption of this speaks to the extent to which *Cultural Catalysis* occurs in the later Movement compared to the earlier one. For Morgan, "postmodernism has enabled and encouraged us . . . to be open to diverse experiences and to feel that that is an authentic part of being Christian." She explains that in the Movement the diversity of such experiences encouraged an ecclesiological approach that embraced the gifts of other traditions in their experiences, perhaps giving some deeper explanation to the experiential ecumenicalism seen in §3.2.2. For Cray, the "bulldozer" effect of postmodern theory upon modernistic epistemology means that "all sorts of foundationalism simply will not do philosophically anymore," helping develop novel approaches to "defending Christian truth and scripture." Cray gives an example of this through highlighting how the overcoming of "Kantian dualism"[12] in the Movement's mid-life encouraged a theology of the arts: the arts not just as a means of communication—as Watson first used them for—but rather "understandings of the faith that you only get if you approach them through the discipline of an art form."

Such later attitudes which embrace the currents of postmodernism in wider culture, and which fan into flame the Movement's pre-existent postmodern characteristics, go a long way to explaining its perceived postmodern nature today, making it understandable how some outside perspectives have viewed the Movement as an expression of postmodernism itself.[13] However, many of the postmodern characteristics catalyzed in growth by postmodern culture in this model are directly traceable to a *Mutual Origins* generation—an anti-modern not postmodern origin. For example, an experiential epistemology, first seen in §3.1.2.2, generated through reaction to church modernism, is catalyzed by missional outreach to wider culture in Gumbel's witness above. Similarly, anti-institutional attitudes seen in Harper's §5.1.2 diatribe against modernism finds cultural catalysis when it comes to Selvaratnam's above choice of where to

---

12. See §2.2.2.
13. See §1.1.1.

church plant. In such examples, the differentiated but connected pathway between generation and subsequent growth seems apparent as part of the hypothesized larger narrative of the Movement's postmodern character. In this narrative the importance of mission in the Movement, which energizes *Cultural Catalysis*, is clear; hypothetically a less missional renewal movement might have also appeared to be less postmodern as a result.

In conclusion, it is clear to see that there is abundant support for recognizing that in the later Movement the *Cultural Catalysis* model has explanative power for describing how many of the Movement's postmodern characteristics, generated through a *Mutual Origins* reaction to modernism within the church, grew into prominently observable facets of its lifeworld through the influence of surrounding culture, and further detail as to how this catalysis works in two subtly different modes (passive and active) emerges as well. However, this is to be tempered by a so far unmentioned observation: that in both David and Mary Pytches's interview responses, not a single pointer to such a model's existence in their leading of renewal can be discerned. Given their impact on the later Movement through New Wine, this gives cause for pause here. Perhaps there is variation of the model's dynamics across the Movement's churches and wider networks over time and location, with St. Andrew's Chorleywood and at least early New Wine on a minimal end of the scale where less *Cultural Catalysis* is seen, and HTB and its wider network of connected churches—with its emphasis on missional pragmatism—on a maximal end. Either way, overall, growth of this model occurs over time, as for the majority in the later Movement *Cultural Catalysis* is now clearly evident.

Two points of reflection emerge out of this that are important for answering questions as to how this model works and what lies at its heart theologically. Firstly, as evidenced in the model's passive mode of operation, it is again seen that *Cultural Catalysis* occurs through the Movement's contact not just with *postmodern* elements of surrounding culture as might be first assumed, but also through contact with *modernistic* elements as well. The former seems more obvious than the latter, postmodernism encouraging postmodernism, which in this study has been explained through sociological analyses of the consumeristic desires of wider culture in §4.1.2.3. The latter, however, has had a growing set of evidence to support it: first theorized in §4.1.2.2 as a consequence of deprivation ideas which described how modernistic cultural elements longed for something better than modernism; first evidenced in §5.1.2 in Harper's commendation of taking advantage of the "unparalleled opportunity" felt by the insufficiency of modernistic individualism; then in §5.2.2 seen in how Watson saw the Movement's emphasis on community meeting an "age of isolation" amid the more general crises of modernity in culture.[14] Seeing this again in the later Movement enables this study to now conclude that, as hypothesized, throughout the Movement's timeline *Cultural Catalysis* works through resonances with both the consumeristic desires of postmodern elements of its surrounding culture *and* with the longings of modernistic elements seeking something new, a double-catalysis in two manners. Such an analysis opens up the question as to whether other wider cultural elements might be part of *Cultural Catalysis*, for example, romantic elements that both the 1981 General Synod report and Charles Taylor highlight,[15] or maybe residual premodern elements that especially interface well with postmodern characteristics because of their strong overlap in nature.[16] Future research into these possibilities could well prove to be fruitful in understanding the Movement's growth.

A second point of reflection arises in discerning what is happening theologically within the Movement, especially in its view of culture, such that such clear manifestations of this model are seen. For example, does the active mode of *Cultural Catalysis* imply that interviewees show a theological appreciation of the value of culture to inform the Movement? Or is culture seen as theologically neutral, or even negative to the Movement's life?

Given the missional energy that impels many of the strongest forms of *Cultural Catalysis* in the later Movement, adaption of Stephen Bevans's work on contextual theology helps highlight potential answers. In *Models of Contextual Theology*,[17] Bevans elucidates six models of missiological theological engagement with culture, yet only two of these models appear to be discernible within the Movement, highlighting a neutral, and even perhaps sometimes negative, view of culture and God's work within it. In the later Movement, *Cultural Catalysis* is largely controlled by a view of culture that sees it as something to be reached with the work of God, and with a form shaped by culture in that outreach, whether in resonance

14. As *Mutual Origins* and *Cultural Catalysis* both have some interaction with the idea of modernism here, it is helpful to differentiate them afresh. In the former, the location is largely different (anti-modernism in the church as opposed to longings in wider culture) and emphasis is different (focused on genesis rather than subsequent growth).

15. §§3.3.2; 4.1.1.2.

16. See §7.2.4.

17. Bevans, *Models of Contextual Theology*.

with postmodern desires within it such as the emphasis on experiential epistemologies in Alpha, or by meeting modernistic deficiencies within it—Gumbel's secularistic "voids." This is at the heart of Bevans's "Translation" model,[18] where Christian truth needs to be translated into culture that is absent of the work of God and needs to receive it. Cray's previously seen usage of the terms "inculturation" and "contextualization" further evidences such an approach,[19] and for most of the seen *Cultural Catalysis* something like a Translation model applies, describing the Movement's theologically neutral view of culture.[20] Postmodernism in culture is at best affirmed as valuable—as in Cray's "bulldozer" comment—yet not any way of God—not "God's bulldozer."

An argument can also be made that attitudes that are more akin to Bevans's "Counter-Cultural" model can also be discerned here,[21] though to a more minor extent, and the differences may be quite subtle. Critiques of modernistic elements of wider culture, to which the Movement's lifeworld provides a winsome alternative option, exhibit negative views of culture that might indicate this. Gumbel's analysis of "a culture that is lacking a spirituality" is an example. Wider culture is not neutral here, but more negatively *deficient*—deficient in spirituality, and by implication in the work of God, not just absent of it. The church stands in direct contrast to this. John Drane, considering the controlling worldview behind the Alpha Course, argues, "a dualistic insistence on some absolute disconnection between human nature and divinity and between Gospel and culture" is "deeply embedded within the charismatic mindset"[22]—something that finds substantiation here.

In this neutral, or even negative, view of culture, postmodernism in culture is at best seen as a *felix culpa* in its resonances with the Movement's nature. Morgan here speaks of the parallels between the timing of Jesus's incarnation and ministry and that of charismatic renewal with their respective cultural contexts that enabled both their messages to "spread," but carefully not of God's precipitation of this timing. Despite the strength of parallelism between the Movement's postmodern characteristics and those of wider culture's, none of Bevans's other models, such

---

18. Bevans, *Models of Contextual Theology*, 37–53.

19. See §6.1.1.

20. See also analysis of Cray's usage of a type of Translation model in Lord, *Network Church*, 242.

21. Bevans, *Models of Contextual Theology*, 117–38.

22. Drane, "Alpha," 382.

as an Anthropological model which would see God at work in culture through the rise of postmodernism, can be seen.[23] This engenders further questions that will be explored in the next chapter, asking whether the Movement is being provoked by this study to embrace a wider and more generous view of culture and God's work within it.[24]

7.1.4 Summary

Insofar as models map the reality of the Movement's lifeworld,[25] there is a relative paucity of evidence to suggest a *Direct Influence* model at work in the later Movement. Combining this with the same being found for the early Movement in chapter 5, it is clear to see that a *Direct Influence* model does not overall provide a substantive answer to CRQ-2; the origins of the Movement's clearly seen postmodern characteristics are not found in the influence of postmodernism upon it. Though evidence indicates that it may have a minor influence in certain parts of its diverse lifeworld from its mid-life onwards, other models and dynamics are responsible.

The same paucity of evidence is not true for *Mutual Origins* and *Cultural Catalysis* models, both of which prove to be strong answers to CRQ-2. Both are evidenced in large measure in the later Movement. While in the earlier Movement only Harper's work directly exhibited evidence of a *Mutual Origins* answer to CRQ-2, there was also evidence of an anti-modern attitude in Watson's work. In the later Movement, a generative reaction to modernism in the church is clear to see across the board, seen both in specific examples of its praxis such as in biblical hermeneutics, and interpretations of specific events such as TTB. The anti-modern drive contained within this explains the prominence of *Criterion One* characteristics of the Movement noted in both parts of its life—an internal postmodern-like drive resulting in an emphasis on them, as predicted in §2.5.3.

Similarly, just as evidence for *Cultural Catalysis* was largely confined to just one of the leaders considered in the early Movement—this time Watson rather than Harper—in the later Movement evidence seen across the breadth of the Movement's life, albeit with contextual variation of strength. Evidence points to both passive and active modes of this

---

23. Bevans, *Models of Contextual Theology*, 54–69.
24. See §8.2.2.2.
25. See §1.1.2.

model's operation highlighting the nuanced way this catalysis works, and substantiates the understanding that catalysis occurs through interaction with the desires of postmodern elements of wider culture *and* with modernistic elements that find its needs met by the Movement.

A large part of the hypothesized overall narrative behind the Movement's observed postmodern character is affirmed by these results. The Movement found a large amount of impetus from an environment of frustration and spiritual dissatisfaction with the effects of modernism in the Church of England, especially in its Evangelical traditions. This dissatisfaction gave rise to searching for, and appropriating of, expressions of faith and theological praxis that were anti-modern. These look to be postmodern characteristics as in essence they had *Mutual Origins* reaction against modernism in a comparable manner to the reaction against modernism in postmodern thought. Subsequently, many of these postmodern characteristics find *Cultural Catalysis* which amplifies their prominence in the life of the Movement through its interaction with elements of its contextual culture that encourage and emphasize them, especially through its missional appeal to culture. In this missional appeal, notable extremes of postmodernistic character are seen as a result, especially the pluralistic missional pragmatism of Millar, Gumbel, and Alpha.

7.2 CRQ-3: PREMODERN RECOVERY

If, as seen above, the Movement's postmodern characteristics stem from a reaction against modernism, a *Mutual Origins* model, an important next question is where it fixes its new destination to in such a reaction, and could this explain its seeming postmodern nature as well? Interview responses affirm that a primary explanatory trajectory involves a return to premodern emphases. Many of these may look like postmodern emphases, or indeed might be understood to be both postmodern and premodern in nature simultaneously—as there are only a limited number of places one can go to in reaction against modernism in postmodern development, many of which have already been experienced in the life of the church previously across the breadth of its history. Such is corroborated through comparison to the same being found in similar movements within the Movement's lifetime, movements which also react against modernism by returning to premodern emphases.

In chapter 6, several observed postmodern characteristics indicated that a premodern recovery impulse continues to be a part of the Movement's later life. Specific examples included the reception within Alpha—via its ecumenical focus—of a Roman Catholic tradition more orientated to received Church tradition and history than charismatic tradition, the recovery of allegorical exegesis as a hermeneutical method, and the emphasis on the usage of stories to mirror Jesus's didactic methodology. Here, under CRQ-3's continued enquiry, the undergirding dynamics behind these examples become clear, augmenting what was found in the early Movement and expanding understanding of their later outworking.

7.2.1 Recovering the New Testament Church

As with Harper and Watson, several interviewees saw the focus of premodern recovery as an attempt to recover the life of the church in the NT, what Harper called "the apostolic age." Notably here, as in the earlier Movement, Old Testament Scriptures play a relatively negligible role, perhaps indicating that the Movement sometimes decontextualizes the NT, seeking to recover its life without appropriate cultural awareness and translation. Millar explains that he never sought to speak about the idea of "the so-called inverted commas charismatic movement," because "I wouldn't use that language, because it seems to me there's nothing to distinguish it from the New Testament Church, and what we are seeking to recover is the New Testament church." Here the recovery of the "New Testament church" and charismatic renewal are identical. However, for others, there is more of a nuanced overlap, with Morgan for example preferring to speak of the predominating "huge desire to recover something of the first-century church experience."

The language used to describe this recovery impulse highlights a range of nuances as to how it operates in the later Movement. For Millar, the idea was of remembrance—that in the life of the Movement, God was saying "you've forgotten about the Holy Spirit," just as he did at the Reformation to a church that had "forgotten" justification by faith. Similarly, he also uses the language of the church being "recalled to its roots" in charismatic renewal. Such language of remembrance and recall speak of a gentler and less judgmental view of recovery than Watson's earlier idea of the church being cleansed from impurities in renewal,[26] and also

---

26. §5.2.3.

Harper's "this" is not "that" of apostolic Christianity.[27] Perhaps some of the force of the earlier imagery and language of charismatic renewal here can be understood as a dialectic response to early opposition to it, as well as an attempt to communicate some of the fresh exhilaration of the newness of it, both of which in the later Movement had waned as renewal was adopted more widely across the church.

This softer tone of language is also employed when discussing the ongoing Evangelical root of such recovery—which is energized by multiple goals. Cray explains that as a "Stott-influenced word Evangelical,"[28] his charismatic experience arose from "the very element in Scripture which taught to expect the action and presence and engagement of the Holy Spirit," and thus it was "a restoration of balance," a "sequence" of discovery he saw others engage with as well. This language of restoration, perhaps paralleling that of remembrance, recovery, and recalling, is surprisingly not recovery for a primarily pragmatic end—as for his St. Michael's predecessor Watson—but for an experiential balance that reflects his desire for a holistic epistemology noted in §6.1.1—which *is* like Watson's. A different deficit was a driving thrust in MacInnes's ministry: adding to previous comments he explains that the lack of personal sanctification through former classical Evangelical engagement with Scripture testified that there was something "very much missing" from it, and the experience of the Spirit as enabled through the challenge of Scripture precipitated the type of holiness it described. For Morgan, the recovery is driven by the pragmatic missional question seen in the early Movement, examining the texts of the early church's life in a new way compared to previous Evangelical engagement, asking cross-contextual missional questions such as, "Why was this so successful with the context of Roman culture?"

In Cleverly's eyes, a desire to recover the NT church is only partially realized in the Movement's lifetime. Critiquing the charismatic movement's fixation with the book of Acts in this, he comments,

> The fact is the book of Acts is full of suffering and death and tears, separation and appalling setbacks, as well as pockets of healing and growth. So, I think the suffering, the opposition, the persecution, the courage required, are usually completely forgotten and underplayed. So, if there is a yearning for the past, it's only a partial yearn.

27. §5.1.3.
28. See §3.1.2.2.

Adding to the vocabulary of this dynamic language of "yearning," Cleverly highlights a critical issue. If there is such a desire for the NT church, it is very much filtered through other desires and contextual factors, meaning charismatic renewal has not reached its end goal in this. Cleverly additionally notes recent contextually driven attentiveness to racial reconciliation in the book of Acts by Nicky Gumbel and Justin Welby,[29] something historically neglected in the predominantly white leadership of the Movement. If such examples can be identified as partly stemming from the influence of a recovery emphasis in charismatic renewal, this shows how this is an ongoing process in the life of the Movement, and one that will perhaps recover some of the emphases Cleverly notes, as well as others not noted. Perhaps the overshadowing power of the experience of the Holy Spirit in such recovery dynamics has hidden other aspects to be recovered, which only latterly in the Movement's life have come to the surface.

7.2.2 Wider Recovery

The central focus of premodern recovery upon the NT age in the later Movement is partially supplemented with desires to recover post-biblical periods of the church's life. Some, like Watson previously, show little desire for this, while others, more like Harper, have wider appreciation; however, none of these latter interviewees are as adamant as Harper in later life about this need in the face of modernism. The evidence in the later Movement sub-divides between an actively pursued recovery of the emphases and insights of other periods, and a more passive shaping by such a desire outworking in some interviewees' personal theologies.

Both Cleverly and Morgan model that at least some of the later Movement actively seek a recovery of a wider breadth of history; yet both lament a lack of this simultaneously. Cleverly comments, "I kind of look to the past, but perhaps to slightly different parts of the past [to others]," and that such wider recovery is "probably a minority pursuit . . . but it needs to become a majority pursuit because the kind of bland sort of normal business of charismatic churches is not going to answer the deepest longings of the human heart." As an example of this, he points to his

---

29. For example, see Gumbel and Gumbel, "Day 167"; Welby, *Power of Reconciliation*, 230.

book on Christian martyrs across church history,[30] written because, "we should learn from the courage of Christians, and their past courage was the great gift that was going to be needed today." Cleverly also broadens this to cover aspects more recently lost that need to be re-found: "the moving of ancient [ethical] boundary stones [to which] we really hope and pray that, that there could be a rediscovery of things that we've sort of jettisoned without realizing how crucial to the health of our children they are." Here, in a novel manner, Cleverly intertwines the existential and ethical imperatives to call for a wider recovery emphasis in the Movement.

Morgan is also pessimistic about who is engaged in such attempts, concluding that recent charismatics "probably aren't looking to the past." As shall be shown, however, she and Cleverly are errant in the strength of such beliefs, no doubt seeking a more theory-impelled approach to this, rather than the more passive manner by which it occurs for the majority. Morgan argues that both the fact that the biblical literature is rightly viewed as having greater authority, and the effect of a postmodern culture that devalues the past, leads to an under-appropriation of the church's broader history, a "losing touch with history." Of importance here, Millar opines that in his experience of renewal, "I don't think we had the same understanding or assurance [as Wimber] that we were standing in a long tradition," and perhaps Morgan's analysis helps illuminate why Wimber's appreciation of premodern eras of church history[31] may not have necessarily transferred to the whole of the later Movement, despite his considerable influence.

As charismatic practitioners, Cleverly and Morgan put into action what they critique as missing in others. Cleverly speaks of his allegorical commentary on the Song of Songs: "I was often digging up, or uncovering, or removing the rubble from the church fathers, and from people of previous centuries who had great insights, which chimed with mine," and that when he did receive new insights from the Holy Spirit, he normatively "found them echoed in the church fathers." Here Cleverly means not just the patristic fathers, but also medieval mystics such as Bernard de Clairvaux and Richard Rolle, whom he places in the same category in expansive appreciation of the past—especially in their understanding of the Holy Spirit as the love and "kiss" of God. Similarly, Morgan

---

30. Cleverly, *Passion That Shapes Nations*.
31. See §3.4.1.2.

speaks of using the prayers of Hildegard of Bingen in leading renewal weekends praying for the coming of the Holy Spirit because they were more palatable for a non-Evangelical audience that she was ministering to, appreciating the power of them. Though Cleverly and Morgan believe themselves to be in a minority in such argued-for appreciation, their very existence as representative leaders in the later Movement may well suggest that this active wider recovery is larger than they suppose. Their independent special regard for medieval mystics may show a certain selectivity of recovery here, with charismatic emphases drawing them especially towards mystics as figures who show similar emphases, especially in their rejection of a purely scholastic approach to the God of their period in favor of a more subjective experiential one—perhaps akin to a modern charismatic rejection of a purely modernistic approach.[32]

This focused desire for a recovery from select moments in the church's history continues a journey of development seen throughout the Movement and does not arise from independent re-discoveries by Cleverly and Morgan, however. It was seen earlier how this was a strong element of Harper's thought and trajectory,[33] and also how the mid-life of the Movement was influenced by Wimber's love for earlier moments of the church's history.[34] To this can be added the influence of Michael Mitton, who as director of the partial successor to the Fountain Trust, Anglican Renewal Ministries, published work on Celtic Christianity in 1995, explaining, "as I explored the Celtic faith . . . I discovered something that I had been searching for during the past twenty years,"[35] which allowed him to weave charismatic emphases with other priorities, including Evangelical bibliocentrism and the depth of Catholic spirituality—a weave he commends to the church as a whole.[36] At a similar time, Guy Chevreau's 1994 defense of TTB, *Catch the Fire*—prefaced and commended by John Arnott and therein influential in the Movement's reception and understanding of it—helped the Movement learn how to evaluate and understand more extreme charismatic phenomena by recovering past insights helpful in defending them. Chevreau draws upon

32. For an analysis of some of the overlaps here, see Castelo, *Pentecostalism*. Such overlaps were noted earlier in the Movement, such as in Hocken, "Charismatics and Mystics."
33. §5.1.3.
34. §3.4.1.2.
35. Mitton, *Restoring the Woven Cord*, 1.
36. Mitton, *Restoring the Woven Cord*, 170.

work from across church history, including Hilary of Poitiers, Basil the Great, Augustine, and Calvin.[37] For nearly a third of the book he explores Jonathan Edwards's experience and work to show that TTB was part of "a well-trodden path,"[38] and concludes his work by expositing the thought of the relatively unknown eighth-century Syrian mystic Joseph Hazzaya.[39] It is easy to see how Mitton, Chevreau, and others help form a continuous chain of development of active premodern recovery in the Movement that Cleverly and Morgan inhabit the later part of, whereby congruently helpful periods of the past are used to bolster or augment present emphases. What is largely unseen in contrast however is moments of recovery that are used to critique and develop the Movement's thinking and praxis; active recovery is of a somewhat biased selectivity.

For most other interviewees, the desire for a wider recovery is much more a passive emphasis in their outworking of renewal and is part of its shaping, rather than a focus of its direction, which remains primarily biblically focused. Cray speaks of how he has become "much more sacramental as a result of my encounter with the Holy Spirit. . . . [M]y experience has opened me to other treasures in the church and other traditions, not just to a rediscovery of the dynamic ministry of the Holy Spirit as in the New Testament." Cray's "openness," while less intense than the active pursuit Cleverly and Morgan enjoin, highlights a wider appreciation which perhaps stems from an original NT recovery emphasis broadening, as the Movement increasingly permeated out its primarily Evangelical background in encounter with other traditions which appreciate a broader range of church history. Cray comments: "The Holy Spirit and renewal gives you a recognition of the most deeply held things of your faith and you discover that Christians of other traditions share them too."

This more passive broadening is perhaps what enables Selvaratnam to draw several direct parallels between Alpha and the practices of other times. For example, in his training on running an Alpha course, he taught how the experience of Alpha was akin to the holistic immersion into a lived community of faith found when a stranger in the Middle Ages "knocked on the door of a monastery," enabling a journey of faith that occurred over a longer period. The small group on Alpha is a band of fellow travelers on "a pilgrimage" in community with you. Overall, "Alpha is a

37. Chevreau, *Catch the Fire*, 7–10, 218–20.
38. Chevreau, *Catch the Fire*, 70–144.
39. Chevreau, *Catch the Fire*, 222–25.

relational form of evangelism, and I think the nearest historic equivalent is either a monastic model or maybe something like the Wesleyan class groups, which were incubators of explored faith." As shall be seen in the next chapter, Selvaratnam takes this type of premodern appreciation to even higher levels in his work on training church planters and medieval guilds, and such wider appreciation exemplifies how this central recovery thrust in the Movement has helped its participants appreciate a wide range of historical insights.

David Pytches, like Watson previously, brings more recent historical events into consideration. Though lamenting the "lack of material" about them that he had access to in ministry, he highlights the importance of Edward Irving and his circle of influence in nineteenth-century London, Douglas Campbell and the 1949 onwards Hebridean Revival, and the experience of his father being filled with the Holy Spirit in the Lowestoft 1921 revival. This, combined with the influence of other more recent events such as the East African revival which was seen to be important at the genesis of the Movement and Watson's charismatic journey, shows that the Movement's recovery trajectory does not need to be limited to what can be characterized as premodern in time period, but perhaps rather premodern in at least epistemology, with powerful subjective experiences of God primary in this.

This can be further seen in Pytches's testimony of his experience of "concentraciones" with the Mapuche tribe in Chile while Bishop there, wherein he experienced the power of church communities regularly coming together in camped communities to sing and worship together before returning to their churches with the overflow of their experiences in them. A forerunner inspiration for the New Wine summer conferences, he shows how premodern influence and appropriation does not just look like learning from premodern periods in Western Church history, but also from areas of the globe that have been less affected by modernism and are perhaps premodern in that sense as well. Morgan similarly testifies that her experiences in Africa on mission were instrumental in causing her "universe to be cracked open," challenging her modernistic worldview assumptions through seeing a non-modern worldview at work, enabling her to gain "freedom" from her modernistic thinking. This is an interesting contrast to the early Movement's global connections. Maiden highlights how Harper also sought to receive from global contexts in early charismatic renewal, especially through invitees to Fountain Trust conferences; however, "the modus operandi was mutual exchange. Anglican charismatics in the West would bring to the table teaching, practices, and resources, while Third World Anglicans could bring spiritual vitality lacking in the West."[40] Now, in the later Movement, teaching *and* practice flow into the West, not just out of it, because of the value of its premodern nature.

7.2.3 The Nature of Premodern Recovery

The thrust of premodern recovery seen in the early Movement continues in the later Movement, continuing a multivalent focus on the primacy of recovery of the New Testament church, but also broadening from this emphasis to embrace other premodern expressions of praxis, in both active imitation and more passive appreciation. The greater range of this story found in the later Movement perhaps indicates the wider exposure of its leaders to the breadth of church history through interactions between the Movement and other traditions in the church as it spread in and through the Church of and in England.[41]

In interview responses this recovery continues to occur in response to modernism, precipitating a going back to go forwards, whether in an Evangelical searching for missing Scriptural experiences and dynamics (MacInnes, Cray), a subsequent openness or appreciation of traditions that emphasize more premodern expressions of faith along the same trajectory (Cray, Selvaratnam), or even an attraction to traditions such as the mystical tradition that arose in a similar reaction to the prevailing conditions of the church in its age (Cleverly, Morgan). Caveating this, however, Morgan also highlights another dynamic perhaps at play. In continuance of her previously cited comment,

> We can only make sense of it by realizing that in modernism, we lost it. And so therefore, it also becomes a going back because we look for theological, logical foundation and the scriptural justification and explanation for it, and we find ourselves in the New Testament.

---

40. Maiden, *Age of the Spirit*, 205.

41. This perhaps parallels Castelo's observation of early Pentecostalism, which in manifestations of the Spirit showed "an impulse . . . to ground their experience and beliefs within the continuous story of the Christian church and not simply within first-century happenings." Castelo, *Pentecostalism*, 43.

Thus, premodern recovery is perhaps not only a response to modernism which leads to renewal experiences and subsequent praxis, but also an attempt to authenticate and justify them. Important for any new movement is the ability to authenticate its existence in terms of what has gone before, and not just to its specific birthing context but also to the wider audience it goes on to appeal to, such as is seen in charismatic renewal's spread in Britain across the denominations and traditions from a more punctiliar origin.[42]

Nonetheless, a *Mutual Origins* described reaction to modernism, leading to premodern recovery, explains how postmodern manifestations in the later Movement are often recovered premodernisms, or at least imitations of them. Ecclesial manifestations of each of the Analytic Criteria can be seen here and in the previous chapter through this mechanism: in a revival of experientialism (*Criterion One*), allegorical hermeneutical approaches (*Criterion Two*), the rhetorical importance of personal story (*Criterion Three*), and David Pytches's appropriating of an experience of premodern communalism from another part of the globe (*Criterion Four*). Though not all the observed postmodern characteristics can be directly evidenced to derive from this mechanic, further support for the importance of this recovery emphasis in explaining their origins and growth in the Movement can be seen by looking to parallel contemporaneous movements which exhibit similar dynamics in their reaction to elements of modernism, exemplifying some of the intertwined nature of postmodernism and the recovery of the past to progress forward.

7.2.4 Parallels of Premodern Recovery

The connection between the Movement's postmodern characteristics and its premodern recovery impetus in reaction to modernism finds corroborating evidence from some parallel proposals and movements, which tread some, if not all, of a similar journey. Here examples are taken from a range of areas, from proposals for postmodern theology, through to twentieth-century paleo-orthodoxy movements, to Emelio Alvarez's proposal for Pentecostal Orthodoxy. These all find commonality in a return to the past in reaction to modernity, with some showing seemingly postmodern character generated as a result.

---

42. See §3.2.2.

As early as 1981, Jürgen Habermas observed in a general sense a growing "alliance of postmodernists with premodernists" in "anti-modernity... circles of alternative culture."[43] In more specifically theological spheres, Nancey Murphy and Brad Kallenberg, noting Stephen Toulmin's proposition that modernity is a giant Ω-shaped detour,[44] explain, "We should not be surprised to discover that postmodern philosophy shares much in common with its premodern cousins (a thesis not pursued here) and that postmodern theology finds a kinship with premodern theology."[45] In the same volume of work, David Ford takes this a step further by suggesting a way forward for postmodern theology that does exactly this, calling for a reappropriation of premodern ideas, some of which are postmodern characteristics under the Analytic Criteria's gaze. Building on parallels in Jewish postmodern theology and the thought of Rowan Williams and Dietrich Bonhoeffer, he suggests a "way forward for postmodern Christian theology," where,

> Key features include the following: being deeply rooted in premodernity (especially in Scriptures and the traditions of their interpretation through commentary, theology, and *"performance" in worship* and *community living*); avoiding the modern tendency to a superiority complex with regard to what preceded it; recognizing that there is no way of avoiding the massive transformations of modernity... and that this calls for a labor of discernment and appropriation.[46]

Ford calls for discerning appropriation of numerous elements, but to note are "performance" in worship and community living, *Criteria Two* and *Three* postmodern manifestations, recovered as premodern features.

John Behr takes this impetus a step further in *The Mystery of Christ*. In its last chapter, entitled "A Premodern Faith for a Postmodern Era," he summarizes, "The approach explored in this book as 'a postmodern reappropriation of a premodern perspective,' where 'postmodern' does not mean the rejection of any claim to absolute truth, but only the rejection (or liberation from) the 'modern' claim to (its) 'truth.'"[47] In this, Behr focuses on explicating salvation history as no longer about what

---

43. Habermas, "Modernity," 14.
44. Toulmin, *Cosmopolis*, 167.
45. Murphy and Kallenberg, "Anglo-American," 39.
46. Ford, "Holy Spirit," 282 (emphasis added).
47. Behr, *Mystery of Christ*, 180–81.

objectively happened, but "rather, it is a way of seeing the scriptures and their description of the world and its history in the light of Christ—it is a *confession*."[48] Here both *Criterion Two* and *Three* emphases emerge out of an attempt to appropriate the past in reaction to the constriction of modernistic historiography, in a manner that blurs the distinction between postmodernism and a desire to recover the premodern, with the latter being a form of the former. Though the proposals of Murphy, Kallenberg, Ford, and Behr for postmodern theology are not definitive proposals, nor would it be appropriate here to evaluate them in terms of other proposed postmodern theologies, they do show strong resonances from a parallel field of study as to how the theological dynamics of premodern recovery in the Movement in reaction to modernism could lead to postmodern emphases as part of the larger hypothesized narrative behind them.

This finds further support in noting resonances in two areas much closer to the Movement's lifeworld, that of Thomas Oden and Robert Webber's paleo-Orthodox and ancient-future faith proposals to Evangelical theology in the mid-twentieth century, and Alverez's recent proposal of Pentecostal Orthodoxy. Oden describes in his theological memoir how, having become disenchanted with the promise of modernity in an analogous manner to Lyotard's analysis of the failure of the modernistic enterprise,[49] he was left asking "After modernity what?" His longing for a postmodern theological stability led to a realization that engendered a wider movement: "I recognized the reasonableness of the ancient consensual Christian tradition. It had a more reliable critical method based on historical consensus . . . it had remained surprisingly stable while passing through innumerable cultures for two millennia."[50] Elsewhere he defines this as *paleo*-orthodoxy to distinguish it from neo-orthodoxy: "The 'paleo' strata of orthodoxy is its oldest layer. For Christians, this means that which is patristic and apostolic."[51] Oden sees this as an ecumenical renewal movement,[52] and it gives extensive theological underpinning through his work.

Paralleling and complementing Oden's work, sparked by his journey towards Episcopalianism from a "Fundamentalist" background,[53] Web-

48. Behr, *Mystery of Christ*, 170.
49. Oden, *Change of Heart*, 163.
50. Oden, *Change of Heart*, 165.
51. Oden, *Rebirth of Orthodoxy*, 34.
52. Oden, *Rebirth of Orthodoxy*, 13.
53. As related in Webber, *Canterbury Trail*.

ber calls for an ancient-future faith to tread the same ground in reaction to modernism, that "the road to the future runs through the past," arguing for a recovery of classical tradition amongst Protestants that has "the power to speak to the postmodern world."[54] As unlike modernistic Evangelical innovations with no connection to the past it "allows what is primary and essential to surface."[55] Webber here, like Oden, strongly parallels the previously explored personal journey that Harper makes in reaction to aspects of modernism in the Church and her theology in seeking to come back to more ancient Christianity.[56] However, as Kenneth Stewart notes, "The theologically broad Anglicanism which Harper *fled* in search of historic Christianity is the very nexus in which Webber claimed to find it."[57] Paradoxically while Harper sought to commend his journey to a more ancient faith in reaction to some of the breadth of Anglicanism, which included more liberal orientations, Webber commends finding ancient faith within that same breadth. Such questions whether Harper could have remained in the Anglican Church if he had been willing to receive some of the riches of other, non-Evangelical, parts of it which emphasize ancient tradition, rather than flee it completely.

In *Pentecostal Orthodoxy*,[58] Alvarez argues that the same dynamic at work in paleo-orthodox movements is "presently working within segments of pentecostalism recovering the Great Tradition [and] is the work of the Spirit and that it constitutes a real phenomenon that deserves attention and identification."[59] Unlike Oden and Webber, this is a not a linear theological recovery, but rather a lived "dynamic move that considers present context, goes back, and returns to develop within a Pentecostal framework,"[60] perhaps modelling some of how this dynamic works in the Movement's lifeworld as well (as well as overlapping with the dialectic nature of this study's own methodology). Paralleling what is observed for the Movement in its premodern recovery, the "initial experience of a crisis of spiritual faith, which many Pentecostals who are recovering the Great Tradition experience, seems to be mainly with an evangelical

---

54. Webber, *Ancient-Future Time*, 11.
55. Webber, *Ancient-Future Faith*, 29.
56. See §5.1.3.
57. Stewart, *In Search*, 73.
58. Alvarez, *Pentecostal Orthodoxy*.
59. Alvarez, *Pentecostal Orthodoxy*, 42.
60. Alvarez, *Pentecostal Orthodoxy*, 54.

rationalism."[61] Alvarez exposits lived experiences of this recovery in segments of Afro-Latino Pentecostalism, adjoining its wider value, while noting the danger of simple mimicry of past tradition in it.[62]

In expositing a specific lifeworld, that of his self-defined Afro-Latino Pentecostalism, Alvarez highlights how the specific lifeworld of another Pentecostal-Charismatic movement, other than the Movement's, can operate in a mode of premodern recovery in reaction to aspects of modernism.[63] Additionally, Alvarez's work on Afro-Latino Pentecostalism shows what it looks like for a different contextualization of such an impulse to be at work—for example, the resultant emphases on clerical dress and Apostolic succession,[64] which are largely unseen in the Movement's manifestation of this impulse. This different contextualization also highlights what it looks like for a shallow mimicking recovery to be at work in a specific lifeworld, calling for a deeper more authentic recovery, provoking similar questions of what can be discerned to be shallow mimicry in some expressions of the Movement's premodern recovery, and where it needs to be led into a deeper authentic recovery if it is to be true to this part of its core identity.[65]

Though none of these contextualized examples explicitly evidence the development of specific postmodern characteristics through recovery impulses, their dynamics speak directly to the Movement's lifeworld because of their respective overlaps with it, whether its Evangelical birthing context (Oden, Webber), Anglican focus (Webber), or Pentecostal-Charismatic spirituality (Alvarez). Combined with the evidence seen from proposals for postmodern theology, they help further substantiate the evidenced hypothesis that many of the Movement's postmodern characteristics find some genesis from an anti-modern premodern recovery dynamic.

---

61. Alvarez, *Pentecostal Orthodoxy*, 78.

62. Alvarez, *Pentecostal Orthodoxy*, 100–135.

63. Of course, Alvarez can be critiqued here in his definition of an ethnically defined type of Pentecostalism that merges two ethnicities, conflating two different ethnic identities in their worshiping practice and theology.

64. Alvarez, *Pentecostal Orthodoxy*, 115, 122.

65. This is considered further in §8.2.2.2.

7.2.5 Summary

The Movement's later lifeworld exhibits the same clear answer to CRQ-3 as its earlier one: its postmodern characteristics are to be contextualized within a trajectory that looks back before the modern period to recover aspects of the church's life and practice that have been lost. Analysis of the later Movement reveals the rich nature of this.

Various ranges of recovery emerge in the later Movement, showing the natural diversification of the outworking of this impulse over time. Firstly, there is a development of a greater range of understanding as to what this impulse is. The semantic range of words used—"remembrance," "recall," "recovery," "restoration," and "yearning"—shows a diversification of ways of understanding this central imperative at the Movement's heart, nearly all of which are of softer tone than both Watson and Harper's language. This may be due to the later wider acceptance of the Movement enabling a less combative posture within its self-understanding. Secondly, there is a greater range in the areas of premodernity that are looked towards in this impulse. Though the NT church's life is still central for most, other periods of the church's history are emphasized: from patristic fathers to medieval mystics, through to revivals that though chronologically of modernity exhibit glimpses of the premodern recovery that the Movement longs for. This growth in range is no doubt encouraged by the Movement's growing contact with traditions that especially prioritize received Christian tradition, as well as perhaps a desire for a type of self-justification that roots charismatic renewal in history. Critically, however, there is an awareness of an incompleteness to this recovery, especially in its shying away from areas that are not normally seen as charismatic priorities, and a certain self-selectivity in the specific historical figures looked to that resonate with charismatic priorities—such as those of the Western mystical tradition. Finally, there is a range in how the recovery impulse outworks in practice, with some actively pursuing it as a priority, while for most it is more a passive shaping of praxis—similar to how active and passive modes were also seen in *Cultural Catalysis* in the later Movement.

Several of the Movement's postmodern manifestations highlighted by CRQ-1's enquiry can be discerned to have been partially yet clearly generated from this recovery impulse, and consideration of further evidence given by interviewees in the later Movement, combined with the analysis of several parallel and overlapping proposals and movements in the twentieth century, additionally substantiates that this premodern recovery is rightly part of the larger narrative behind the Movement's perceived postmodern nature. Many seemingly postmodern characteristics are generated by a reaction against elements of modernism in the church in a *Mutual Origins* manner, leading to a desire to recover areas of its life from before modernism—no doubt originally stemming from some of its Evangelical roots that prioritized the church's NT lifeworld, but subsequently broadening out to other parts of the church's history. Here, Toulmin's insight applies to the Movement, the postmodern and premodern converge. *Cultural Catalysis* subsequently in interplay with these dynamics grows these postmodern characteristics to become key marks of the Movement's existence in a wider cultural interaction. Though this description is complex, it makes best sense of the evidence seen in the last few chapters and represents the complexity of a reality that does not follow linear paths of single models and ideas at work.

Two further questions for future research are generated by this analysis. Firstly, how might the underlying dynamics of *Cultural Catalysis* relate to the Movement's premodern recovery impulse? For example, does a partial desire for a return to premodern times within culture in reaction to modernity catalyze this in the Movement in a manner akin to the *Cultural Catalysis* of the Movement's postmodern characteristics by postmodern cultural desires? Secondly, where has premodern recovery in the Movement been attempted but failed, either due to a surface-level attempt at mimicry rather than authentic inhabitation—as seen in Alvarez's analysis of Afro-Latino Pentecostalism—or because the continuing modernistic aspects of the Movement quench or undermine such attempts?

7.3 CONCLUSION

This chapter has provided a crucial conclusion to the investigation of the Movement's lifeworld, showing how its later life convincingly evidences ongoing contentions as to how CRQs-2 and 3 are answered. It has added vital understanding as to how postmodern characteristics seen throughout the timeline of the Movement have come to be, reaffirming the fact that overall, they are not directly generated by the *Direct Influence* of postmodernism, but rather through modes of the *Mutual Origins* model, further encouraged in growth by *Cultural Catalysis*. The direction of the anti-modernistic impulse of the *Mutual Origins* model is often directed towards premodern recovery; given that many premodern and postmodern characteristics converge, this further explains some of the strong overall postmodern character that outside observers have seen, and cements in this larger narrative behind the Movement's perceived postmodern nature.

What has been particularly important is the level of clarity and detail to these mechanisms that this chapter elucidates. Some signs of how a *Direct Influence* mechanism may be at work later in the life of the Movement are seen through a small minority of its leader's reception of postmodern ideas, yet in no way undermining the argument that this is not how its postmodern characteristics have formed overall. A *Mutual Origins* model is now seen to be strongly at work across the Movement's life, how this generates postmodern characteristics is made clear by examples of it in action being seen, and the tension of a Movement that remains modernistic in several ways yet anti-modernistic in others is further highlighted. A *Cultural Catalysis* model similarly is now seen to be strongly evidenced across the Movement's lifeworld, and active and passive modes of its action are distinguishable—in clear interaction with both postmodern and modern elements of wider culture. Additional reflection on this model's operation in the later Movement brings clarity to its theological view of culture which is further explored in the next chapter.

Elucidated granularity on the outworking of premodern recovery highlights multiple aspects of its operation in the Movement's life. The semantic range of description shows how it is understood by its leaders in a softer manner that points to a less combative posture. Relatedly the means of its outworking is distinguished between active recovery and a more passive shaping of informed praxis. The development of this impulse from its original Evangelical origins is seen by the broader range of periods of church history looked to outside the NT—yet the nature of specific periods, figures, and themes looked to highlights a selectivity that is shaped by the Movement's core renewal priorities.

The scene is now set to ask about the implications of these findings for the Movement itself, and more broadly for charismatic renewal in a postmodern context, to which this study's concluding chapter now turns.

8

Conclusion and Challenges

8.1 SUMMATIVE CONCLUSION

THE POSTMODERN NATURE OF charismatic renewal has often been posited, yet without substantiation. Part of the solution to this disparity is found through studying this question within a well-defined localized context—the Charismatic Movement in the Church of England. This study has shown that the Movement exhibits multiple postmodern characteristics throughout its lifetime, which vary in strength and nature. However, deeper analysis reveals that it is incorrect to call it a postmodern movement in a general manner. A better narrative describes how such characteristics come about through a more complex interaction with modern, anti-modern, postmodern, and premodern themes.[1] In this, there is little direct shaping of the Movement by a postmodernism that generates its postmodern characteristics; rather three other dynamics are responsible. Firstly, they are birthed through a reaction to the felt deficiencies of modernism within the church creating an anti-modern drive. Manifestations of this drive strongly overlap in nature with postmodern manifestations due to the commonality by which the latter are also generated through a reaction to modernism in the history of philosophical enquiry. Secondly,

---

1. Though it is tempting to label such a complex mix—such as the label "paramodern" that Kenneth Archer gives to the early Pentecostal movement that inhabits variously modern, premodern, and anti-modern characteristics and impulses—to do so risks the danger of covering over the nuances of the dynamics generating the Movement's mixed characteristics that are important to discern. See Archer, *Pentecostal Hermeneutic*, 33.

this anti-modern drive helps impel a sustained desire for the recovery of premodern emphases, several of which have significant similarities and overlaps with postmodern ones—as the way forward past modernism is found to be the way back to before modernism. Thirdly, the Movement's interaction with elements of its wider cultural context—especially through missional outreach to modernistic and postmodernistic elements of it—encourages the growth of these postmodern characteristics due to appealing resonances and parallels with them, amplifying their size.

These conclusions have arisen through the application of a modified version of Cartledge's Spirit-Dialectic methodology to study the Movement, driven by the enquiry of three Central Research Questions (CRQs). This journey of this is best summarized in relation to each of the CRQs.

8.1.1 CRQ-1: Postmodern Characteristics

CRQ-1 enquired as to the extent the Movement displays postmodern characteristics. Analysis in response to this question shows that while the Movement exhibits postmodern characteristics, it is inappropriate to call the Movement postmodern in either a general or absolute manner. This is corroborated by the variable nature of the Movement's postmodern characteristics over time: some like postmodern communication wax and wane; others such as anti-clericalism decrease and disappear; others such as spiritual and allegorical exegesis appear clearly only later; and still others, like missional pragmatism, increase over time. The Movement's postmodern character is variable and differs depending on which Criterion-angle it is viewed through, with neither a sense of postmodern progression nor regression over time, indicating that a more complex description of the Movement is needed.

In such a description, CRQ-1's enquiry reveals that *Criterion One* postmodern characteristics are often the most strongly exhibited characteristics across the Movement's timeline, which, as theorized in §2.5.3, suggests an internal postmodern-like drive at work to produce them. On two occasions the postmodern characteristics described under other criteria are seen to directly flow from *Criterion One* ones: *Criterion Two* subjective exegesis of Scripture in the 1981 General Synod report,[2] and

---

2. See §3.3.2.

Criterion Three emphases on personal testimony in the later Movement.[3] This identified drive is an anti-modernistic drive that generates postmodern characteristics from a changed epistemological orientation, and which lies at the heart of the *Mutual Origins* model explored under CRQ-2.

8.1.1.1 Criterion One: A Non-Foundational Epistemology

Criterion One characteristics are often the strongest and most consistently evidenced ones throughout the Movement's life. However, a lack of relativism, and consistent emphases on a rational epistemology, limits its overall *Criterion One* character. In the early Movement (chapter 5) both Harper and Watson held to the importance of a rational epistemology, yet also critiqued its dominance, as do interview responses in the later Movement (chapter 6). The most thoroughgoing alternative epistemological emphasis focuses on experiential knowledge, prized throughout the Movement's lifetime. This was clearly seen in analyzed historical events (chapter 3): the Movement's birth in a context of frustration with Evangelical hermeneutics lacking in experience of God; the Fountain Trust's experiential ecumenicalism; and the Movement's attraction to Wimber's theological system which synthesized the experiential-pragmatic and rational-theological. Deeper analysis in later chapters (chapters 5–7) confirmed what was seen in these events: the normative position of an experiential emphasis held in parallel with a rational one—even when the former is temporarily promoted above the latter by events.

Additionally, pragmatic epistemological emphases are prominent throughout. In the early Movement, Harper exhibits this generally in approach, while Watson does so especially in missiological method. In the later Movement, this pragmatism is most obviously seen in the latter sphere. Gumbel (chapter 6) is a key example, whose missional pragmatism is even stronger than Watson's. Conversely, however, emotional emphases are relatively absent in the Movement: strongly argued against by Harper and Watson, some appreciation is seen in the later Movement by interviewees, yet with concern about emotionalism.

These epistemological emphases were held in a hierarchical manner in the early Movement by Harper, while Watson combined them more in a parallelism—the only approach then evidenced in the later Movement.

3. See §6.2.3.

The locus of this epistemology consistently encompassed fresh emphasis on embodiment in a postmodern manner. Additionally, pluralistic tendencies that inhabit some postmodern epistemological character are seen in ecumenicalism for Watson, and in mission in the later Movement—especially for Gumbel who inhabits a pragmatic missional pluralism that sublimates differing theological traditions for the sake of mission.

Despite these strong manifestations, some *Criterion One* characteristics find active curtailment. This was seen in the reaction to critiques of experiential ecumenicalism that led the early Movement to re-emphasize a rational epistemology, integration of which was perhaps why Wimber's theological system was positively received in the Movement's midlife (chapter 3). Similarly, the outbreak of the "Toronto blessing" brought critique against its supra-rational nature, with considered reflection leading to an acceptance of this critique's validity. Throughout awareness is exhibited of when experiential and pragmatic emphases go too far, and limits are sought to mitigate this (chapters 5, 6). Such curtailments, added to a lack of epistemological relativism—perhaps only glimpsed in Watson's ecumenicalism—describe limits to the Movement's overall *Criterion One* character, which nonetheless is the strongest and most consistently seen.

8.1.1.2 Criterion Two: Discontinuities between Signifiers and Signified

The Movement's *Criterion Two* postmodern characteristics are overall weaker than *Criterion One* ones, and, apart from in biblical exegesis, wane over time. General Synod's 1981 report highlighted the Movement's new approach to biblical exegesis that exhibited *Criterion Two* manifestations (chapter 3). Such was argued against in the early Movement, yet by the later Movement a developed method of spiritual and allegorical exegesis is clearly seen (chapter 6). The report's observation perhaps sits midway between the two, capturing a moment of development with concern.

However, all other manifestations of this criterion wane over time. In the early Movement evidence of *Criterion Two* is partially seen in Watson's understanding of prophecy and for Harper in glossolalia (chapter 5); however, there is much less evidence in the later Movement for both (chapter 6). Watson's initial usage of postmodern communication, a strong postmodern characteristic, fades in emphasis in the later Movement, as does his understanding of the performative nature of language—something also exhibited by Harper. Throughout this study, hypothesized postmodern rhetorical calls to break with past narratives are unseen in the Movement (chapter 4). Combining this with the waning of most other manifestations, the Movement's overall weak postmodern character under *Criterion Two*'s gaze is apparent.

8.1.1.3 Criterion Three: Metanarratives and Micronarratives

Similarly, *Criterion Three* characteristics are relatively weakly seen in the Movement. However, dissimilarly, those that are exhibited are more consistently seen throughout its timeline. General Synod's report suggested that the Movement's focus on personal testimony is an aspect central to its praxis (chapter 3). Investigation of the early Movement showed that Harper had a strong emphasis on both individual and community testimony as a means of spreading and facilitating charismatic renewal (chapter 5). However, with Watson, the picture is mixed, with no comment on community narratives, and a limiting of the value of personal testimony to evangelism. In the later Movement interviewees emphasize both the importance of personal and communal testimony like Harper, yet in a relatively tamer manner (chapter 6). Confirming the General Synod report's suggestion that this focus is linked to *Criterion One* experiential emphases, this tamer emphasis on testimony is perhaps due to the later spread of initial charismatic renewal that its initial usage sought to propagate through testimony of experiences of it.

Throughout the Movement's timeline, more explicitly postmodern manifestations of *Criterion Three* fail to be seen: testimony is never raised to the importance of Christian micronarratives of faith—indeed, in the later Movement there is evidence that this possibility was guarded against; micronarratives are not related to ruptures with wider culture in postmodern impetus—though Harper touches on this; and testimonies are not seen to be stereotypically formed to fit a larger metanarrative in a postmodern manner.

8.1.1.4 Criterion Four: The Importance of Community

The Movement exhibits moments of acute postmodern character through *Criterion Four* manifestations in its timeline, yet simultaneously in juxtaposition with directly opposite tendencies. Throughout the Movement's life, importance is given to communities in a postmodern manner, finding early expression in attempts to create charismatic communal living—with mixed success (chapters 3, 5); Cray suggests their failure was due to modernizing individualizing forces, highlighting how postmodern and modernistic characteristics coexist in the Movement (chapter 7). Later, a valuing of community occurs differently, for example in Alpha table groups (chapter 6). In such communities themselves, communal interpretation was initially prized. Both Harper and Watson highlight this (chapter 6), and historically the attractiveness of Wimber's every-member ministry played into this (chapter 3). This is also seen in the later Movement, though held in a wider spectrum of strength (chapter 7).

Throughout the Movement bishops, as authority holders, are highly regarded. However, in its early life Harper—and to a similar though lesser extent Watson—launched strong attacks on regular clergy in an anti-authoritarian manner that is probably the *strongest* postmodern manifestation in the whole of the Movement's timeline (chapter 5). Nonetheless, by the later Movement this attitude disappears, indicating the priority of contextually driven factors behind it: perhaps a need to find antagonists to renewal to give it energy and an attractive subversive story.

Structurally, the Fountain Trust's initial strong emphasis against separation from denominational structures (chapter 3) is consistently reinforced throughout the Movement's life—especially with regards potential alternatives such as New Wine (chapter 6). However, a General Synod report comment on the sub-cultural creation of additional structures to Anglican ones on the local level highlights something of perceived *Criterion Four* character here (chapter 3), and indeed smaller structural changes at the local level are seen throughout the Movement's timeline in new leadership structures, becoming normative in the later Movement.

Overall, the Movement can often be described more clearly as postmodern under *Criterion Four*'s gaze compared to that of *Criterion Two* and *Three*'s—its early anti-authority emphases especially witnesses to this. Yet the variable strength of relevant manifestations indicates that the magnitude of the Movement's overall *Criterion Four* postmodern character still lies behind its *Criterion One* magnitude.

8.1.2 CRQ-2: Models of Influence

CRQ-2 examines potential models of relationship between the Movement and its wider cultural context that explain the above characteristics. Herein, little evidence is seen for a *Direct Influence* model to explain the generation of the Movement's postmodern characteristics; what evidence there is indicates the potential minor influence of postmodern philosophy and its sociological reception later in its life. Conversely, clearly evidenced is a *Mutual Origins* model which describes the characteristics' generation as part of a reaction to modernism in the church, just as postmodernism was a reaction to modernism in the philosophical realm—the parallel nature of these explaining the similarities perceived in individual postmodern characteristics. Similarly, *Cultural Catalysis* is consistently evidenced throughout the Movement's timeline, and increasingly so, such that two different modes of its operation can be later distinguished. Here, evidence indicates that the catalysis of postmodern characteristics is not just through interaction with postmodern elements of culture, but also with modernistic ones feeling their own inherent limitations.

8.1.2.1 Direct Influence

The Movement's above postmodern characteristics are unlikely to be largely generated by the *Direct Influence* of postmodernism upon it, whereby postmodern thought is directly received into the Movement through its cultural context, and thus its postmodern characteristics formed under its influence. However, such may have a minor role to play at times. This is despite General Synod's report fearing that the Movement inhabited "Christianised existentialism" (chapter 3); the actual language used, through the clarificatory insights of chapter 2, indicate that a postmodern influence was in view in this alarm.

Sociological and anthropological scholarship fails to suggest any likelihood of this model in the Movement (chapter 4). In the early Movement (chapter 5), Harper adamantly argues against any import from wider philosophical and cultural trends and thought. Though Watson showed an awareness of facets of postmodernism in the breakdown of cultural narratives, he shows no indication of drawing thought from postmodern philosophy—though showing some ability to receive it more indirectly through his adoption of postmodern communicative practices. The later Movement exhibited growth in the awareness of postmodern philosophy in some quarters, yet only a minor role for its active reception into praxis for one interviewee (chapter 6). Overall, there is little appetite or evidence for the direct reception of postmodern ideas into the Movement.

8.1.2.2 Mutual Origins

This study has consistently shown that the dynamics of a *Mutual Origins* model are the key manner through which the Movement's postmodern characteristics are generated, describing how the Movement reacts to forms of modernism in a similar fashion to the reaction to modernism found within postmodernism, causing postmodern-looking characteristics to be generated within the Movement. Therein, it illuminates an anti-modern internal drive within the Movement—the exact postmodern-*like* one that explains the strength of the Movement's *Criterion One* character. The overlap between an anti-modern trajectory and a postmodern one is strong, §§2.2–3 describing how in philosophical enquiry the latter came about through the former; hence generated anti-modern characteristics of the Movement look strongly postmodern under CRQ-1's analysis.

Sociological and anthropological insights helped establish explanative backgrounds to this (chapter 4). When applied to the Movement, the secularization thesis, and related developments of it by Berger and Taylor, highlighted the likelihood of the *Mutual Origins* model at work, as does Cox's thesis of a "Primal return" in reaction to modernism. Additionally, the anthropological conceptualization of play explains how the Movement, in some of its pentecostal-like spirituality, forms in reaction to modernism more generally, holding out hope of a broader epistemology that rejects modernistic dualisms in a return to experiential affective knowledge. Such insights also brought potential understanding to how this model's dynamics spring directly from within the life of the Movement's individual participants, stemming from embeddedness in the universe (Taylor), correlating to a longing for innate purpose and significance (Cox), expressed in playful fashion (Droogers, Vondey).

Analysis of historical events supports these theoretical predictions (chapter 3). The Movement was partly birthed out of reaction to negative aspects of modernism in both the dry formalism of the church at the time, and modernistic hermeneutics in Evangelical parts of the Church of England. Wimber's substantial influence on the mid-life of the Movement was readily received as he critiqued Enlightenment thought as the barrier to inhabiting a supernatural "biblical" worldview. Later, considered response to the events of the "Toronto Blessing" from some leaders within the Movement actively warned against the danger of Enlightenment rationalism in stopping the Spirit's work. Indeed, in anthropological perspective, the events of TTB highlighted an embodiment emphasis that was a reaction against a modernistic environment (chapter 4).

Deeper qualitative analysis of the Movement's lifeworld reveals the thoroughgoing presence of a *Mutual Origins* model throughout its timeline. Harper's work showed that the early Movement strongly exhibited a critique of modernism in the church, which charismatic priorities were to stand against, as well as the opinion that the breakdown of modernism in culture was an opportunity for charismatic renewal (chapter 5). Tempering this, however, he recognized that many of the negatives of rationalistic epistemologies arose in the church before the Enlightenment period. Additionally, his contemporary Watson, while showing some anti-modern views, did not directly connect them to the Movement. However, in the later Movement, several postmodern characteristics were directly seen to be generated in part from a reaction to prevalent modernisms, including embodied emphases, allegorical exegesis, and understandings of glossolalia (chapter 6). Additionally, clear reactions to modernism at the heart of charismatic renewal were espoused by most directly interviewed about it—interpretation of events around TTB and changed hermeneutical approaches directly confirmed to be part of this dynamic (chapter 7). While the Movement retained modernistic elements throughout its life—occasionally limiting some postmodern characteristics such as overfocuses on emotion and experience—anti-modern reactions are a key to understanding its lifeworld, clearly generating some of its postmodern characteristics. A *Mutual Origins* model is central to the overall narrative explaining the Movement's postmodern character.

8.1.2.3 *Cultural Catalysis*

Many of the Movement's postmodern characteristics, first generated through a *Mutual Origins* model, found subsequent growth through *Cultural Catalysis*; interactions between the Movement and two cultural elements, modern and postmodern, caused such characteristics to be appreciated and actively encouraged, often in the missional context. As this occurs after their initial generation, unsurprisingly more of this model is seen later in the Movement than earlier.

No signs of this model were seen in initial historical explorations of the Movement (chapter 3)—unsurprising given the relative inability of purely historical approaches to excavate cultural dynamics. However, when sociological insights are brought to bear (chapter 4), predictions of its vital explanatory contribution to the Movement's perceived postmodern nature are seen. Deprivation theories suggest catalysis through the Movement's contact with *modernistic* elements of culture and their longings, which postmodern characteristics of the Movement meet as a salve; while ideas of religious consumerism conversely suggest catalysis through contact with *postmodern* elements of culture and their desires being directly met by the Movement's postmodern characteristics.

These predictions are met in qualitative analysis of the Movement's lifeworld. In the early Movement, while Harper's work showed some initial evidence of *Cultural Catalysis* by both modern and postmodern elements of culture, Watson's work exhibited firmer evidence (chapter 5): postmodern characteristics of emphases on embodiment (*Criterion One*), postmodern communication (*Criterion Two*), and community (*Criterion Four*), were all amplified through mission to culture. Such catalysis was more widespread in the later Movement, such that it was seen in the growth of a variety of postmodern characteristics (chapter 6); it was again identified to result from missional interaction with both modern and postmodern elements of culture, and now later clearly seen to operate in two different modes—passive and active (chapter 7). Bringing these findings into conversation with contextual theology highlighted a theological neutral, if not negative, view of wider culture in the Movement.

8.1.3 CRQ-3: Premodern Recovery

CRQ-3 in essence asked the open-ended "what else" question: what else, other than the above model-based answers to CRQ-2, is important in understanding the Movement's postmodern character? What other trajectories of movement and influences, and whence do they come from? Here, early in this study, importation of postmodern character through Pentecostal influences in the Movement's genesis was both theorized as an answer (chapter 2) and then largely disproved, as was the potential of similar importation from American Episcopalian renewal (chapter 3). Instead, consistent, repeated, and building evidence is seen that a desire for premodern recovery within the Movement is a key answer to CRQ-3. In development of the *Mutual Origins* model, an anti-modernistic impulse impels a desire for the recovery of premodern emphases, many of which have significant similarities and overlaps with postmodern ones, such that the two are sometimes identical—as the way forward past modernism is found to be the way back to before it. This recovery develops from an initial NT focus to a broader recovery of the premodern life of the church and gives important explanatory power to the prevalence of postmodern characteristics in the Movement—many are premodern not postmodern in base nature.

Initial historical explorations of the Movement highlighted preliminary signs of this (chapter 3). The Movement's Evangelical birthing context reveals a desire for the recovery of NT experiences behind its seeking of renewal, notably within a biblical hermeneutic which, tired with rationalism, in anti-modern impulse sought to retrieve the past. General Synod's report helps confirm this trajectory, suggesting that the primary reason the Movement emerged was an impetus to recover the supernatural life of the NT church. Wimber's later influence on the Movement imparted both confidence in it about living the NT witness, and likely some of Wimber's own wider interest in premodern forms of faith and praxis. Sociological and anthropological analysis helped substantiate and contextualize such observations (chapter 4). Cox's thesis of a "primal" turn to a repressed primal spirituality at the heart of pentecostal-like renewal movements, generated from a reaction to modernistically controlled cultures and religions, speaks to this; and an understanding of playful spiritualities further illuminates how in reaction to modernism movements like the Movement enable a return to repressed premodern spiritualities.

Qualitative lifeworld analysis reveals the richness and development of this premodern recovery desire. In the early Movement (chapter 5), the primary focus of premodern recovery upon the life of the NT church is clear: Watson believed it met the breakdown of modernism in culture that brought it to a receptive state to such premodern "pure" Christianity. Similar was seen in Harper's work, but in Harper's journey toward the Antiochian Orthodox church he also commended a temporally broader desire to recover a premodern Orthodox tradition that had preserved primitive Christianity in the face of the negative effects of modernism in the wider church. This temporally broader approach was seen clearly in the later Movement, which while holding to the primacy of NT recovery, sought the praxis of other periods of Western Church history as well, from patristic to monastic to especially mystical periods (chapter 7). For some this was an active pursuit, while for most a more passive shaping of praxis. Additionally, evidence of the Movement looking to premodern praxis in the present global church indicates that not just temporal location matters here, present cross-global expressions of premodernism are valued as well.

Various "postmodern" characteristics are clearly observed to be generated through an attempted recovery of premodern praxis: in the early Movement emphases on experience (*Criterion One*) and community (*Criterion Four*); in the later Movement a pragmatic ecumenical reception of tradition into the Movement (*Criterion One*), a desire to return to premodern allegorical exegesis in reaction to modernistic hermeneutics (*Criterion Two*), and a desire to recapture Jesus's model of storytelling (*Criterion Three*). Additionally, consideration of parallel and overlapping theological proposals and movements in the twentieth century (chapter 7) supports the idea that this anti-modern premodern recovery impulse likely lies at the heart of many more of the Movement's postmodern characteristics, which are more appropriately to be understood as a retrieval of premodern praxis in various manners whereby the premodern and postmodern converge in nature. Herein, the final element of the overall narrative behind the Movement's perceived postmodern nature, which this study aimed to elucidate, is established.

Concluding these findings, it is helpful to see the identified elements of this larger narrative in action. This can be done through consideration of two separate postmodern characteristics of the Movement. The Movement's *Criterion One* experiential epistemological emphasis was first seen to be generated through a *Mutual Origins* model (§3.1), which follows a desire to recover premodern NT experiences of God according to Cray's interview responses (§7.2.1), and through *Cultural Catalysis* is amplified in size in the later Movement through missional outreach (§6.2.1). Similarly, the Movement's *Criterion Four* emphases on community finds life through a *Mutual Origins* impulse in their power to overcome modernistic individualism according to Watson (§5.2.1.4), which retrieves premodern praxis according to his contemporary Harper (§5.1.3) and later in the Movement grows in prominence through *Cultural Catalysis* in Alpha's table groups (§6.2.4). Not only can this explanative narrative be substantiated through evidence for *each* part of it, but also through tracking individual postmodern characteristics through *every* part of it.

8.2 REFLECTIONS, RECOMMENDATIONS, AND FURTHER RESEARCH

8.2.1 Reflections on Initial Observations

Returning to where this study began, its conclusions suggest that relevant commentators often probably wrongly identify charismatic renewal as postmodern in nature, and this misidentification comes from two dynamics at work in renewal. Firstly, that in a reaction against modernism, renewal charts a path to recover premodern praxis which often looks postmodern because the two strongly overlap in nature. Secondly, postmodern elements of wider culture do not generate renewal's postmodern characteristics, but they do encourage (catalyze) their growth from nascence from the above reaction, which can look like a direct generative influence from outside perspective.

This helps nuance and correct the previous observations with which this study began in §1.1. To Fernando's view that the "charismatic movement is one expression of the postmodern thirst for spiritual experience to replace dry, ultrarationalistic religion,"[4] Fernando is likely to only be partially correct. When it comes to the example of the Movement, ideas of postmodern thirst are not seen within it. Few postmodern ideas or desires drive its development. However, a better phrased "anti-modern drive" that reacts against "dry, ultrarationalistic religion" is clear to see. In contrast, Michael Green's more nuanced observation—"The charismatic movement has significant parallels with postmodernism and speaks powerfully to the postmodern scene"[5]—is more fully justified by this study. Such "parallels" are explained by the *Mutual Origins* model seen throughout the Movement's life, and the fact that it "speaks powerfully to the postmodern scene" is indeed a core reason certain postmodern characteristics grew in prominence through *Cultural Catalysis* in its later life. Green's intuitive observation is corroborated, and perhaps his core inhabitation of the Movement's lifeworld is part of what enabled this, unlike Fernando who speaks more from outside perspective.

---

4. Fernando, *Sharing the Truth*, 25.
5. Green, *When God Breaks In*, 136.

The potential "cause for alarm" in General Synod's 1981 report, a concern about the possibility of "a seed of the rise of the movement" being found in a "direct causal link" between the Movement and what can be later identified as postmodern cultural trends, is not warranted.[6] Throughout this study, little evidence has been seen of a *Direct Influence* model at work, so the language of a *causal* link is inappropriate. However, as seen through *Cultural Catalysis*, a link that later encouraged the growth of certain postmodern characteristics in the Movement is very appropriate to talk about and is consistently evidenced. Here Maiden's follow-on reflection that charismatic renewal "may have little to do directly with Sartre, Derrida and Foucault, but it undoubtedly reflected developing notions of authenticity from the mid-century"[7] finds mixed corroboration. Maiden is likely correct in saying there is no direct link to the postmodern philosophers Derrida and Foucault, something this study especially sought to detect in lifeworld investigations. The question of Sartre is unknown, but in a similar vein unlikely apart from Watson's knowledge of his work as seen in §5.2.2. "Notions of authenticity," are touched on in §4.1.1.2 in Taylor's work suggesting a *Mutual Origins* model. However, Taylor does not relate these to "developing notions of authenticity from the *mid-century*" but rather the residual propagation and then amplification of nineteenth-century Romanticism. Maiden perhaps needs to show greater awareness of sociological analyses like Taylor's. So too should Percy show greater nuance of understanding, who in his list of postmodern trends that charismatic renewal copies only really hits the mark with "pluralism." However, this is not, in Percy's language, a "copying," but part of a missional pragmatism generated from an expanded epistemology in reaction to the restrictions of modernistic epistemologies.

Finally, in Quebedeaux's work on the charismatic movement—which comes closest to analyzing renewal in an appropriate manner—the observation of the "non-rational" and an "Anti-Institutionalism" in surrounding culture that helped make charismatic renewal attractive is only partly corroborated.[8] The "non-rational" was seen to be an attractive *Criterion One* characteristic in *Cultural Catalysis* within the Movement, alongside other characteristics. However, "Anti-Intuitionalism" is repeatedly missing from the Movement's lifeworld when exploring potential *Criterion Four* characteristics. This study both extends the range of

6. Buchanan, *Charismatic Movement*, 41–42. See also §3.3.2.
7. Maiden, *Age of the Spirit*, 233.
8. Quebedeaux, *New Charismatics*, 181–89.

Quebedeaux's observations as to what is potentially attractive about charismatic renewal to surrounding cultural elements and challenges them.

8.2.2 Reflections on the Study

8.2.2.1 Methodological Reflections

In §1.2, Cartledge's Spirit-Dialectic methodology was selected as a suitable methodology to investigate the CRQs, under two significant modifications. The fruit of these modifications both justifies them and signposts to future research a clear avenue of potential adaptation of Cartledge's methodology in a heuristic, contextual, profitable manner.

The first modification concerned the dimensions of the lifeworld being investigated, where it was argued that there was a need to investigate the Movement's praxis over its entire timeline, as well as the present, enabling a richer understanding of the present, which is always composed of seen and unseen influences and dynamics from the past. This modified approach has paid dividends in the outcome of this study. By looking at the Movement's lifeworld historically, trajectories of movement that extend into the present have been identified. Among others: the catalyzation of postmodern characteristics through the Movement's interaction with surrounding culture through a growing missional pragmatism in some quarters of the Movement; the growing emergence of a richer premodern recovery emphasis that goes beyond the bounds of just the NT church and into other areas of church history; and the change in seeming postmodern attitude to regular clergy from the era of Watson and Harper to today.

This not only enables a richer understanding of the Movement's present but also enables an understanding of its future, as these trajectories continue to outwork into it. For example, premodern recovery in the Movement that enables future growth is likely to find broader and richer expressions. What began with the early NT Church and was seen to expand towards the recovery of the praxis of medieval mystics, monastic movements, and Celtic Christianity among others, will likely expand even further to include other helpful rediscoveries, perhaps beyond the bound of Western Christianity as Harper trailblazed.

The second modification of Cartledge's methodology involved, rather than using a pre-defined theological system, developing an appropriate theological system to investigate the Movement's lifeworld in a dialectical relationship between the two—*ecclesial postmodernism*, derived from the nature of the lifeworld investigation itself. Again, this has paid dividends, enabling the creation of a base system of ecclesial postmodern manifestations in chapter 2, which found expansion through the work of chapter 4, enabling precise categories to be formed for qualitative analysis of the Movement's lifeworld in chapters 5–7 through documentary and interview analysis. Such a methodology equipped lifeworld analysis with a specificity that enabled a comparison of postmodern characteristics along its timeline, something that would have been otherwise lacking, and equips future researchers to use this system in investigating other similar Pentecostal-Charismatic movements.

8.2.2.2 Pneumatological Reflections

In §1.2.1 it was seen that Cartledge's Spirit-Dialectic methodology drives the researcher to vital pneumatological questions to enable fruitful kingdom growth both for the researcher and the church that they are part of, based on the assumption that God is at work through the research process. Three questions enable this: "(1) what is the Holy Spirit doing in this context?; (2) how does this activity relate to the work of the Holy Spirit revealed in Scripture; (3) what is the Spirit saying to the church?"[9]

These broad questions can be simultaneously answered by bringing a key aspect of this study into conversation with the work of two theologians engaged within it, Wolfgang Vondey and Mark Cartledge himself. By considering the strong parallels between the rise of postmodernism in both philosophical fields and its cultural outworking and of the postmodern characteristics of charismatic renewal, it is argued here that the Spirit brings to the church generally, the Movement specifically, and indeed to myself as a researcher, an appreciation of God's work in culture in the playful interface between church and culture, which calls for a development of tools to discern such playful moments.

Such an idea flies in the face of central views within the Movement, which inhabits, at best, a neutral view of culture in *Translation* models of contextualization, and sometimes a more negative one, a *Counter-Cultural* model.[10] Culture is at best devoid of God's activity, or at worst against it. Scriptures that would corroborate such assessments include,

9. Cartledge, *Practical Theology*, 30.
10. See §7.1.3.

for example, the Johannine assessment that "the whole world lies in the power of the evil one" and Pauline encouragement to "not be conformed to this world"[11]—the Spirit is not at work in culture, it belongs to another power and way of thinking.

This perspective lies at the heart of Cartledge's recent work, *The Holy Spirit and Public Life*. In it, he attempts to formulate "a renewed understanding of how the Holy Spirit guides [the church's] interaction with society,"[12] and does so by mining the "Paraclete sayings" of John 14–16 to form a crucial frame of reference to help the church engage in public theology. The narrative of this frame is one of a clash of worldviews,[13] and indeed a conflict rooted in the "*conflict* with the world that is presupposed in John's Gospel."[14] In this conflict context, "just as the Spirit brokers a relationship between the disciples and the Trinity after Christ's departure, so the church brokers a relationship between Christ and the world by means of the Spirit."[15]

Though Cartledge shows awareness of *Translation* model approaches in his view that in Public theology "theological language needs translation in order to be understood,"[16] and also awareness of the correlational approaches of Paul Tillich and David Tracy,[17] the underlying approach is of a negative assessment of the possibility of God's work in culture and society (which Cartledge seems to combine in the Johannine usage of the word "world")[18]—as found in *Counter-Cultural* models. Though he encourages the church to neither be subordinate nor superordinate to society, but to "walk alongside it,"[19] simultaneously he tellingly warns, "There is always a critical distance between the world of the Spirit and human activity (call it a 'Barthian moment'!). This critical distance is something that disciples of Christ need to discern and cultivate through self-critical awareness."[20] Though later in his work Cartledge exhibits a more positive appreciation of God's work in the wider renewal of creation—which the

---

11. 1 John 5:19; Rom 12:2.
12. Cartledge, *Holy Spirit*, 3.
13. Cartledge, *Holy Spirit*, 28.
14. Cartledge, *Holy Spirit*, 32.
15. Cartledge, *Holy Spirit*, 37.
16. Cartledge, *Holy Spirit*, 6.
17. Cartledge, *Holy Spirit*, 7.
18. Cartledge, *Holy Spirit*, 3.
19. Cartledge, *Holy Spirit*, 21.
20. Cartledge, *Holy Spirit*, 39.

church is called to attend to—he leaves open the question of how his more negative assessment of culture fits within this view.[21]

In this analysis, Cartledge self-identifies as an "Anglican priest, shaped by the tradition and worshiping practices of the Church of England, yet influenced also by Pentecostal and charismatic spirituality . . . deeply rooted in Anglican theology and liturgy, especially its Evangelical tradition."[22] It is perhaps therefore not unreasonable to say that Cartledge acts as recent academic representation of the Movement's axiomatic view that precludes the Spirit's work in culture apart from the church.

However, such perhaps does not pay sufficient attention to the work of the Spirit in culture, as adduced from this study's results. If the Holy Spirit can be said to have been at work in the Movement to bring it past its limiting and frustrating modernistic heritage to more postmodern emphases, and if wider culture also witnessed a movement along a similar path—as the *Mutual Origins* model describes—then could not the same agent within culture perhaps be ascribed to be at work as is in the church to this end, the Holy Spirit? Perhaps even that culture was being prepared for the church's charismatic life as a fuller more winsome experience of God through a convergence of journeys?

A contrast to Cartledge's approach is found in Vondey's previously considered work, *Beyond Pentecostalism*, which critiques ecclesiologies that place the Church as a subject and culture as an object in missionary endeavor as formulated within a Christendom understand of ecclesial structure and identity, where "church and culture are seen as two distinct realms, and it is their association and integration that is presented as the chief problem. Ecclesiology is the subject but not the object of consideration."[23] This is how many of the interviewees viewed the relationship between church and culture.[24] For Vondey, the rise of a Classical Pentecostalism, which in being event and movement-orientated does not fit a standardized Christendom narrative of ecclesiological development of history and tradition, highlights the insufficiencies of such Christendom ecclesiology[25] and the need for a post-Christendom one where there is a greater understanding of "the theological identity and

21. Cartledge, *Holy Spirit*, 67–68.
22. Cartledge, *Holy Spirit*, 10.
23. Vondey, *Beyond Pentecostalism*, 159.
24. And arguably an axiom of this study's analysis of them in using Bevans's models in §7.1.3.
25. Vondey, *Beyond Pentecostalism*, 150–58.

role of culture."[26] By considering various global pentecostalisms, he sees ecclesiologies that have developed to recognize "the Holy Spirit is seen as present not only in the church but in some way also in the environments of cultures, societies, and religions,"[27] and thus it is appropriate to reverse the previous orientation such that the Church can be seen as object and culture as the subject of post-Christendom ecclesiology.[28]

In this approach Vondey recognizes the dangers of syncretism such that "the Christian community seeks cultural relevance at the cost of theological commitment," and therefore calls for "spiritual discernment as an ecclesiological tool . . . located both in the church directed toward culture and in the culture directed toward the church."[29] Vondey perceives such as possible e through Amos Yong's idea of discernment as both a gift of the Spirit and attention to the world such that it occurs in "the interplay of church and world."[30] The ecclesiological implications of this approach are expanded through Suurmond's notion of play,[31] which he says proposes "that the structures of the church should be seen as the movement of the Spirit where the world is brought into relationship with God and the faithful," such that "Pentecostals recognize the play of Word and Spirit also outside of the churches in other cultures and religions, abolishing the divisions between holy and worldly, church and culture." Here, "the discernment of these encounters is not performed by the church on the world" but comes through an engagement between church and world in a playful attitude that interacts with ethical demands and concrete situations anew in each situation.[32]

The application of such an approach to the Movement could be profound. Given the observed significant parallels between the Movement and postmodern elements of culture, could they be viewed as the work of the Holy Spirit to bring about a church as an object in an interface with culture, with the fulfilment of the Spirit's work in culture as the subject

---

26. Vondey, *Beyond Pentecostalism*, 158.

27. Vondey, *Beyond Pentecostalism*, 165.

28. Vondey could be described to inhabit something of Bevans's Anthropological model where God sets his agenda by his work in culture, or at least a Synthetic model that includes this emphasis, as opposed to Cartledge's inhabitation of a Counter-Cultural model. See Bevans, *Models of Contextual Theology*, 54–69, 88–102, 117–38.

29. Vondey, *Beyond Pentecostalism*, 165.

30. Vondey, *Beyond Pentecostalism*, 167.

31. See §4.2.1.

32. Vondey, *Beyond Pentecostalism*, 168.

of said interface?[33] The Movement, which, as seen, exhibits postmodern character in combination with continuing modernistic character, does indeed seem to be the exact right fit for a general culture that also contains both in its makeup as well.[34] Discernment of the specific works of the Spirit in this uniting work could be safeguarded in this playful interface, yet not through constriction to a universal paradigm, but through playful discernment in a case-by-case basis for each one of the postmodern characteristics and points of contact discerned under CRQ-1 in this interface.

Such a playful interface and discernment might be seen in Scripture by moving away from the Johannine framing texts that Cartledge looks to and instead looking to an example of the interface between Christian faith and Athenian culture seen in Acts 17:16–33, which helps recognize less of a polarity in the locus of God's work. A possible reading here is that Paul recognizes God's work in Athenian history and culture, pointing to a historical artefact embedded in it (v. 23) and recognizing native philosophy (v. 28) as not just "points of contact" but perhaps also the prevenient work of God by the Spirit.[35] Such things are to be understood in the context of recognizing God's prevenient work that "allotted the times of their existence and the boundaries of the places where they would live, so that they would search for God and perhaps grope for him and find him" (vv. 26b–27). The result of this playful interface, which engages his audience's imagination in a novel way, is that Paul is enabled to present the coming of Christ as the fulfilment of this work of witness (vv. 29–31) on their cultural ground, drawing some into the community of faith (v. 34).

Vondey's argument poses the question as to whether churches of the Movement, stirred by the postmodern resonances seen in this study, might be challenged to inhabit a more expansive ecclesiology and pneumatology which sees possibilities of the Spirit at work in both the church and culture simultaneously for the sake of Christ's purposes for the latter?

33. This could be seen as part of the true "escapism" the Movement is enabled to offer to the world to experience the reality of God, which Jaichandran and Madhav were seen to describe in §2.5.1.

34. Its premodern characteristics perhaps similarly resonate, though this has not been explored within the bounds of this study.

35. Keener recognizes that Paul probably quotes from the writings of Epimenides and Aratus out of their original contexts. Following the line of argument here, this could tantalizingly suggest Paul's recognition of divine self-revelation puncturing these philosophical traditions despite themselves. Keener, *Acts*, 3:2657–64.

A work to be discerned on a case-by-case basis? Perhaps a key challenge the Spirit issues from amid this study.

For the Movement to inhabit this paradigm, further work on how case-by-case discernment might be achieved is needed to give security to such a new approach. Vondey highlights Yong's work here, and his argument that the best context for discernment of the church community is through engagement with the public square where all voices (including that of other faiths) can be invited into the situation seems logical, due to the need to look at discernment through both directions of the church-culture interface if it is to be serious to the possibility of God's work in the totality of culture as subject and church as object.[36] However, this may be too far a leap for many in the Movement. A stepping stone towards this may be to instead first concentrate on developing specific analytic tools to discern God's work in culture which discern movements in culture towards Kingdom of God ideals, seen as potential ripple effects of the Spirit at work in this interface. Yong's suggestion that the hermeneutics of culture requires the incorporation of all humanistic and anthropological sciences is again perhaps a logical yet too large a step in the development of such tools.[37] Instead, taking Acts 17 as a possible starting model, first steps might involve developing tools to discern the Spirit's action, especially in philosophical and historical movements and events, noting moments of radical change and/or discontinuity, asking whether they have upon them the fingerprints of the Spirit's action through conversation with the Movement's own experiences of change and discontinuity in its birth and subsequent growth.

8.2.3 Recommendations for Renewed Praxis

This study has brought unique understanding to the nature of the Charismatic Movement in the Church of England and impels several recommendations for its continued life as a result. Such recommendations must be contextualized in the wider questions raised about the Movement's future given its now seventy-year history, its relatively successful dissemination across the breadth of the Church, and arguably a lack of clear paradigmatic events in the last twenty years. Where does it go from here? Has it lived out its life and intended purpose like other movements in

---

36. Yong, *Spirit-Word-Community*, 303.
37. Yong, *Spirit-Word-Community*, 302.

the church's history? In partial answer to some of these questions, three recommendations are made for its ongoing life to bring it further growth, purpose, and contribution for the future. Primarily directed towards the Movement, they have subsequent implications for the wider church; even if the Movement's relatively depleted momentum today means that some might not call it a "movement," such recommendations can also be framed in terms of recommendations to charismatic "tradition" in the Church of England, noting that their implementation would indeed give a sense of dynamic movement again. These recommendations are made as encouraging imperatives: *inhabit, re-form*, and *contribute*.

8.2.3.1 Inhabit an Integrated Praxis

Through this study's insights, a possibility is opened up for the Movement to inhabit its unique nature more explicitly in a self-aware manner for missional purposes. If the Movement's growth and influence are at least partially the work of the Spirit, whose nature is marked by bringing a measure of creativity,[38] then this will be a fruitful endeavor. It is a uniquely formed movement that retains many modernistic characteristics, integrates postmodern and premodern characteristics, and therein, as has been seen, often relates to its wider cultural context in a winsome manner. However, this is not a call to judiciously inhabit certain observed aspects, such as its richer epistemology or emphasis on premodern recovery, but to inhabit in an integrative holistic manner the multiple aspects of its nature, which this study helps the Movement to identify.

An example of this in action can be seen in Selvaratnam's *The Craft of Church Planting: Exploring the Lost Wisdom of Apprenticeship*, published shortly after his interview for this study. Within its thesis on how to train church planters, Selvaratnam models nearly the entire spectrum of this study's findings, showing postmodern character under every criterion, motivation through a *Mutual Origins* dynamic, and an emphasis on premodern recovery which develops from this.

Selvaratnam argues for a model of training church planters in apprentice guilds, arguing that his model allows for an expanded approach

---

38. This can be seen, for example, in the case of Bezalel in the OT (Exod 31:3–5). From considering this passage and others, Gutherie makes the argument that the Holy Spirit enables a creativity that augments human creativity, giving fresh and restored vision in the context of human freedom to create as unique individuals. Gutherie, *Creator Spirit*, 95–132.

to learning that goes beyond propositional and conceptual knowledge towards a holistic strategy that comes through being able to answer not just "What is important?" and "Why is this important?" but also "Is this worth doing?" and "If so, how well?"[39]—an epistemology that goes beyond the rational to incorporate pragmatic and experiential knowledge, *Criterion One* manifestations. A guild approach imparts the crucial structure for church planting, enabling creativity that goes beyond stereotypical concepts of it—such as art, music, and drama—to incorporate other communicative activities;[40] resonances with Watson's *Criterion Two* communicative practices abound, rooted in mentor-apprentice relationship in guilds which enable transfer of "tacit knowledge . . . information that is difficult to pass to another person using writing or verbal communication . . . because tacit knowledge is located within the relationship between people."[41] The personal stories and experiences of mentors come to the fore in a *Criterion Three* manner as "knowledge is context-specific and based upon creative experience and the experimentation of the mentor."[42] Such guilds enable learning through a community of practice, a structure that he contrasts with traditional theological training institutions in a *Criterion Four* mood, emphasizing communal discernment and learning "through an understanding of training that focuses more on learning than institutional instruction, and learning from a social rather than cognitive perspective."[43]

These postmodern characteristics are motivated by a strong reaction against a modernistic model of church and training in a *Mutual Origins* dynamic. He sets his thesis in juxtaposition with a declining Church of England in need of renewal—though his solution is not charismatic renewal, but rather "to renew the craft of church planting to release a fresh phase of mission innovation and growth that will renew the church and birth new churches."[44] This is in contrast to "modern methods for training leaders [which] have been significantly shaped by industrial and post-industrial organizational worldviews," while, "by contrast, the

---

39. Selvaratnam, *Craft of Church Planting*, 86.
40. Selvaratnam, *Craft of Church Planting*, 151.
41. Selvaratnam, *Craft of Church Planting*, 92.
42. Selvaratnam, *Craft of Church Planting*, 134.
43. Selvaratnam, *Craft of Church Planting*, 90.
44. Selvaratnam, *Craft of Church Planting*, 185.

craft model is in close harmony with the organic metaphors of the New Testament."[45]

This premodern recovery of a non-modernistic methodology is not just restricted to the NT. Selvaratnam throughout calls for a recovery of another period: "For approximately 700 years, spanning the High and Late Middle Ages occupational guilds were the most important example of apprentice-style training in England."[46] His great hope is "as the Church continues to rediscover the ancient practices of starting and revitalizing Christian communities, the ministry of the church planter will become a more common and normal form of ministry."[47] Here it might be critiqued that such a guild approach originally gave way to the modernistic university approach for good reason, especially in the latter's ability to further knowledge through academic research. However, his argument still holds valuable insights in practice, and issues a challenge to church planting training today.

This integration of aspects of elements of nearly all the observed conclusions of this study, by a practitioner and leader within the later Movement, shows the potential of what can happen when its postmodern characteristics, and the impulses behind them, combine. For Selvaratnam this occurs intuitively—he writes from deep inhabitation of the Movement's lifeworld. However, here, explicitly identifying underlying dynamics in Selvaratnam's work enables other practitioners not only to build on his work in a manner congruent with its essential inspiration but also to be inspired to apply a similar integrated approach to other areas in a manner that keeps with the grain of the Spirit's work in the Movement. For example, what might a similarly constructed approach look like for urban estate evangelism, for enacting creation concern, or for a whole range of other areas of mission today? If, as has been argued above, the Spirit has been simultaneously at work both in the Movement and wider culture to precipitate a vital meeting point between the two in postmodern resonances, then attempts to reformulate church mission around the work of the Spirit to this end continues the trajectory of this work and reaps its full missional benefits.

---

45. Selvaratnam, *Craft of Church Planting*, 167–68.
46. Selvaratnam, *Craft of Church Planting*, 71.
47. Selvaratnam, *Craft of Church Planting*, 173.

8.2.3.2 *Theologically Re-form Praxis*

A key facet of the Movement's nature observed throughout its timeline is how much it has been led by events and experiences rather than theological discovery, innovation, and reflection. Chapter 3 showed historically how the latter aspect, important to many in the Movement, often lagged behind and had to play catch-up with the former.[48] A consequence of this is that there are specific aspects of praxis in the Movement identified in this study that require greater theological reflection and critique to ensure safe and continued effective praxis, and there is a call issued to the Movement herein. This is not a call to grand theological "reform," but rather to "re-form" these aspects: to not lose their value in a drastic theological reformation, but to see them formed afresh with deeper theological awareness. This is a different response to Smail's 1990s lament of "a movement in desperate need of a theology,"[49] rather an encouragement to deeper informed theological exposition and formation in some key practices and assumptions. From what this study has seen two clear examples of this need can be readily identified.

Firstly, the Movement's pluralistic missional pragmatism. First seen with Watson,[50] this is seen most clearly in the later missional approaches of Millar, Gumbel, and HTB/Alpha. A pragmatic embrace of multiple traditions and labels, all with their own valuable truths, seeks to negate any conflict between their inherent theologies for the sake of the adoption of Alpha as wide across the church as possible. This approach translates downwards to the table groups on Alpha, which are places where multiple and competing truths are encouraged to be aired and posited for the sake of missional progress.[51]

This approach has had obvious fruitfulness. However, as noted, it can lead to unsatisfying lowest common denominator theologies that are destined to cause problems when key divisive issues, which previously had been sublimated into a silence that enabled pragmatic unity, raise their head. An example is seen in Atherstone's historical analysis of Alpha, which exposes how Alpha has avoided disputed topics like the sacraments from its beginning—to many an onlooker's consternation.[52] The

---

48. See especially §§3.2.3; 3.3.1; 3.4.2.
49. Smail, "Cross," 49.
50. See §5.2.1.1.
51. See §6.1.1.
52. Atherstone, *Repackaging Christianity*, 147–48.

issue is seen clearest in Alpha's handling of human sexuality. Atherstone notes how the 1994 version of *Searching Issues*, a companion resource book for Alpha, included a chapter on "What is the Christian attitude to human sexuality," "under the assumption that it was possible to describe "*the* Christian attitude," but within a decade any broad consensus among the churches had disappeared, in the Anglo-American world at least."[53] This resulted in first the softening and shrinking of the content in this section in subsequent editions of the book, before eventual deletion of sections on both homosexuality and sex before marriage in the 2013 edition.[54] It is unsurprising, therefore, to find that churches within the HTB network, heavily shaped by Alpha, significantly struggle when trying to deal with questions this area of Christian discipleship raises, most notably (relatively) recently at St. Luke's Church, Kentish Town.[55] A pragmatic missional silence serves to harm rather than help, and questions remain as to how silence will affect the whole network in the context of *Living in Love and Faith*, whose conclusions are being implemented across the Church of England at the time of writing. Much remedial work needs to be done to reintegrate theological understanding into current praxis to avoid wide-scale instances of what was seen at St. Luke's. Failure to do so will not serve LGBTQI+ Christians within such churches wondering what is believed about them in those churches, nor the wider ecumenical unity that HTB/Alpha seeks to maintain for the sake of mission. This takes even more importance given the recent decision of several key leaders within the HTB network, including HTB's last and present vicars, to sign—in personal capacity alone—multiple letters issued by "The Alliance" organization strongly opposing proposals and developments perceived to go against more traditional views of human sexuality.[56]

A second area where theological re-forming is called for is in the Movement's recovery of premodern forms of spirituality and practice. Consideration of Alvarez's work highlighted the danger of mixed motivations when retrieving and recovering ancient practice: that of "mimicry" rather than authentic contextual inhabitation.[57] Deeper theological embeddedness is needed so that such recovered practices are neither

53. Atherstone, *Repackaging Christianity*, 183.
54. Atherstone, *Repackaging Christianity*, 185.
55. Williams, "After Coming Out."
56. Alliance, "Letters."
57. §7.2.4.

shallow nor temporary fads but are deeply inhabited and re-appropriated contextually.

A positive example of this in practice can be seen in the attempted recovery of "Lectio Divina" as a way of reading, meditating upon, and praying Scripture. For several years in the charismatic context, it has been adopted as an exciting new but ancient practice.[58] More recently Pete Greig, the cofounder of 24-7 Prayer International and former Director of Prayer for Alpha and HTB, has written extensively on it, appearing to heed critical voices that lament surface-level recovery of its practice. Raymond Studzinski laments in his work on the practice: "This tool cannot simply be extracted from the centuries when it was first developed and appropriated without some critical awareness and sensitivity,"[59] something Greig seems to understand to a certain extent. Greig shows awareness of its ancient roots, the important Benedictine context of its formation as a practice, and importantly its nebulous methodology that was only later systematized by the Carthusian Guigo II into the commonly known four steps of *lectio*, *meditatio*, *oratio*, and *contemplatio*. This leads to a remark of contextual nuance before going any further into recovering the practice: "Please note that it took six hundred years for *lectio divina* to be systematized in this way, so you shouldn't feel constrained to take Guigo's process too rigidly."[60] Greig shares how he often finds the steps are more points of reference to things that might happen in the practice, and not necessarily in a certain order, explaining, "*Lectio divina* is meant to be a delightful relational exchange, never a rigid religious straightjacket."[61]

This stands in contrast to Cleverly's teaching of it in his commentary on the Song of Songs. Published seven years prior to Greig's book, he introduces the practice mid-way through it, a "time honoured approach" which he proposes is undertaken through a simple four-step process without Greig's awareness and therefore contextual nuance in application.[62] Potentially Greig—who writes the foreword to Cleverly's book—aware of attempts to teach a simple systematized version of the practice, deliberately seeks to root his version of it deeper in its historical context

---

58. This writer was first taught a basic four-step version of it at St. Aldates Church, Oxford, in 2004.
59. Studzinski, *Reading to Live*, 18.
60. Greig, *How to Hear God*, 75–76.
61. Greig, *How to Hear God*, 76.
62. Cleverly, *Song of Songs*, 121–22.

and formation, enabling a deeper inhabitation of it, no doubt leading to a longer-lasting and more effective fruitfulness.

These examples show how the Movement ought to be challenged to pause, look at its praxis, and involve itself in theological reflection and development of it. As a largely event-to-event-based movement,[63] the lack of momentous events in recent years allows space to do this well. It can address inherent dangers in some of its more postmodern characteristics, such as in elements of its missional pragmatism,[64] and can also cultivate its fruitful inclinations to be more fruitful, as seen in Greig's work. Its cross-denominational and ecumenical relationships allow it to do this in conversation with other traditions of the church which are more theologically grounded and worked out than it, and it can take advantage of the experiential unity in the Spirit it has with others to have an openness to the voice of critical friends to help enable this.[65] This would have the added advantage of enabling charismatic renewal to be more catholic as a result in the future, more of a gift to the universal church, while losing none of its distinctiveness.

8.2.3.3 Contribute to Wider Theological Progress

Despite the above theological needs of the Movement, its observed nature also gives it a potentially unique voice to contribute to wider theological discussions. At the heart of the Movement's postmodern character is its epistemological breadth and holism; in analysis under *Criterion One*'s gaze it has been seen that while upholding a commitment to rational epistemology, it also variously incorporates experiential, pragmatic, and sometimes emotional epistemologies, in embodied contexts. This foundational root of its postmodern character offers a wider gift to the church's theology.

This can be seen through consideration of Simeon Zahl's work, *The Holy Spirit and Christian Experience*. Writing from both doctrinal and historical theological perspectives, Zahl argues, firstly, that experience cannot be excluded as a fundamental component of theological inquiry, even though "in modern Christian theology, 'experience' has often been explicitly excluded and suppressed as a legitimate dimension

---

63. See chapter 3's explanation of this.
64. See above and Morgan's and Cleverly's critiques in §6.2.1.
65. See §3.2.

of theological reflection."⁶⁶ His second claim is that the reintegration of this experiential component occurs in a pneumatological key, such that "the doctrine of the Holy Spirit thus provides compelling justification for attending to lived experience in Christian theology, and supplies a powerful theological language for engaging in such attention."⁶⁷ As Zahl's arguments outwork, he integrates consideration of experience in combination with emotional elements, "through a focus on affect and emotion, I provide fresh arguments for why issues of embodiment and subjectivity are matters of core rather than peripheral significance for Christian theology."⁶⁸ It is clear that Zahl's argument hinges on a broader theological epistemology that incorporates the rational, the experiential, and the emotional, with an embodied emphasis—*Criterion One* marks of the Movement's observed epistemology.

The outworked thrust of Zahl's argument is novel and convincing, motivating a desire for a wider application of his insights. Through a retrieval of the thought of Melanchthon, Luther, and Augustine, he shows how a pneumatologically focused exploration of the context of embodied experience and emotion enables the uncovering of more fully orbed understandings of soteriological issues. For example, he shows how such an approach solves hamartiological questions about the ongoing plausibility of the traditional Christian doctrine of sin in modern discourse and society. By expanding the concept of sin past questions of moral culpability "which have become disconnected from bodies and from experiences,"⁶⁹ he shows how past understandings of sin were "substantially about desires and feelings, not just behaviors,"⁷⁰ with the dividend of understanding that such experiences are more stable across cultures and contexts than recently supposed, "indicating that early and premodern Christian views are less implausible than has been assumed."⁷¹ Zahl similarly applies this approach to other soteriological issues, and at the end of his work he comments on possible wider applications of his methodology: "Particularly fruitful here would be the set of activities associated with the Spirit's work of supporting and guiding the mission of the church, including vocation and calling, miracles and healing, day-to-day communication

66. Zahl, *Holy Spirit*, 2.
67. Zahl, *Holy Spirit*, 3.
68. Zahl, *Holy Spirit*, 6.
69. Zahl, *Holy Spirit*, 162.
70. Zahl, *Holy Spirit*, 163.
71. Zahl, *Holy Spirit*, 234.

between God and Christians, and gifts of the Spirit like speaking in tongues."[72]

The Movement's lifeworld epistemology broadly maps the major elements of Zahl's approach, with a Spirit-focused praxis which inhabits a broader epistemology which pays attention to experiential, and at times emotional, aspects of knowledge in a bodily locus, and which is engaged in forms of premodern retrieval of praxis. Theologians and theology emerging out of the Movement would therefore be apposite, if not ideally suited, to using Zahl's insights and methodology to contribute to wider doctrinal progress, especially in the above areas he identifies, which are all within the Movement's lifeworld experiences. This is somewhat unsurprising, as Zahl recognizes that a key influence behind his argument comes from his interest in Pentecostal and charismatic theology, which he believes has unique insights to gift theological endeavor: "One significant aim of this book is to help establish conditions for a more fruitful engagement between Pentecostal and charismatic theologies and mainstream academic theology than currently tends to be elicited."[73] Zahl represents one who has allowed his charismatic interests to impel valuable theological contributions to the mainstream academy, and his example challenges the Movement to produce, or at least influence, theologians who are willing to "own" their lifeworld influences to create novel and fruitful theological insights.

The challenge to the Movement is to nurture and develop such theologians not just for its own theological re-formation, but also for wider theological contribution. Though some theologians engaged with in this study are examples of this,[74] there are relatively few making current mainstream academic contributions given the size and impact of charismatic renewal in the Church of England. Similarly, dedicated streams of theological output from the Movement, such as Anglican Renewal Ministry's *Skepsis* theological supplements, have long since disappeared. Some of this is due to its inherent nature as an event led rather than theologically driven movement, and some due to the partial sublimation of the distinct renewal movement into the wider church. Nonetheless, recognition of this is a call for a concerted effort to ameliorate this, revealing the riches and implications of the Spirit's work in its midst for others.

72. Zahl, *Holy Spirit*, 236.
73. Zahl, *Holy Spirit*, 6.
74. For example, Cartledge, Lord, and Cray.

In turn, this may well lead to a challenge from the Movement to the academy and theologians such as Zahl, calling for a greater explicit integration of lifeworld insights into academic theology—something Zahl, despite his background, seems hesitant to do. As a positive example of this, Helen Collins's recent work models a theology self-consciously done explicitly from within the Movement, which engages beyond itself, modelling this new manner of integration.[75] Encouragement for such approaches can also be taken from scholars within Pentecostalism who have increasingly contributed to wider theology in recent decades, such as Amos Yong, Wolfgang Vondey, Veli-Matti Kärkkäinen, and Frank Macchia. This additionally touches on the wider ongoing conversation about integrating doctrinal and practical theology, which Swinton argues is crucial to a full understanding of God's outworked self-revelation.[76] Perhaps theologians from the Movement can uniquely bridge the divide and integrate theological fields here.

8.2.4 Further Questions

This study's unique approach to analysis and theological reflection on the Movement's lifeworld begets several further research questions which merit future exploration. Responses to them potentially enable further avenues for renewed praxis. These questions arise from consideration of this study's methodology, the lifeworld being analyzed, and its relationship to wider contexts.

1. How might this study's findings about the Movement be augmented by further studies focused on participant ethnography and other leaders of the Movement?

2. How might this study's central question about postmodern nature, with its resultant methodology, be applied to other Pentecostal-Charismatic movements in Britain and globally? Does such application form a larger picture of the dynamics identified, showing some form of universality, or highlight the relative uniqueness of the Church of England context in this frame?

---

75. Collins, *Charismatic Christianity*, 1–5.

76. Swinton, "Empirical Research," 86–89. See also Ward, *Introducing Practical Theology*, 123–24.

3. What other elements of wider culture, apart from modern and postmodern ones, encourage the growth of the Movement's postmodern characteristics? Especially, do premodern and romantic elements add significant contributions to *Cultural Catalysis*?

4. Where has premodern recovery in the Movement been attempted but failed, either due to an attempt of mimicry rather than authentic inhabitation, or because the continuing modernistic aspects of the Movement quench or undermine such attempts? How might the Movement "try again" in these attempts in a more self-aware manner?

5. What do developed tools of discernment of the Spirit's work in both wider culture and the Movement in playful interfaces between the two look like? What might using them enable in missional endeavors that "keep in step with the Spirit"?[77]

6. How might the wider Church of England appreciate and incorporate the contributions of the Movement into its wider life and self-understanding through understanding its postmodern characteristics, building on its early reflections in its 1981 General Synod report? Could it be better equipped to reach culture as a result?

8.3 FINAL REMARKS

This study represents an original contribution to the body of Pentecostal-Charismatic research on localized charismatic movements. It has modelled a new method of analyzing such movements through consideration of postmodern characteristics and themes, thereby exposing previously hidden dynamics behind the surface of one particular movement—the Charismatic Movement in the Church of England. This has furthered the body of research on charismatic renewal in Britain, and models how such an exploration may be undertaken for other specific charismatic movements globally. It has improved previous observations about the Movement's postmodern nature, generated important recommendations for revised praxis in the Movement, and highlighted multiple areas for fruitful further study.

More generally, as well as equipping the wider theological field to ask questions of the postmodern nature of other localized

77. Gal 5:16.

Pentecostal-Charismatic movements, through this study the wider field is enabled to use the descriptor "postmodern" with greater nuance and awareness, incorporating considerations of "anti-modern" and "pre-modern" descriptors and themes into a richer description. This richer theology not only appreciates the complex nature of associated cultural currents, but also speaks better of the God who brings renewal to the church in every age in a manner befitting it.

APPENDIX 1

Ecclesial Postmodernism System

THE TRANSCONTEXTUAL SYSTEM EMPLOYED in this study, ecclesial postmodernism, is mapped by the following manifestations of the Analytic Criteria, keyed to where in this study they are identified.

CRITERION ONE: A NON-FOUNDATIONAL EPISTEMOLOGY

Manifestation	Location
Experiential Spiritual Epistemology	§2.5.2
Emotional Spiritual Epistemology	§2.5.2
Pragmatic Spiritual Epistemology	§2.5.2
Pluralism in Faith Discourse	§2.5.2
Relativism in Faith Discourse	§2.5.2
Embodied Epistemological Locus	§4.2.3.2

CRITERION TWO: DISCONTINUITIES BETWEEN SIGNIFIERS AND SIGNIFIED

Manifestation	Location
Discontinuities in Spiritual Gifts: Usage of Prophetic Language and Signs	§2.5.2; §4.2.3.1
Discontinuities in Spiritual Gifts: In Glossolalia	§2.5.2; §4.2.3.1
Spiritual and Allegorical Exegesis of Scripture	§2.5.2
Usage of Performative Language	§4.2.3.1
Postmodern Communication Methods	§5.2.1.2

CRITERION THREE: METANARRATIVES AND MICRONARRATIVES

Manifestation	Location
Authority of Personal Testimony	§2.5.2
Authority of Corporate Testimony	§2.5.2
Calls to Break with Previous Cultural Metanarratives	§4.2.2
Ritual Stereotypical Shaping of Testimonies	§4.2.3.1

CRITERION FOUR: THE IMPORTANCE OF COMMUNITY

Manifestation	Location
Emphasis on Community	§2.5.2
Communal Interpretation (Especially in Spiritual Gift Usage)	§2.5.2; §4.2.1
Suspicion of Authority	§2.5.2
De-emphasizing of Institution	§2.5.2
New Organizations and Structures	§2.5.2

APPENDIX 2

Categories for Documentary Content Analysis

CRQ investigated	Research Question	Key Categories for Analysis
CRQ-1: Postmodern Characteristics	How fully are each of the four sets of Analytic Criteria manifestations seen in the lifeworld of the Movement?	*Criterion One* - Emotional Epistemology - Experiential Epistemology - Pragmatic Epistemology - Embodied Ritual Emphasis - Relativity and Pluralism *Criterion Two* - Prophetic Language & Signs - Glossolalia and its Link to Reality - Ritual Language - Allegorical or Spiritual Biblical hermeneutics *Criterion Three* - The Importance of Personal Testimony - Corporate Narratives and Identity - Clash with Cultural Narratives *Criterion Four* - Communities & Interpretation - Networks & their Origins - Anti-Clericalism & Suspicion of Authority - Anti-Institution/Establishment - Communal Pragmatism - New Ecclesiological Structures

CRQ-2: Models of Relationship	Is there any evidence of the influence of either postmodern philosophy, or similar philosophies, upon the Movement in the period considered?	- Direct References to Philosophy/Philosophers - References to cultural beliefs - The Influence of External Thinkers or Influencers
	Is there an espoused anti-modern emphasis in the Movement, and where does this come from?	- Anti-modern Sentiments - Distrust of the Enlightenment's Fruit - Distrust Modernism in the Church
	Is there a shaping of the Movement to appeal to postmodern culture in its life as either congruent to it or fulfilling a felt lack or need? If so, is this an active or passive shaping?	- Analysis of Postmodernism's Presence and Nature in Cultural Attitudes & Thoughts. - Evangelism and Mission in Light of Postmodern Culture
CRQ-3: Premodern Recovery	Can desire for the recovery of premodern emphasis and expressions of spirituality be seen in the life of the Movement? If so, does this connect to an anti-modern sentiment or trajectory of travel?	- Exploration of Premodern Worldviews - Emphasis on Recapturing NT/OT Christianity - Valuing of Past Over Present Understanding

Bibliography

Adams, Daniel. "Toward a Theological Understanding of Postmodernism." *CrossCurrents* 47 (1997) 518-30.
Aisthorpe, Steve. *The Invisible Church: Learning from the Experiences of Churchless Christians.* Edinburgh: Saint Andrew, 2016.
Albrecht, Daniel. *Rites in the Spirit: A Ritual Approach to Pentecostal/Charismatic Spirituality.* Sheffield: Sheffield Academic, 1999.
The Alliance. "Letters." https://alliancecofe.org/letters/.
Alvarez, Emilio. *Pentecostal Orthodoxy: Toward an Ecumenism of the Spirit.* Downers Grove, IL: InterVarsity, 2022.
Anderson, Allan. *An Introduction to Pentecostalism: Global Charismatic Christianity.* 2nd ed. Cambridge: Cambridge University Press, 2014.
———. "Revising Pentecostal History in Global Perspective." In *Asian and Pentecostal: The Charismatic Face of Christianity in Asia*, edited by Allan Anderson and Edmond Tang, 147-73. London: Regnum International, 2005.
Anderson, Perry. *The Origins of Postmodernity.* London: Verso, 1998.
Archer, Kenneth. *A Pentecostal Hermeneutic for the Twenty-First Century: Spirit, Scripture, and Community.* London: T&T Clark, 2004.
Association of Vineyard Churches. "Board Report." Association of Vineyard Churches, 1995.
Atherstone, Andrew. *Repackaging Christianity: Alpha and the Building of a Global Brand.* London: Hodder Faith, 2022.
Atherstone, Andrew, et al. "Lloyd-Jones and the Charismatic Controversy." In *Engaging with Martyn Lloyd-Jones: The Life and Legacy of "the Doctor,"* edited by Andrew Atherstone and David Ceri Jones, 114-55. Nottingham: Apollos, 2011.
Atherstone, Andrew, et al. *Transatlantic Charismatic Renewal, c. 1950-2000.* Leiden: Brill, 2021.
Barling, Michael. "Editorial: Unless a Grain of Wheat Dies." *Renewal* 89 (1980) 2-3.
Barth, Karl. *Protestant Theology in the Nineteenth Century: Its Background and History.* Grand Rapids: Eerdmans, 2002.
Bauman, Zygmunt. *Intimations of Postmodernity.* London: Routledge, 1992.
———. *Liquid Modernity.* Cambridge: Polity, 2012.
Bax, Josephine. *The Good Wine: Spiritual Renewal in the Church of England.* London: Church House, 1986.
Bebbington, David. "Charismatics, Pentecostals, and Contemporary Culture." In *Transatlantic Charismatic Renewal, c. 1950-2000*, edited by Andrew Atherstone et al., 240-51. Leiden: Brill, 2021.

———. "Epilogue—Charismatics, Pentecostals, and Contemporary Culture." In *Transatlantic Charismatic Renewal, c. 1950-2000*, edited by Andrew Atherstone et al., 240-51. Leiden: Brill, 2021.

———. *Evangelicalism in Modern Britain: A History from the 1730s to the 1980s*. London: Routledge, 1993.

Beckford, James. "Religion, Modernity, and Post-Modernity." In *Religion: Contemporary Issues: The All Souls Seminars in the Sociology of Religion*, edited by Bryan Wilson, 11-23. London: Bellew, 1992.

Behr, John. *The Mystery of Christ: Life in Death*. New York: St. Vladimir's Seminary Press, 2006.

Bellah, Robert N. "New Religious Consciousness and the Crisis in Modernity." In *Varieties of Civil Religion*, by Robert N. Bellah and Phillip E. Hammond, 167-87. Eugene, OR: Wipf & Stock, 2013.

Berger, Peter L. "A Friendly Dissent from Pentecostalism." *First Things: A Monthly Journal of Religion and Public Life* 227 (2012) 45-50.

———. *The Heretical Imperative: Contemporary Possibilities of Religious Affirmation*. Garden City, NY: Anchor, 1979.

———. *The Sacred Canopy: Elements of a Sociological Theory of Religion*. Garden City, NY: Doubleday, 1969.

Best, Steven, and Douglas Kellner. *The Postmodern Turn*. New York: Guilford, 1997.

Bevans, Stephen B. "Models of Contextual Theology." *Missiology: An International Review* 13 (1985) 185-202.

———. *Models of Contextual Theology*. Rev. and expanded ed. Maryknoll, NY: Orbis, 2002.

Bialecki, Jon. "Affect Intensities and Energies in the Charismatic Language, Embodiment and Genre of a North American Movement." In *The Anthropology of Global Pentecostalism and Evangelicalism*, edited by Simon Coleman et al., 95-108. New York: New York University Press, 2015.

Blumhofer, Edith L. "Alexander Boddy and the Rise of Pentecostalism in Great Britain." *Pneuma* 8 (1986) 31-40.

Bonnington, Mark. *Patterns in Charismatic Spirituality*. Cambridge: Grove, 2007.

Bosch, David J. *Transforming Mission: Paradigm Shifts in Theology of Mission*. Maryknoll, NY: Orbis, 2011.

Boulton, Wallace. *The Impact of "Toronto": Reports from Renewal Magazine*. Crowborough: Monarch, 1995.

Bourdieu, Pierre. "Intellectual Field and Creative Project." *Social Science Information* 8 (1969) 89-119.

Bradfield, Cecil. *Neo-Pentecostalism: A Sociological Assessment*. Lanham, MD: University Press of America, 1979.

Brady, Michael, *Emotional Insight: The Epistemic Role of Emotional Experience*. Oxford: Oxford University Press, 2013.

Bray, Gerald Lewis. *The History of Christianity in Britain and Ireland: From the First Century to the Twenty-First*. Nottingham: Apollos, 2021.

Brian, Stephen. "The Alpha Course: An Analysis of Its Claim to Offer an Education Course On 'The Meaning of Life.'" PhD diss., University of Surrey, 2003.

Brown, William. "Theology in a Postmodern Culture: Implications of a Video-Dependent Society." In *The Challenge of Postmodernism: An Evangelical*

Engagement, edited by David Dockery, 158–68. 2nd ed. Grand Rapids: Baker Academic, 2001.
Bruce, Steve. *God Is Dead: Secularization in the West*. Oxford: Blackwell, 2002.
Buchanan, Colin. *The Charismatic Movement in the Church of England*. London: General Synod of the Church of England, 1981.
———. *Encountering Charismatic Worship*. Grove Worship 51. Bramcote: Grove, 1977.
———. *St. John's College Nottingham: From Northwood to Nottingham*. Nottingham: St. John's College, Nottingham, 2013.
———. *Taking the Long View: Three and a Half Decades of General Synod*. London: Church House, 2006.
———. "What Are You Doing About It?" *Renewal* 103 (1983) 26–27.
Burghardt, Gordon M. "Defining and Recognizing Play." In *The Oxford Handbook of the Development of Play*, edited by Peter Nathan and Anthony D. Pellegrini, 10–18. Oxford: Oxford University Press, 2010.
Byassee, Jason. *Northern Lights: Resurrecting Church in the North of England*. Eugene, OR: Cascade, 2020.
Caputo, John. D. *What Would Jesus Deconstruct? The Good News of Postmodernism for the Church*. The Church and Postmodern Culture. Grand Rapids: Baker Academic, 2007.
Cargal, Timothy B. "Beyond the Fundamentalist–Modernist Controversy: Pentecostals and Hermeneutics in a Postmodern Age." *Pneuma* 15 (1993) 163–87.
Cartledge, Mark. "Can Theology Be Practical? Part II: A Reflection on Renewal Methodology and the Practice of Research." *Journal of Contemporary Ministry* 3 (2017) 5–19.
———. "Charismatic Prophecy: A Definition and Description." *Journal of Pentecostal Theology* 2 (1994) 79–120.
———. *Encountering the Spirit: The Charismatic Tradition*. London: Darton, Longman, and Todd, 2006.
———. *The Holy Spirit and Public Life: Empowering Ecclesial Praxis*. Lanham, MD: Fortress Academic, 2022.
———. *The Mediation of the Spirit: Interventions in Practical Theology*. Grand Rapids: Eerdmans, 2015.
———. *Narratives and Numbers: Empirical Studies of Pentecostal and Charismatic Christianity*. Leiden: Brill, 2017.
———. "A New Via Media: Charismatics and the Church of England in the Twenty-First Century." *Anvil* 19 (2000) 271–93.
———. "Practical Theology." In *Studying Global Pentecostalism: Theories and Methods*, edited by Allan Anderson et al., 268–85. Berkeley: University of California Press, 2010.
———. *Practical Theology: Charismatic and Empirical Perspectives*. Carlisle, UK: Paternoster, 2003.
———. *Testimony in the Spirit: Rescripting Ordinary Pentecostal Theology*. Burlington: Ashgate, 2010.
———. *Testimony: Its Importance, Place, and Potential*. Cambridge: Grove, 2002.
Castelo, Daniel. *Pentecostalism as a Christian Mystical Tradition*. Grand Rapids: Eerdmans, 2017.
Catholic Herald. "Papal Preacher Says Christian Churches Are Drawing Closer Together." May 11, 2015. https://web.archive.org/web/20241002224802/https://

catholicherald.co.uk/papal-preacher-says-christian-churches-are-drawing-closer-together/.
Chevreau, Guy. *Catch the Fire: The Toronto Blessing: An Experience of Renewal and Revival*. London: Marshall Pickering, 1994.
Christianity Today. "Wimber's Wonders." Feb 9, 1998. https://www.christianitytoday.com/1998/02/wimbers-wonders/.
The Church of England. *Crockford's Clerical Directory 2016/17*. London: Church House, 2015.
———. *Mission-Shaped Church: Church Planting and Fresh Expressions of Church in a Changing Context*. London: Church House, 2004.
The Church of England, General Synod, and The Church of England, Information Office. *Report of Proceedings*. Vol. 9. London: Church Information Office, 1978.
———. *Report of Proceedings*. Vol. 13. London: Church Information Office, 1982.
Cleverly, Charlie. *The Passion That Shapes Nations*. Eastbourne: Victor, 2005.
———. *The Song of Songs: Exploring the Divine Romance*. London: Hodder and Stoughton, 2015.
Coleman, Simon. *The Globalisation of Charismatic Christianity: Spreading the Gospel of Prosperity*. Cambridge: Cambridge University Press, 2000.
———. "Materializing the Self: Words and Gifts in the Construction of Charismatic Protestant Identity." In *The Anthropology of Christianity*, edited by Fenella Cannell, 163–84. Durham, NC: Duke University Press, 2006.
———. "Voices: Presence and Prophecy in Charismatic Ritual." In *Practicing the Faith: The Ritual Life of Pentecostal-Charismatic Christians*, edited by Martin Lindhardt, 198–219. New York: Berghahn, 2011.
Collins, Helen. *Charismatic Christianity: Introducing Its Theology Through the Gifts of the Spirit*. Grand Rapids: Baker Academic, 2023.
Collins, Randall. *Interaction Ritual Chains*. Princeton: Princeton University Press, 2005.
Cox, Harvey. *Fire from Heaven: The Rise of Pentecostal Spirituality and the Reshaping of Religion in the Twenty-First Century*. Cambridge: Da Capo, 2001.
Cray, Graham. "Methods of Communication and Contextualisation." *World Evangelization (Lausanne)* 80 (1997) 14–15.
———. "On Not Knowing the End at the Beginning." *Journal of Missional Practice* 2 (2013) 1–12.
———. *Postmodern Culture and Youth Discipleship: Commitment or Looking Cool?* Pastoral Series 76. Cambridge: Grove, 1998.
Csordas, Thomas J. *Language, Charisma, and Creativity: The Ritual Life of a Religious Movement*. Berkeley: University of California Press, 1997.
Davie, Grace. "Believing Without Belonging: Is This the Future of Religion in Britain?" *Social Compass* 37 (1990) 455–69.
———. "Is Europe an Exceptional Case?" *International Review of Mission* 95 (2006) 247–58.
Davis, Richard, and W. Paul Franks. "Against a Postmodern Pentecostal Epistemology." *Philosophia Christi* 15 (2013) 383–99.
Davison, Andrew, and Alison Milbank. *For the Parish: A Critique of Fresh Expressions*. London: SCM, 2010.
Deininger, Matthias. *Global Pentecostalism: An Inquiry into the Cultural Dimensions of Globalization*. Hamburg: Anchor Academic, 2014.

Derrida, Jacques. *Of Grammatology*. Translated by Gayatri Chakravorty Spivak. Corrected ed. Baltimore: Johns Hopkins University Press, 1997.

———. *Of Spirit: Heidegger and the Question*. Translated by Geoffrey Bennington and Rachel Bowlby. Chicago: University of Chicago Press, 1989.

Derrida, Jacques, and Jean-Luc Marion. "On the Gift: A Discussion between Jacques Derrida and Jean-Luc Marion. Moderated by Richard Kearney." In *God, the Gift, and Postmodernism*, edited by John D. Caputo and Michael J. Scanlon, 54–78. Bloomington: Indiana University Press, 1999.

Dillon, Michele. *A Handbook of the Sociology of Religion*. Cambridge: Cambridge University Press, 2003.

Dingemans, Gijsbert. "Practical Theology in the Academy: A Contemporary Overview." *Journal of Religion* 76 (1996) 82–96.

Dixon, Patrick. *Signs of Revival*. Rev. ed. Eastbourne: Kingsway, 1995.

Dobbelaere, Karel, and Liliane Voyé. "From Pillar to Postmodernity: The Changing Situation of Religion in Belgium." *Sociological Analysis* 51 (1990) S1–S13.

The Doctrine Commission of the Church of England. *We Believe in God: A Report*. London: Church House, 1987.

———. *We Believe in the Holy Spirit: A Report*. London: Church House, 1991.

Drane, John. "Alpha and Evangelism in Modern and Post-Modern Settings." In *The Alpha Phenomenon: Theology, Praxis, and Challenges for Mission and Church Today*, edited by Andrew Brookes, 370–84. London: Churches Together in Britain and Ireland, 2007.

Droogers, André F. "Essentialist and Normative Approaches." In *Studying Global Pentecostalism: Theories and Methods*, edited by Allan Anderson et al., 30–50. Berkeley: University of California Press, 2010.

———. *Play and Power in Religion: Collected Essays*. Berlin: de Gruyter, 2011.

Eagleton, Terry. "Awakening from Modernity." *Times Literary Supplement*, Feb. 20, 1987.

Ecclestone, Kathryn, and Dennis Hayes. "Affect: Knowledge, Communication, Creativity, and Emotion." Beyond Current Horizons program report, 2008. https://repository.derby.ac.uk/item/9393v/affect-knowledge-communication-creativity-and-emotion.

Elliott, Esther. "Worship Time: The Journey Towards the Sacred and the Contemporary Christian Charismatic Movement in England." PhD diss., University of Nottingham, 1999.

England, Edward. *David Watson: A Portrait by His Friends*. Crowborough: Highland, 1985.

Erickson, Millard J. *Truth or Consequences: The Promise and Perils of Postmodernism*. Westmont, IL: Intervarsity, 2001.

Fernando, Ajith. *Sharing the Truth in Love: How to Relate to People of Other Faiths*. Grand Rapids: Discovery House, 2001.

Feuerbach, Ludwig. *The Essence of Christianity*. Translated by George Elliot. Buffalo: Prometheus, 1989.

Ford, David F. "Holy Spirit and Christian Spirituality." In *The Cambridge Companion to Postmodern Theology*, edited by Kevin J. Vanhoozer, 269–90. Cambridge Companions to Religion. Cambridge: Cambridge University Press, 2003.

Foster, Richard. "The Rise of the Charismatic Movement in the UK." In *Pentecostals and Charismatics in Britain: An Anthology*, edited by Joe Aldred, 23–38. London: SCM, 2019.

Foucault, Michel. *Discipline and Punish: The Birth of the Prison*. Translated by Alan Sheridan. New York: Vintage, 1995.

———. *Madness and Civilization: A History of Insanity in the Age of Reason*. Translated by Richard Howard. New York: Vintage, 1988.

———. *Power/Knowledge: Selected Interviews and Other Writings, 1972-1977*. Translated by Colin Gordon. New York: Pantheon, 1980.

The Fountain Trust. "Fountain Trust 1. Eclectics Group, 1963–1971." Calisphere, University of Southern California. https://calisphere.org/item/6f2bb319369ef5c930c9ad1d1336210f/.

———. "Fountain Trust 2. Theological Workshops. 1969–1979." University of Southern California Digital Archive. http://digitallibrary.usc.edu/cdm/ref/collection/p15799coll14/id/143903.

———. "Fountain Trust Advisory Council Minutes 1969–1979." Calisphere, University of Southern California. https://calisphere.org/item/9b145f56e503757a6f8d62c853850c7c/.

The Fountain Trust, and The Church of England Evangelical Council. "Gospel and Spirit, 1977." Calisphere, University of Southern California. https://calisphere.org/item/11a19f945237d1ea9308c526f0b17b37/.

Frestadius, Simo. *Pentecostal Rationality: Epistemology and Theological Hermeneutics in the Foursquare Tradition*. London: Bloomsbury, 2019.

Goodman, Nelson. *Ways of Worldmaking*. Indianapolis: Hackett, 1978.

Green, Michael. *Adventure of Faith: Reflections on Fifty Years of Christian Service*. London: HarperCollins, 2001.

———. "Awakening to the Reality of God." *Renewal* 53 (1981) 13–14.

———. Review of *The Charismatic Movement in the Church of England*, by Colin Buchanan. *Renewal* (1981) 20–21.

———. *When God Breaks In: Revival Can Happen Again*. London: Hodder and Stoughton, 2014.

Greig, Pete. *How to Hear God: A Simple Guide for Normal People*. Grand Rapids: Zondervan, 2022.

Grenz, Stanley J. *A Primer on Postmodernism*. Grand Rapids: Eerdmans, 1996.

———. "Ecclesiology." In *The Cambridge Companion to Postmodern Theology*, edited by Kevin J. Vanhoozer, 252–68. Cambridge Companions to Religion. Cambridge: Cambridge University Press, 2003.

———. *Renewing the Center: Evangelical Theology in a Post-Theological Era*. 2nd ed. Grand Rapids: Baker Academic, 2006.

Grenz, Stanley J., and John R. Franke. *Beyond Foundationalism: Shaping Theology in a Postmodern Context*. Louisville: Westminster John Knox, 2001.

Grossmann, Siegfried. *Stewards of God's Grace*. Exeter, UK: Paternoster, 1981.

Guardiani, Francesco. "The Postmodernity of Marshall McLuhan." *McLuhan Studies* 1 (1991) 141–62.

Guest, Mathew. *Evangelical Identity and Contemporary Culture: A Congregational Study in Innovation*. Milton Keynes, UK: Paternoster, 2007.

Gumbel, Nicky. *Questions of Life*. 4th ed. Eastbourne: Kingsway, 2003.

———. *Telling Others: The Alpha Initiative*. Eastbourne: Kingsway, 1994.

Gumbel, Nicky, and Pippa Gumbel. "Day 167: Following and Not Opposing God." https://bibleinoneyear.org/en/classic/167/.

Gunstone, John T. A. "An Anglican Evaluation." In *John Wimber: His Influence and Legacy*, edited by David Pytches, 224–36. Guildford, UK: Eagle, 1998.

———. *Greater Things Than These*. Leighton Buzzard: Faith, 1974.

———. *Meeting John Wimber*. Crowborough: Monarch, 1996.

———. *Pentecostal Anglicans*. London: Hodder and Stoughton, 1982.

———. *Signs and Wonders: The Wimber Phenomenon*. London: Daybreak, 1989.

Gutherie, Steven. *Creator Spirit: The Holy Spirit and the Art of Becoming Human*. Grand Rapids: Baker Academic, 2011.

Habermas, Jürgen. "Modernity Versus Postmodernity." Translated by Seyla Ben-Habib. *New German Critique* (1981) 3–14.

Harcourt, Paul. *Greater Things: The Story of New Wine So Far*. London: SPCK, 2019.

Harper, Jeanne. *Visited by God: The Story of Michael Harper's 48 Year-Long Ministry*. Cambridge: Aquila, 2013.

Harper, Michael. *As at the Beginning: The Twentieth Century Pentecostal Revival*. London: Hodder and Stoughton, 1965.

———. *Beauty or Ashes?* Hounslow: Hounslow, 1979.

———, ed. *Bishops' Move*. London: Hodder and Stoughton, 1978.

———. "Editorial: A Narrowing of the Divide." *Renewal* 55 (1975) 2–4.

———. "Editorial: Ministry of Encouragement." *Renewal* 19 (1969) 2–4.

———. "Editorial: Simplicity at the Centre." *Renewal* 84 (1979) 2–4.

———. *Equal and Different: Male and Female in Church and Family*. London: Hodder and Stoughton, 1994.

———. *A Faith Fulfilled*. Ben Lomond: Conciliar, 1999.

———. *Glory in the Church: A Guidebook to Christian Renewal, Advent to Whitsunday*. London: Hodder and Stoughton, 1974.

———. *Jesus the Healer*. Guildford, UK: Highland, 1992.

———. *Let My People Grow: Ministry and Leadership in the Church*. London: Hodder and Stoughton, 1977.

———. *The Love Affair*. London: Hodder and Stoughton, 1982.

———. *A New Way of Living: How the Church of the Redeemer, Houston, Found a New Life-Style*. London: Hodder and Stoughton, 1973.

———. *None Can Guess*. London: Hodder and Stoughton, 1971.

———. "The Orthodox Contribution to Christian Unity in Europe." Oct. 2002. https://web.archive.org/web/20190530075630/http://harperfoundation.com/files/The_Orthodox_contribution_to_Christian_unity_in_Europe.pdf.

———. "The Orthodox Way." https://web.archive.org/web/20190530092625/http://harperfoundation.com/files/The_Orthodox_way.pdf.

———. *Power for the Body of Christ*. Eastbourne: Kingsway, 1981.

———. *Prophecy: A Gift for the Body of Christ*. Lowestoft: Green and Company, 1964.

———. "Screwtape Returns to His Desk." https://web.archive.org/web/20190530074602/http://harperfoundation.com/files/Screwtape_returns_to_his_desk.pdf.

———. *Spiritual Warfare*. London: Hodder and Stoughton, 1970.

———. *That We May Be One*. London: Hodder and Stoughton, 1983.

———. *These Wonderful Gifts!* London: Hodder and Stoughton, 1989.

———. *This Is the Day: A Fresh Look at Christian Unity*. London: Hodder and Stoughton, 1979.

———. *The True Light: An Evangelical's Journey to Orthodoxy*. London: Hodder and Stoughton, 1997.
———. *Walk in the Spirit*. Rev. ed. Guildford, UK: Highland, 1985.
———. *You Are My Sons*. London: Hodder and Stoughton, 1979.
Harvey, David. *The Condition of Postmodernity: An Enquiry into the Origins of Cultural Change*. Cambridge: Blackwell, 1990.
Hassan, Ihab. *The Postmodern Turn: Essays in Postmodern Theory and Culture*. Columbus: Ohio State University Press, 1987.
Heard, James. "Re-Evangelising Britain? An Ethnographic Analysis and Theological Evaluation of the Alpha Course." PhD diss., King's College London, 2008.
Ho Yan Au, Connie. "Grassroots Unity and the Fountain Trust International Conferences: A Study of Ecumenism in the Charismatic Renewal." PhD diss., University of Birmingham, 2008.
Hocken, Peter. "Charismatics and Mystics." *Theological Renewal* 1 (1975) 11–17.
———. "David Pytches." In *The New International Dictionary of Pentecostal and Charismatic Movements*, edited by Stanley M. Burgess and Eduard M. Van der Maas, 1013. Grand Rapids: Zondervan, 2003.
———. "David Watson." In *The New International Dictionary of Pentecostal and Charismatic Movements*, edited by Stanley M. Burgess and Eduard M. Van der Maas, 1186. Grand Rapids: Zondervan, 2003.
———. "Fountain Trust." In *The New International Dictionary of Pentecostal and Charismatic Movements*, edited by Stanley M. Burgess and Eduard M. Van der Maas, 646. Grand Rapids: Zondervan, 2003.
———. *Streams of Renewal: The Origins and Early Development of the Charismatic Movement in Great Britain*. Rev. ed. Carlisle, UK: Paternoster, 1986.
Holland, David. "On the Volatile Relationship of Secularization and New Religious Movements: A Christian Science Case." In *Secularization and Religious Innovation in the North Atlantic World*, edited by David Hempton and Hugh McLeod, 103–20. Oxford: Oxford University Press, 2017.
Hollenweger, Walter J. *Pentecostalism: Origins and Developments Worldwide*. Peabody, MA: Hendrickson, 1997.
Howard, Roland. *Rise and Fall of the Nine O'Clock Service: A Cult Within the Church?* London: Mowbray, 1996.
HTB Church. "Leadership Conference, 2015." https://www.youtube.com/watch?v=TlR8ZrV4Hzw.
Hunt, Stephen. *The Alpha Enterprise: Evangelism in a Post-Christian Era*. Aldershot: Ashgate, 2004.
———. "The Anglican Wimberites." *Pneuma* 17 (1995) 105–18.
———. "Deprivation and Western Pentecostalism Revisited: Neo-Pentecostalism." *PentecoStudies* 1 (2002). http://glopent.net/pentecostudies/online-back-issues/2002/hunt2002-2.pdf/view.
———. "'Doing the Stuff': The Vineyard Connection." In *Charismatic Christianity: Sociological Perspectives*, edited by Stephen Hunt et al., 77–96. Basingstoke: Macmillan, 1997.
———. *History of the Charismatic Movement in Britain and the United States of America: The Pentecostal Transformation of Christianity*. New York: Mellen, 2009.
———. *Religion and Everyday Life*. London: Routledge, 2005.

Hutchinson, Mark, et al. "Introduction—The Evidence of Things Unseen: The Transatlantic Charismatic Movement in the Postwar Period." In *Transatlantic Charismatic Renewal, c. 1950-2000*, edited by Andrew Atherstone et al., 1–18. Leiden: Brill, 2021.

Huyssen, Andreas. "Mapping the Postmodern." In *The Post-Modern Reader*, edited by Charles Jencks, 40–72. London: Academy, 1992.

Huyssteen, J. Wentzel van. *Essays in Postfoundationalist Theology*. Grand Rapids: Eerdmans, 1997.

Jackson, Bill. *The Quest for the Radical Middle: A History of the Vineyard*. Cape Town: Vineyard International, 1999.

———. "A Short History of the Association of Vineyard Churches." In *Church, Identity, and Change: Theology and Denominational Structures in Unsettled Times*, edited by David Roozen and James Nieman, 132–40. Grand Rapids: Eerdmans, 2005.

Jaichandran, Rebecca, and B. D. Madhav. "Pentecostal Spirituality in a Postmodern World." *Asian Journal of Pentecostal Studies* 6 (2003) 39–61.

Kay, William K. *Apostolic Networks in Britain: New Ways of Being Church*. Milton Keynes, UK: Paternoster, 2007.

Kay, William K., and Anne E. Dyer. *European Pentecostalism: A Sociological Perspective*. Leiden: Brill, 2011.

Keener, Craig S. *Acts: An Exegetical Commentary*. 4 vols. Grand Rapids: Baker Academic, 2014.

———. *Spirit Hermeneutics: Reading Scripture in Light of Pentecost*. Grand Rapids: Eerdmans, 2016.

Komonchak, Joseph. "Theology and Culture at Mid-Century: The Example of Henri De Lubac." *Theological Studies* 51 (1990) 579–602.

Ladd, George E. *A Theology of the New Testament*. Guildford, UK: Lutterworth, 1975.

Leach, John. *Encountering Vineyard Worship*. Cambridge: Grove, 2016.

Lederle, Henry I. "Life in the Spirit and Worldview: Some Preliminary Thoughts on Understanding Reality, Faith, and Providence from a Charismatic Perspective." In *Spirit and Renewal: Essays in Honor of J. Rodman Williams*, edited by Mark W. Wilson, 22–33. Sheffield: Sheffield Academic, 1994.

———. *Theology with Spirit: The Future of the Pentecostal and Charismatic Movements in the Twenty-First Century*. Tulsa, OK: Word and Spirit, 2010.

Lindhardt, Martin. Introduction to *Practicing the Faith: The Ritual Life of Pentecostal-Charismatic Christians*, edited by Martin Lindhardt. New York: Berghahn, 2011.

———. "Narrating Religious Realities: Conversion and Testimonies in Chilean Pentecostalism." *Suomen Antropologi* 34 (2009) 25–43.

Lings, George, and Paul Perkin. *Dynasty Or Diversity? The HTB Family of Churches*. Sheffield: Church Army, 2002.

Lints, Richard. *The Fabric of Theology: A Prolegomenon to Evangelical Theology*. Grand Rapids: Eerdmans, 1993.

Lloyd-Jones, David M. *Knowing the Times: Addresses Delivered on Various Occasions, 1942–1977*. Edinburgh: Banner of Truth Trust, 1989.

Lord, Andrew. *Network Church: A Pentecostal Ecclesiology Shaped by Mission*. Leiden: Brill, 2012.

———. *Transforming Renewal: Charismatic Renewal Meets Thomas Merton*. Eugene, OR: Wipf & Stock, 2015.

Lubac, Henri de. *The Drama of Atheist Humanism*. San Francisco: Ignatius, 1995.

Luhrmann, Tanya. "Metakinesis: How God Becomes Intimate in Contemporary U.S. Christianity." *American Anthropologist* 106 (2004) 518–28.
Lyon, David. *Postmodernity*. Milton Keynes, UK: Open University Press, 1994.
Lyotard, Jean-François. *The Postmodern Condition: A Report on Knowledge*. Minneapolis: University of Minnesota Press, 1984.
Maiden, John. *Age of the Spirit: Charismatic Renewal, the Anglo-World, and Global Christianity, 1945–1980*. Oxford: Oxford University Press, 2023.
Martin, David. *Forbidden Revolutions: Pentecostalism in Latin America and Catholicism in Eastern Europe*. London: SPCK, 1996.
———. *The Future of Christianity: Reflections on Violence and Democracy, Religion and Secularization*. Farnham: Ashgate, 2011.
———. *On Secularization: Towards a Revised General Theory*. Farnham: Ashgate, 2005.
Mather, Anne. "The Theology of the Charismatic Movement in the Church of England from 1964 to the Present Day." PhD diss., University of Wales, 1983.
McBain, Douglas. *Fire Over the Waters: Renewal Among Baptists and Others from the 1960s to the 1990s*. London: Darton, Longman, and Todd, 1997.
———. "Mainline Charismatics: Some Observations of Baptist Renewal." In *Charismatic Christianity: Sociological Perspectives*, edited by Stephen Hunt et al., 43–59. Basingstoke: Macmillan, 1997.
McCance, Dawne. *Derrida on Religion: Thinker of Differance*. London: Routledge, 2009.
McDonnell, Kilian. "Holy Spirit and Pentecostalism." *Commonweal* 89 (1968) 198–204.
———. *Presence, Power, Praise: Documents on the Charismatic Renewal*. Collegeville, MN: Liturgical, 1980.
McGrath, Alister E. "Evangelical Anglicanism: A Contradiction in Terms?" In *Evangelical Anglicans: Their Role and Influence in the Church Today*, edited by Richard T. France and Alister E. McGrath, 10–21. London: SPCK, 1993.
———. *A Passion for Truth: The Intellectual Coherence of Evangelicalism*. Leicester: Apollos, 1996.
McGuire, Meredith B. "Words of Power: Personal Empowerment and Healing." *Culture, Medicine, and Psychiatry* 7 (1983) 221–40.
McLeod, Hugh. *The Religious Crisis of the 1960s*. Oxford: Oxford University Press, 2007.
McLuhan, Marshall. *Understanding Media: The Extensions of Man*. London: Routledge, 1964.
Mellor, Philip, and Chris Shilling. *Re-Forming the Body: Religion, Community, and Modernity*. London: SAGE, 1997.
Meyer, Birgit. *Translating the Devil: Religion and Modernity Among the Ewe in Ghana*. Edinburgh: Edinburgh University Press, 1999.
Milbank, John. *Theology and Social Theory: Beyond Secular Reason*. Oxford: Blackwell, 1990.
Miller, Donald E. *Reinventing American Protestantism: Christianity in the New Millennium*. Berkeley: University of California Press, 1997.
———. "Routinizing Charisma: The Vineyard Fellowship in the Post-Wimber Era." In *Church, Identity, and Change: Theology and Denominational Structures in Unsettled Times*, edited by David A. Roozen and James R. Nieman, 141–62. Grand Rapids: Eerdmans, 2005.
Mitton, Michael. *Restoring the Woven Cord: Strands of Celtic Christianity for the Church Today*. London: Darton, Longman, and Todd, 1995.

Morgan, Alison. *The Wild Gospel: Bringing Truth to Life.* Oxford: Lion Hudson Limited, 2012.
Morris, Brian. *Religion and Anthropology: A Critical Introduction.* New York: Cambridge University Press, 2006.
Morris, Jeremy. "Secularization and Religious Experience: Arguments in the Historiography of Modern British Religion." *The Historical Journal* 55 (2012) 195–219.
Mumford, John. "The Global Vineyard—Meet John Mumford." Mar. 3, 2016. https://vineyardusa.org/library/the-global-vineyard-meet-john-mumford/.
Murphy, Nancey, and Brad Kallenberg. "Anglo-American Postmodernity: A Theology of Communal Practice." In *The Cambridge Companion to Postmodern Theology*, edited by Kevin J. Vanhoozer, 26–41. Cambridge Companions to Religion. Cambridge: Cambridge University Press, 2003.
Murray, Iain H. *David Martyn Lloyd-Jones: The Fight of Faith 1939–1981.* Edinburgh: Banner of Truth Trust, 1990.
Noel, Bradley. *Pentecostal and Postmodern Hermeneutics: Comparisons and Contemporary Impact.* Eugene, OR: Wipf & Stock, 2010.
———. "Pentecostal and Postmodern Hermeneutics: Comparisons and Contemporary Impact." PhD diss., University of South Africa, 2007.
Oden, Thomas C. *A Change of Heart: A Personal and Theological Memoir.* Westmont, IL: InterVarsity, 2014.
———. *The Rebirth of Orthodoxy: Signs of New Life in Christianity.* New York: HarperCollins, 2003.
O'Farrell, Clare, *Foucault: Historian or Philosopher?* New York: St. Martin's, 1989.
Padgett, Deborah. *Qualitative Methods in Social Work Research.* 3rd ed. Los Angeles: SAGE, 2016.
Patel, Jitesh. "Postmodernism and the Charismatic Movement in the Church of England." PhD diss., Lambeth RDT, 2024.
Pennington, Basil. *The Song of Songs: A Spiritual Commentary.* Woodstock: SkyLight Paths, 2004.
Percy, Martyn. "The City on a Beach: Future Prospects for Charismatic Movements at the End of the Twentieth Century." In *Charismatic Christianity: Sociological Perspectives*, edited by Stephen Hunt et al., 205–28. Basingstoke: Macmillan, 1997.
———. "Sweet Rapture: Subliminal Eroticism in Contemporary Charismatic Worship." *Theology and Sexuality* 1997 (1997) 71–106.
———. *Words, Wonders, and Power: Understanding Contemporary Christian Fundamentalism and Revivalism.* London: SPCK, 1996.
Pfeil, Gretchen. "Imperfect Vessels: Emotion and Rituals of Anti-Ritual in American Pentecostal and Charismatic Devotional Life." In *Practicing the Faith: The Ritual Life of Pentecostal-Charismatic Christians*, edited by Martin Lindhardt, 277–305. New York: Berghahn, 2011.
Phillips, Gary. "Religious Pluralism in a Postmodern World." In *The Challenge of Postmodernism: An Evangelical Engagement*, edited by David Dockery, 131–43. 2nd ed. Grand Rapids: Baker Academic, 2001.
Poewe, Karla. "On the Metonymic Structure of Religious Experiences: The Example of Charismatic Christianity." *Cultural Dynamics* 2 (1989) 361–80.
Poirier, John C. "Pentecostalism as a Product of the Enlightenment." *Pneuma* 44 (2022) 497–524.

Poloma, Margaret M. *The Assemblies of God at the Crossroads: Charisma and Institutional Dilemmas*. Knoxville: University of Tennessee Press, 1989.

———. "Toronto Blessing." In *The New International Dictionary of Pentecostal and Charismatic Movements*, edited by Stanley M. Burgess and Eduard M. Van der Maas, 1149–52. Grand Rapids: Zondervan, 2003.

Porter, Matthew. *David Watson: Evangelism, Renewal, Reconciliation*. Cambridge: Grove, 2003.

———. "The Missiological Influence of David Watson on Evangelicalism in the Church of England." MA thesis, University of Sheffield, 2000.

Pytches, David. *Come Holy Spirit: Learning How to Minister in Power*. 2nd ed. London: Hodder and Stoughton, 1995.

———. "David Pytches." In *Meeting John Wimber*, edited by John Gunstone, 40-52. Crowborough: Monarch, 1996.

Pytches, David, and Brian Skinner. *New Wineskins: A Plea for Radical Rethinking in the Church of England to Enable Normal Church Growth to Take Effect Beyond Existing Parish Boundaries*. Guildford, UK: Eagle, 1991.

Pytches, Mary. *There Is Still More: Reaching for More of the Kingdom*. Maidstone: River, 2011.

Quebedeaux, Richard. *New Charismatics II: How a Christian Renewal Movement Became a Part of the American Religious Main-Stream*. New York: Harper and Row, 1983.

———. *The New Charismatics: The Origins, Developments, and Significance of Neo-Pentecostalism*. New York: Doubleday, 1976.

Randall, Ian M. *Evangelical Experiences*. Carlisle, UK: Paternoster, 1999.

Reardon, Bernard. "Romanticism." In *The Blackwell Encyclopedia of Modern Christian Thought*, edited by Alistair E. McGrath, 573–79. Oxford: Blackwell, 1995.

ReSource. "History, Vision, and Values." https://www.resourcingrenewal.org/history-vision-values.

Richardson, Rick. *Reimagining Evangelism: Inviting Friends on a Spiritual Journey*. Milton Keynes, UK: Scripture Union, 2007.

Richter, Philip J. "'God Is Not a Gentleman!' The Sociology of the Toronto Blessing." In *The Toronto Blessing—Or Is It?*, edited by Stanley E. Porter and Philip J. Richter, 5–37. London: Darton, Longman, and Todd, 1995.

Ringer, Fritz. "The Intellectual Field, Intellectual History, and the Sociology of Knowledge." *Theory and Society* 19 (1990) 269–94.

Robbins, Joel. "Anthropology." In *Studying Global Pentecostalism: Theories and Methods*, edited by Allan Anderson et al., 156–78. Berkeley: University of California Press, 2010.

———. "The Globalization of Pentecostal and Charismatic Christianity." *Annual Review of Anthropology* 33 (2004) 117–43.

Rookmaaker, Hans. *Modern Art and the Death of a Culture*. London: Inter-Varsity, 1970.

Rorty, Richard. *Consequences of Pragmatism: Essays 1972–1980*. Minneapolis: University of Minnesota Press, 1982.

———. *Philosophy and the Mirror of Nature*. Princeton: Princeton University Press, 2009.

Rosenau, Pauline. *Post-Modernism and the Social Sciences: Insights, Inroads, and Intrusions*. Princeton: Princeton University Press, 1992.

Ryder, John. "The Use and Abuse of Modernity: Postmodernism and the American Philosophic Tradition." *Journal of Speculative Philosophy* 7 (1993) 92–102.
Saunders, Teddy, and Hugh Sansom. *David Watson: A Biography*. London: Hodder and Stoughton, 1992.
Schaeffer, Francis A. *Francis A. Schaeffer Trilogy*. Leicester: InterVarsity, 1990.
Seligman, Adam, et al. *Ritual and Its Consequences: An Essay on the Limits of Sincerity*. Oxford: Oxford University Press, 2008.
Selvaratnam, Christian N. *The Craft of Church Planting: Exploring the Lost Wisdom of Apprenticeship*. London: SCM, 2022.
Shin, Yoon. *Pentecostalism, Postmodernism, and Reformed Epistemology: James K. A. Smith and the Contours of a Postmodern Christian Epistemology*. Lanham, MD: Lexington, 2021.
Silverman, David. *Interpreting Qualitative Data*. 6th ed. Los Angeles: SAGE, 2020.
Smail, Thomas A. "The Cross and the Spirit: Towards a Theology of Renewal." In *Charismatic Renewal: The Search for a Theology*, by Thomas A. Smail et al., 49–70. London: SPCK, 1993.
Smith, Graham Russell. "The Church Militant: A Study of 'Spiritual Warfare' in the Anglican Charismatic Renewal." PhD diss., University of Birmingham, 2011.
Smith, James K. A. *Thinking in Tongues: Pentecostal Contributions to Christian Philosophy*. Grand Rapids: Eerdmans, 2010.
———. *Who's Afraid of Postmodernism? Taking Derrida, Lyotard, and Foucault to Church*. Grand Rapids: Baker Academic, 2006.
Snyder, Jon. "Translator's Introduction." In *The End of Modernity: Nihilism and Hermeneutics in Post-Modern Culture*, by Gianni Vattimo, vi–il. Translated by Jon Snyder. Cambridge: Polity, 1988.
Stanley, Brian. *The Global Diffusion of Evangelism: The Age of Billy Graham and John Stott*. Nottingham: InterVarsity, 2013.
St. Hild College. "Christian Selvaratnam: About Christian." https://sthild.org/christian-selvaratnam.
Stark, Rodney, and William S. Bainbridge. "Towards a Theory of Religion: Religious Commitment." *Journal for the Scientific Study of Religion* 19 (1980) 114–28.
Steven, James. "'Worship in the Spirit': A Sociological Analysis and Theological Appraisal of Charismatic Worship in the Church of England." PhD diss., King's College London, 1999.
———. *Worship in the Spirit: Charismatic Worship in the Church of England*. Milton Keynes, UK: Paternoster, 2002.
Stewart, Kenneth J. *In Search of Ancient Roots: The Christian Past and the Evangelical Identity Crisis*. London: Apollos, 2017.
Stiller, Brian. "Growing up Pentecostal: Unconsciously Postmodern in a Consciously Modern World." Lecture. Northwest University, Kirkland, WA. Feb. 8, 2007.
Stott, John R. W. *The Baptism and Fullness of the Holy Spirit: An Explanation to All Christians*. London: Inter-Varsity Fellowship, 1964.
Studzinski, Raymond. *Reading to Live: The Evolving Practice of Lectio Divina*. Collegeville, MN: Liturgical, 2009.
Stuhr, John J. *Pragmatism, Postmodernism, and the Future of Philosophy*. New York: Routledge, 2003.
Sullivan, Emmanuel. *Can the Pentecostal Movement Renew the Churches?* London: British Council of Churches, 1972.

Suurmond, Jean-Jacques. "The Church at Play: The Pentecostal/Charismatic Renewal of the Liturgy as Renewal of the World." In *Pentecost, Mission, and Ecumenism: Essays on Intercultural Theology, Festschrift in Honour of Professor Walter J. Hollenweger*, edited by Jan Jongeneel, 247–59. Frankfurt: Lang, 1992.

———. *Word and Spirit at Play: Towards a Charismatic Theology*. Translated by John Bowden. London: SCM, 1995.

Swinton, John. "Empirical Research, Theological Limits, and Possibilities." In *The Wiley Blackwell Companion to Theology and Qualitative Research*, edited by Peter Ward and Knut Tveitereid, 81–90. Chichester: Wiley-Blackwell, 2022.

———. "What Comes Next? Practical Theology, Faithful Presence, and Prophetic Witness." *Practical Theology* 13 (2020) 162–73.

Swinton, John, and Harriet Mowat. *Practical Theology and Qualitative Research*. 2nd ed. London: SCM, 2016.

Tanner, J. Paul. "The History of Interpretation of the Song of Songs." *Bibliotheca Sacra* 154 (1997) 23–46.

Tarnas, Richard. *The Passion of the Western Mind: Understanding the Ideas That Have Shaped Our World View*. London: Pimlico, 1996.

Taylor, Charles. *A Secular Age*. Cambridge: Belknap, 2007.

Teraudkalns, Valdis. "New Charismatic Churches in Latvia as Examples of Postmodern Religious Subculture." *International Review of Mission* 90 (2001) 444–54.

Tester, Keith. *The Life and Times of Post-Modernity*. London: Routledge, 1993.

Thiselton, Anthony. *The Holy Spirit: In Biblical Teaching, Through the Centuries and Today*. London: SPCK, 2013.

Toulmin, Stephen. *Cosmopolis: The Hidden Agenda of Modernity*. New York: Free, 1990.

Tveitereid, Knut, and Pete Ward. *The Wiley Blackwell Companion to Theology and Qualitative Research*. Chichester: John Wiley and Sons, 2022.

Urquhart, Colin. *When the Spirit Comes*. London: Hodder and Stoughton, 1974.

Van Gelder, Craig. "Postmodernism as an Emerging Worldview." *Calvin Theological Journal* 26 (1991) 412–17.

Veith, Gene. *Postmodern Times: A Christian Guide to Contemporary Thought and Culture*. Wheaton, IL: Crossway, 1994.

Vondey, Wolfgang. *Beyond Pentecostalism: The Crisis of Global Christianity and the Renewal of the Theological Agenda*. Grand Rapids: Eerdmans, 2010.

Wakefield, Gavin. *Alexander Boddy: Pentecostal Anglican Pioneer*. Carlisle, UK: Paternoster, 2006.

Walker, Andrew. "Pentecostal Power: The 'Charismatic Renewal Movement' and the Politics of Pentecostal Experience." In *Of Gods and Men: New Religious Movements in the West*, edited by Eileen Barker, 89–105. Macon, GA: Mercer University Press, 1983.

———. "Recovering Deep Church: Theological and Spiritual Renewal." In *Remembering Our Future: Explorations in Deep Church*, edited by Andrew Walker and Luke Bretherton, 1–29. London: Paternoster, 2007.

———. *Restoring the Kingdom: The Radical Christianity of the House Church Movement*. 4th ed. London: Hodder and Stoughton, 1998.

———. "Thoroughly Modern: Sociological Reflections on the Charismatic Movement from the End of the Twentieth Century." In *Charismatic Christianity: Sociological Perspectives*, edited by Stephen Hunt et al., 17–42. Basingstoke: Macmillan, 1997.

Walker, Thomas. *Renew Us by Your Spirit*. London: Hodder and Stoughton, 1982.

Wallis, Roy. *The Elementary Forms of the New Religious Life*. London: Routledge, 1984.

Ward, Pete. *Introducing Practical Theology: Mission, Ministry, and the Life of the Church*. Grand Rapids: Baker Academic, 2017.

Watson, Anne. "The Third Wave Has Only Just Begun." In *Riding the Third Wave: What Comes After Renewal?*, edited by Kevin Springer, 63–73. Basingstoke: Marshall Pickering, 1987.

Watson, David. "David Watson." In *My Path of Prayer: Personal Glimpses of the Glory and the Majesty of God Revealed through Experiences of Prayer*, edited by David Hanes, 85–95. Worthing: H. E. Walter, 1981.

———. *Discipleship*. London: Hodder and Stoughton, 1981.

———. *Fear No Evil: A Personal Struggle with Cancer*. London: Hodder and Stoughton, 1984.

———. Foreword to *Celebration of Discipline: The Path to Spiritual Growth*, by Richard Foster. London: Hodder and Stoughton, 1980.

———. *Hidden Warfare*. Bromley, UK: STL, 1972.

———. *I Believe in Evangelism*. London: Hodder and Stoughton, 1976.

———. *I Believe in the Church*. London: Hodder and Stoughton, 1978.

———. *In Search of God*. London: Falcon, 1974.

———. *Is Anyone There?* London: Hodder and Stoughton, 1979.

———. *Live a New Life*. London: InterVarsity, 1975.

———. *My God Is Real*. London: Falcon, 1970.

———. *One in the Spirit*. London: Hodder and Stoughton, 1973.

———. *Start a New Life*. Malton: Gilead, 1981.

———. *You Are My God: An Autobiography*. London: Hodder and Stoughton, 1983.

Watson, David, and Jean Watson. *Through the Year with David Watson: Devotional Readings for Every Day*. London: Hodder and Stoughton, 1982.

Watson, David, and Simon Jenkins. *Jesus: Then and Now*. Tring: Lion, 1983.

Webber, Robert. *Ancient-Future Faith: Rethinking Evangelicalism for a Postmodern World*. Grand Rapids: Baker, 1999.

———. *Ancient-Future Time: Forming Spirituality through the Christian Year*. Grand Rapids: Baker, 2004.

———. *Evangelicals on the Canterbury Trail: Why Evangelicals Are Attracted to the Liturgical Church*. Harrisburg. PA: Morehouse, 1985.

Weber, Max. *From Max Weber: Essays in Sociology*. Translated by Hans Heinrich Gerth and C. Wright Mills. Oxford: Oxford University Press, 1946.

Welby, Justin. *The Power of Reconciliation*. London: Bloomsbury, 2022.

Western, Simon. *Leadership: A Critical Text*. 3rd ed. London: SAGE, 2019.

Wilkinson, Michael, and Peter Althouse. *Catch the Fire: Soaking Prayer and Charismatic Renewal*. Ithaca, NY: Cornell University Press, 2014.

Williams, Don. "Theological Perspective and Reflection on the Vineyard Christian Fellowship." In *Church, Identity, and Change: Theology and Denominational Structures in Unsettled Times*, edited by David Roozen and James Nieman, 163–87. Grand Rapids: Eerdmans, 2005.

Williams, Hattie. "After Coming Out, 'I Had PTSD Symptoms' Says Lay Leader in Church-Plant." *Church Times*, Feb. 12, 2021. https://www.churchtimes.co.uk/articles/2021/12-february/news/uk/after-coming-out-i-had-ptsd-symptoms-says-lay-leader-in-church-plant.

Williams, Peter. "Editorial: 'A Very Horrid Thing'?" *The Churchman* 96 (1982) 195–96.

Williams, Rowan. *Looking East in Winter: Contemporary Thought and the Eastern Christian Tradition*. Bloomsbury, 2021.

Wimber, Carol. *John Wimber: The Way It Was*. London: Hodder and Stoughton, 1999.

Wimber, John, and Association of Vineyard Churches. "Refreshing, Renewal, and Revival." Vineyard Reflections: John Wimber's Leadership Letter, Aug. 1994.

Wimber, John, and Kevin Springer. *Power Evangelism*. Rev. ed. London: Hodder and Stoughton, 1992.

Winter, Ralph D. "The Two Structures of God's Redemptive Mission." *Missiology* 2 (1974) 121–39.

Yong, Amos. *Discerning the Spirit(s): A Pentecostal–Charismatic Contribution to Christian Theology of Religions*. Eugene, OR: Wipf & Stock, 2019.

———. "Radically Orthodox, Reformed, and Pentecostal: Rethinking the Intersection of Post/Modernity and the Religions in Conversation with James K. A. Smith." *Journal of Pentecostal Theology* 15 (2007) 233–50.

———. *Spirit-Word-Community: Theological Hermeneutics in Trinitarian Perspective*. Eugene, OR: Wipf & Stock, 2006.

Zahl, Simeon. *The Holy Spirit and Christian Experience*. Oxford: Oxford University Press, 2020.

Zichterman, Joseph. "The Distinctives of John Wimber's Theology and Practice Within the American Pentecostal-Charismatic Movement." PhD diss., Trinity Evangelical Divinity School, 2010.

Ziefle, Joshua. *David du Plessis and the Assemblies of God: The Struggle for the Soul of a Movement*. Leiden: Brill, 2013.

www.ingramcontent.com/pod-product-compliance
Lightning Source LLC
Chambersburg PA
CBHW071241230426
43668CB00011B/1533